GW01110945

MATADORS

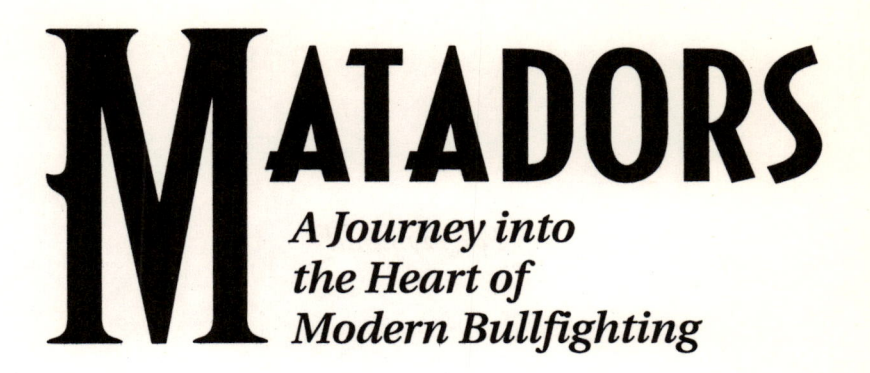

MATADORS
A Journey into the Heart of Modern Bullfighting

EAMONN O'NEILL

MAINSTREAM PUBLISHING
EDINBURGH AND LONDON

For my family

Copyright © Eamonn O'Neill, 1998
All rights reserved
The moral right of the author has been asserted

First published in Great Britain in 1998 by
MAINSTREAM PUBLISHING COMPANY (EDINBURGH) LTD
7 Albany Street
Edinburgh EH1 3UG

ISBN 1 84018 147 8

No part of this book may be reproduced or transmitted in any
form or by any means without written permission from the
publisher, except by a reviewer who wishes to quote brief passages
in connection with a review written for insertion in a newspaper,
magazine or broadcast

A catalogue record for this book is available from the British Library

Photographs by Eamonn O'Neill, unless otherwise credited
Typeset in Adobe Garamond
Printed and bound in Great Britain by Butler & Tanner Ltd

Contents

1.	The Immortals	7
2.	An Act of God	17
3.	A Very Spanish Gesture	34
4.	Indefensible but Irresistible	40
5.	A Very Disagreeable Labyrinth	59
6.	The *Novilleros*	70
7.	The Rising Sun Kid	88
8.	Where it all Started	99
9.	Hemingway and Nirvana	115
10.	Friend, I Must Kill You	139
11.	A Chic Night Out	159
12.	A *Sobresaliente* in Burgos	169
13.	*¡Fiesta!*	192
	Acknowledgements	224

Bullfighting is not a sport. It was never supposed to be. It is a tragedy. A very great tragedy...

Ernest Hemingway, the *Toronto Star Weekly*, 20 October 1923

It is not the same to talk of bulls as to be in the bullring

Spanish proverb

ONE

The Immortals

I was lost in a cloud of dust and, for a moment, I couldn't see any way out.

Somewhere in the middle of the Andalucian countryside, in southern Spain, the car I was travelling in swerved round a corner.

Another tobacco-coloured dirt track unfolded in front of us like a stained old ribbon. Olive trees came and went in a blur on either side of the car. What scenery I did manage to glimpse looked like a rain-spoiled watercolour. It was difficult to make out anything properly. The windscreen was covered in thick yellow dirt. The ultramarine blue sky appeared every so often, then promptly vanished again. When I did catch a glimpse of the sun, it served only to blind me with its diamond-white brightness. The world flew by in snatches and fragments. The faster we went, the slower everything seemed to be happening. The wipers and windscreen wash were useless – they just turned everything into a muddy cake-mix. A few moments earlier I had to get my bearings by fixing a field of olive trees against the umber hills. But we turned a corner, accelerated along another dirt track and I failed. I was lost again inside a cloud of dust which was enveloping us like a bad mood. I was discovering that one field of olive trees tended to look very much like another.

'Did I tell you that I was once Lawrence of Arabia?'

My host, who was driving the car, jerked his head round when he asked me this. The sound of the tyres on the road's surface was deafening so he had to raise his voice to drown out the noise. I shook my head in response. He smiled and opened his mouth, then closed it quickly, his attention momentarily diverted by a huge pothole which suddenly appeared on the road in front of us. He grabbed the steering-wheel of the sleek brown Mercedes and swerved. We avoided the hole by a couple of inches. Then he turned to me again to continue his tale.

'Yeah, I was Lawrence of Arabia – well, Peter O'Toole's double in the film anyway. They shot it in this area. Over thirty-five years ago. Jesus, time flies!'

The man telling me all this was John Fulton.

From his businesslike appearance – sky-blue short-sleeved silk shirt, smart linen khaki-coloured trousers and soft burgundy loafers – you would never have guessed what occupation John was engaged in for the greater part of his life. You might have said he was an accountant on the verge of retiring perhaps, or even a suntanned international lawyer. Possibly a well-groomed schoolteacher who taught English and Spanish. You would definitely have suggested he might be a doctor, one who loved Seville and Spain so much that he'd stayed on to set up his own practice treating the very rich travellers who passed through the city. But if you said any of these you'd be wrong. Wrong by a mile. Wrong by a hundred miles. My host was in fact a retired bullfighter – an ex-*matador de toros*. And an exceptional one to boot. John Fulton was – and still is, according to the record books – the only American ever to graduate to the rank of full matador on Spanish soil.

John was born in Philadelphia in 1932. His father was Italian, a handsome man who loved athletics and had been something of a cycling champion in his youth. His pretty, vibrant-looking mother was also an immigrant, from Hungary. Now in his mid-sixties, John was tall, good-looking in a distinguished kind of way, well built, with slicked-back grey hair. He had old-fashioned good manners. He tended to be shy until his love of a good story and a good time took over; then he would open up to tell me how his devoted parents brought him up on stories of heroes: David and Goliath, King Arthur and the Knights of the Round Table and, inevitably, Lawrence of Arabia. One day he walked into a cinema in Philadelphia to see a film called *Blood and Sand* starring Tyrone Power. What he saw on the screen that afternoon changed his life for ever. It was a film about bullfighting.

'I saw a man with a cape and something marvellous happened,' said John. He shook his head at the memory, as if it had all just happened the day before. Seeing that old movie was the beginning of a long quest to become a bullfighter. By the time I caught up with him he had been revered and respected within the international bullfighting community for nearly four decades. 'If you want to learn about bullfighting, go to Seville and find a man named John Fulton,' I was repeatedly told by everyone I'd spoken to.

So that's exactly what I did.

Two days after first making contact with John I found myself in the countryside outside of Seville. More than any other part of the country, Andalucia is filled with the clichéd images of Spain – the flamenco dancers, the tiled palaces, the fields of sunflowers, the wineskins, the open-topped carriages, the noisy tapas bars and, above all, the bulls and the matadors who kill them.

While I battered and bounced around the Andalucian countryside in John Fulton's car, the city of Seville scratched itself awake after another siesta. Along the street of the Catholic Kings the blank-faced waiters read their newspapers and yawned. Outside on the street itself the fat-bellied taxi-drivers manually shoved their vehicles down the street, saving petrol, their shoulders to the door, one hand on the steering-wheel. Then they stretched and talked about money, women, football, politics and bulls. Old men in woollen trousers slept beneath the skinny, dried-out trees next to the river. The vast holy places in the city centre were empty now. Watery wine-coloured splashes from the stained-glass windows spilled all over the floor of the cathedral. The odd die-hard tourist flitted through the shadowed interior, examining the altars and the gold icons. Across the street a pot-bellied foreman bellowed at his workers. They sweated in heavy blue boilersuits and pleaded with the owner of a nearby bar to turn up the radio so they could hear the football match commentary. Across the street from the builders' pipe-filled trench, next to the city's archives, the fat, blind lottery-ticket seller, her radio and handbag strapped around her creaking chair, thumbed her sheaves of tickets and mouthed her second-last decade of the rosary. Then she began the daily ritual of shifting her pitch to the other side of the street to avoid the early-evening sun's piercing rays. Like the rest of her city, she only moved when the shadows moved.

It was a typical Sevillian summer's day.

Somewhere to the south of the city I was rattling along a dirt track in John's airy, expensive vehicle.

'O'Toole was something else. One night we got drunk together in Seville where David Lean was using the Plaza de España as a location for the British HQ in Cairo. I was supposed to keep an eye on O'Toole. He tended to get bored out of his skull, though – desert fever or something, probably – and when that happened, anything was liable to go down. Anyway, we ended up wandering around the city together late at night. Out of the blue we came upon a pet shop and there were little yellow chicks in the window inside a sort of cage. O'Toole started crying and saying he had to, just had to, free those poor little chicks from such awful oppression. He could be very theatrical sometimes, you know. Maybe he was just staying in character – "Lawrence Frees the Chickens" or something. Who knows.'

Our car lurched round another corner. I was still lost. There wasn't a road sign to be seen. The thick dust billowed behind us. John kept talking as we drove.

'Anyway, to cut a long story short, he somehow managed to kick the window of the pet shop in. There was glass everywhere and the little chicks were all over the damn place. I couldn't believe my eyes. It was surreal. Needless to say, O'Toole was laughing his head off.'

'What did you do?' I found myself clutching madly at a handle on the door as we shot over a large bump in the road. For a long moment we were airborne.

'Run like hell,' John replied, grinning as the car hit the track again with a whack.

'What about the chicks?'

'Who knows? Crazy. Haven't seen Peter for years. I miss him. What a great guy. Remind me to give you the long version of the tale about the night I was in a car with Omar Sharif and O'Toole coming back from Málaga. Utter chaos. O'Toole was driving like a madman. At one point I decided, "This is it, I'm definitely going to die . . . it's all over." Strangely, the moment I thought that, I felt fine. Really calm. Facing death can be oddly liberating.'

I knew what he meant. For the past forty-eight hours I'd been lying drugged up to my eyeballs in a darkened room. I'd eaten something which had disagreed with me. Huge blotches appeared on my body in the most intimate places and I shook violently for two hours. A local doctor arrived at seven in the morning and gave me lots of painful injections in my bum; at least they made the blotches vanish, the shakes stop and put me to sleep for two days. I had vague memories of him asking me if I'd 'seen a canary'. A *canary*? Is the man mad, I thought? 'Seen a canary? Seen a canary?' he kept asking. I actually gave the question some serious thought. Maybe this was the Spanish equivalent of the miners who used to take canaries down the mines – if the canary died, the miners knew it was time to leave because deadly fumes were on their way. In my case perhaps if I'd seen a canary I was at death's door. If I hadn't seen anything then I was okay. Or maybe it was the other way round. Whatever the reason I hadn't a clue what canaries had to do with my allergic reaction to Spanish food.

'You Scot? Scotland? Seen Canary! Seen Canary!'

He mimed a man shooting. Then he mimed a man playing golf. All this was taking place at the foot of my sick-bed. Maybe if I'd been healthier I'd have got it quicker. Eventually, through a pleasantly overwhelming cortisone-induced haze, I cracked it.

'Ah, Sean Connery!'

'Yes! Yes! Marbella! He live there! Bond!' he beamed. Then suddenly his forehead furrowed, he coughed and waved a huge bill at me. 'No cheques or credit cards. Please just cash. I wait.'

Just over two days later, after our short, bumpy journey, John Fulton and I arrived at our dusty destination. It was called the Hacienda El Pablo and it lay half an hour's drive south of Seville. Lush green trees stood guard around the brilliant white building. I shielded my eyes when I got out of the car, looking up at the gold-coloured tiles on the roof. A rusting weathervane was perched on top of a little square tower. It didn't look as if it had seen a gust of wind or a drop of oil in centuries. My host led the way towards the rear of the building. The air was thick and still, without even the slightest whisper of a breeze. The place seemed completely deserted.

We walked around a courtyard until I saw a small white stone archway. John ducked through. I followed him and found myself in front of a red wooden fence. I could hear some faint, almost imperceptible sounds. I peered over the fence.

There in front of me was a small private bullring. The sand was a bright, rich orange colour and it was surrounded by a low white and flame-red brick wall. Seats stretched back for VIP guests, where a few people were watching the scene beneath them. They were framed by vast lines of dark-green olive groves and, off in the dusty distance, the hazy light-blue horizon.

I blinked and took it all in.

Thirty young men, some stripped to the waist and sweating in the evening sun, stood on the sand. Their ink-black shadows fell on the ground like a row of pine trees on the horizon. Slowly they all went through the moves that a matador makes when he's in a bullfight. As one boy held a red cape, whether it was the large fighting cape or the shorter blood-red *muleta*, another slowly acted out the role of the bull. Some held their hands like horns, the way we all did as children, while others used real bull horns which they held up to their shiny black hair. Every one of them was deadly serious. They wore old sweatshirts and sweatpants and baggy T-shirts stained with sweat and dust. Two-thirds of the young men trained in the crescent of shade which hung in an arc over half the ring. A few, following their instincts, danced and shuffled into the hot light, oblivious to anything except their moves and their form. No one spoke. A strange hush hung in the oppressive heat of the evening air. All I could hear was the swish of a cape as it brushed the sand, or the brief metallic scrape of a sword as it touched the floor of the bullring.

Off to the left of the ring I saw a hose which ran with crystal clear water. Every so often one of the men, sweating like a horse, broke away from the group and held his head under the hose. Then, soaked and cooled, he returned to the training again.

I had heard that if you wanted to make a go of it in the world of bullfighting, places like this were one of the starting points. It was where you first got your hands on the capes, where you first felt the weight of a sword in the palm of your hand and where you first tried to control the threat of the bull in the semi-public setting of a proper ring.

Some of the boys looked awkward – they were shy and stood off to the side by themselves. It was here that their private dreams had to be hauled out of their heads, transformed into action and put on display, flaws and all, for their patrons and peers to see. It was easier for some than for others. One thin, though solidly muscled gypsy boy refused to join the group. Occasionally he eyed up everyone from beneath the thick curtain of his coal-black hair as he self-consciously went through a series of difficult-looking passes with a large cape. When he'd finished he walked off back into the shadows, where he leaned against the wall. Although he'd been carrying out the moves slowly, the intensity of his concentration had taken its toll. Hidden in the shade I could see his sweat-stained chest pumping up and down as he gasped for oxygen. When the whites of his eyes made contact with mine he stared for a moment then averted his gaze down towards the sand. For some reason he looked ashamed at being caught even trying.

I watched all this for ten minutes or more without saying a word. Then John Fulton silently signalled me to come and join him on the other side of the ring where he had been standing in the shadows with another man.

'Eamonn, this is Professor Manuel Chavez,' he said. 'He is one of the men who look after these young aspiring matadors. We were just talking about how important it is for the boys playing the role of the bull to be good at their job. They must become one with the thoughts of the bull – they must act out the role realistically. It's not a game. It's very, very important.' John whispered when he spoke.

We paused for a brief moment while I looked back out at the boys training. Those playing the role of the bull charged slowly and deliberately at their fellow trainee-matadors. Their companions with the capes moved very gracefully and carefully when the boy acting as the bull came towards them.

Everyone concentrated. No one laughed or joked.

They were doing it half for themselves and half for their small audience which included me, my host and the patron of the hacienda I'd just been introduced to. I shook hands with the man and he bowed. He must have been about sixty-five. I noticed how powerful and rough his hand felt when I shook it. His face was lined and heavy and he had the thick neck of a weightlifter. I caught a glimpse of a silver chain which disappeared into dense chest hair. He reminded me of a famous actor whose name I suddenly couldn't remember. He spoke to me in gravelly tones which I had trouble understanding. I nodded and turned to John. He understood my predicament immediately.

'Oh, he says he saw the look on your face. Yes, he knows. Everyone remarks on it. He says he very much enjoyed doubling for Anthony Quinn.'

'I've wanted to be a bullfighter for as long as I can remember.'

That was the first thing José Manuel, one of the young men who trained at the hacienda, said to me when I met him. He was nineteen and a college student studying administration and business in Seville. But his first love was bullfighting.

'Why do you want to be a bullfighter?'

'The money, the glamour, the fame and the women.' José gave an impish smile then straightened himself up. He furrowed his brow in an effort to look older and more serious. A layer of sweat gathered on his forehead.

'Have you fought already?' I asked.

'Yes, three times as a *novillero* – a novice professional – and I hope eventually to graduate to become a full, first-class matador.'

'How often do you train here?'

'Three times a week. A bus paid for by a patron picks us up in Seville and brings us out here.'

'What do you think people from other countries think about Spaniards like you who want to become bullfighters?'

'Bullfighting is such a part of our culture. Foreigners probably think anyone who does it is crazy. They also think it's cruel and dangerous, but they don't understand either the culture or the tradition.'

He shrugged and bowed his head. His friends ignored us and continued with their training as if I wasn't there.

'Do you ever worry about the thought of being seriously injured or dying in a bullfight?' I asked.

He pondered the question for a moment, then his face broke out in a cheeky smile. 'Nah, I don't fear dying. I have respect for death. But fear? Nah!'

I nodded, scribbled down his reply in my notebook and shook

José's hand. Our little group watched him as he plodded back to the bullring to resume his training. I also said my goodbyes to Professor Chavez – his title was an honorary one, given to him as a mark of his experience and to acknowledge the high respect in which he was held; in much the same way I heard John Fulton being referred to as *Maestro* Fulton. The professor offered me a drink on the terrace by the swimming-pool but I declined. He threw up his arms and shrugged dramatically. I hoped I hadn't offended him. I appreciated his help and knew visitors weren't usually welcomed into the matadors' training class.

As I was leaving I noticed a young woman who was also training with a cape and a sword. She had been banished to a piece of waste ground behind the bullring where the rest of the aspirants were. She looked somewhat lonely. But with the help of a boy she slowly went through all the moves and the motions. Her pretty, freckled face was twisted into a mask of deadly determination.

A few moments before I spoke to young José I'd noticed John Fulton chatting to a young boy who seemed to be having trouble carrying out a certain pass with the large pink-and-yellow cape. I asked what was wrong.

'His feet – he can't keep them on the ground. They should be flat. Nowadays it's the fashion to lift or arch one. They seem to think it looks better. Just a fad.' He looked irritated.

'Is that bad?' I wondered why he seemed so disappointed by the spectacle of the young man lifting up his feet instead of planting them flat and square.

'Young would-be matadors are too quick to copy those that are already in the big time. All too often they pick up their bad habits. No one is keen to learn the real basics any more. They just want to make money quickly. Everyone wants a short-cut to fame and fortune in this game,' he replied as we slowly trudged our way out of the hacienda. My shirt was burning up under the evening sun and rivers of sweat rolled down my back.

I stopped to wipe my forehead. 'Do places like this turn up stars – young guys who'll make it into the big time?'

'Occasionally. Very occasionally. If you know what you're after you might spot a diamond in the rough. That's what patrons of a place like this hope for. That's why they invest in renting the hacienda, invest their time, pay for a bus to bring the boys out from the city – half of them won't be able to afford the fare, remember – and provide them with basic equipment. Down the line they may even buy a few bulls and lay on a fight. They're always hoping they'll spot somebody with a real gift. But that's a hard thing to do. Even when you do spot somebody it's still a long, long road. And it's all uphill.'

'They certainly looked confident enough,' I remarked as I took one last backwards glance at the young men standing on the sand. They reminded me of hopeful boxers I'd seen and trained with in Scotland: defiant and desperate.

'Well, that's youth. You aren't looking at the type of confidence that comes from someone knowing their art inside out and back to front. No, what you're looking at is the confidence of youth, the natural God-given stuff we're all born with. But eventually that goes . . . in time.' He paused and stared into the white, sunbleached distance. 'And always, remember one thing . . .'

'What's that?' I asked.

He opened the car door and jabbed the ignition key in my direction. 'Always remember that all young matadors, every single one of them, think they are immortal.'

TWO

An Act of God

My journey to Spain to research the world of bullfighting wasn't exactly prompted by the fact that a childhood friend of mine once owned a dog called Rusty. But, if you can bear with me, I'll briefly explain how the two are, in my mind at least, forever linked.

I was about six years old before I first became aware that something called bullfighting even existed. The events leading up to that discovery are indelibly printed in my memory.

I must have been attending primary school for a year or so when my friend's dog, Rusty, suddenly vanished. When you're six, the thought of your friend's favourite mutt disappearing is a very big thing in your life. My pal was distraught. It obsessed him, and the rest of us, for weeks – where had the poor old thing gone? Had it drowned? Had it been run over? None of us was certain. Eventually my friend's father said that he'd learned that a local farmer had shot the dog because it was always chasing his cattle and annoying them. When my pal heard this he went nuts.

Over time, our ghoulish six-year-old minds got the better of us and we decided that if the dog had been shot then there was a fair chance that its partially decomposed body might still be lying in the farmer's field somewhere. We were kids: maggot-ridden things were of enormous interest to us. And so we all trooped off on an expedition to find the dead dog. Three hours later we'd given up. We'd scoured every corner of the field where the cows usually grazed and we hadn't found even the faintest sign of a dead dog.

What we did spot in an adjoining field, however, was a huge bull.

We sat on the fence surrounding this field and flung stones at the bull. It never budged an inch.

Someone had a box of matches and set a gorse-hedge alight in an effort to frighten the creature: it just grazed quietly and didn't take the slightest interest in our presence. We gave up annoying it and decided to head home. But, just as we moved off, one of my friends noticed that the rear gate to the bull's field was lying open. We all turned round in time to see the bull amble slowly towards the opening. Then it seemed, and I stress *seemed*, to gather some speed. A cry went up. We all ran like hell . . .

I have a vague memory of looking over my shoulder and seeing the bull only yards behind me – but that can't be true. I know it can't, but almost three decades later I still have the odd nightmare about it. When I was running and my little heart was thumping in my chest, I knew that the bull was after me; it was me that it wanted to trample and impale on its horns. I just knew it instinctively.

A friend later confirmed my fears about the bull's deadly intentions when we all sat sweating and shaking and swapping lies about how it nearly caught us: 'You were definitely the one it was after!' I was gravely informed.

The others nodded sagely.

'How come?' I was bewildered. They all seemed to know something I didn't. I felt very confused and left behind.

Everyone shook their heads in disgust. 'Are you stupid?'

I didn't think I was stupid but at six these things are still debatable. They all slowly pointed to my jumper.

'Eh?' I just didn't get it. Had the bull been trying to kill me because it didn't like my jersey?

One of my friends, a thick-set, well-fed-looking character spoke up: 'The colour! Your jersey! Look at it! It's red! Bulls hate red! It's the colour of blood . . . That's why they go for it. Have you never seen a bullfight from Spain? The bulls go for the big red bathtowel the guy waves and, eh, then he dives out of the way and it, eh, kills him at the end. Sometimes the guy kills it, but mostly *it* kills *him*! There's bucketloads of blood everywhere. Guts hanging out. Heads on the sand. People scream and run away. It's some stuff. I've seen loads of them. They're great!'

The boy telling us this had been to Majorca once on a package holiday. We were stunned into silence with his knowledge and we walked back home quietly thinking deep thoughts about an arena washed in blood and covered in decapitated bodies.

Later, in the bathroom at home, I used the large floral bathtowel as a cape and tried to envisage the sink charging at me like a big bull. I imagined the shiny brass taps were large, sharp horns on which I could end up impaled if I wasn't very careful.

In the intervening years I always used to look up encyclopaedias to see if they had a listing in the Bs for either 'Butch Cassidy' or 'Bullfighting'. Not surprisingly, I was usually out of luck on the former but occasionally I got lucky with the latter. Once I came across a really good, clear colour photograph of a matador and a bull. I cut the picture out and stuck it to my headboard next to some dinosaurs I'd snipped from the D listing. My second-oldest sister, Geraldine, was horrified when she discovered her encyclopaedia had been mutilated like this. She was really mad and complained to my parents. They told me off and banned me from any more book-cutting. I hadn't realised that my sister's book had been a school prize.

I felt awful about destroying parts of the book so I told my sin to the priest the next time I went to Confession. He had trouble hearing me and I had to shout out the word 'bullfighter' to him in the confessional. I was very embarrassed and felt sure everyone waiting to go in had heard me. 'Cutting up books? Bullfighters? That's not very holy, Eamonn, is it?' he asked. I sat in the darkness and said nothing.

It was always shocking to realise that the priest knew exactly who you were by your voice. Even if you dropped it a few octaves he always could identify you. It was very unsettling. The air was stale and he always smelled of cigarettes.

Eventually I left the confessional, said my penance and went home. I spent days wondering whether the 'That's not very holy' pronouncement was directed at the defacement of the book or at bullfighting. Eventually I decided, generally speaking, he'd meant the book, so I carried on looking up the Bs for bullfighting with a relatively clear conscience.

*

When I was about eleven years old one of my five sisters, Kate, the third eldest, went to Spain to teach English. I was incredibly impressed and her departure left a mark on me. I missed her terribly. She was one of the few people in the world I knew who owned a rucksack. This rucksack, an old green canvas affair that looked as if it had been to Tibet and back on some great adventurer's shoulders, had caught my imagination. I used to slip it on my back and imagine myself disappearing off over the horizon to somewhere very hot. On Saturday mornings, at a very early hour while everyone else slept, I stuffed the rucksack with old clothes and hitchhiked up and down the living-room while I watched Open University programmes. After my sister took this weatherbeaten rucksack to Spain, at last I knew for certain that it had been somewhere foreign. It could, in my mind, finally hold up its head amongst other rucksacks. Thereafter, I convinced myself that I could smell Spain off its fraying canvas and that the yellow stain on the bottom came from the bright sand of a bullring and not from the tin my father had used to paint the bathroom walls.

On one of her visits home from Madrid, Kate seemed to have changed. I couldn't put my finger on how or why, but from my child's perspective she seemed different. Different in a mysterious and very good way. Even her skin had changed after being exposed to sunshine for long periods. And you could tell that she was excited about all the new things she'd seen and done. She also spoke Spanish. I was dazzled by this ability and loved hearing her wrap her tongue around strange place-names, her Spanish friends' names and the peculiar phrases she'd picked up.

She'd brought me back some gifts, one of which was a colourful poster featuring three matadors: a guy called 'El Cordobés', someone called 'Paco Camino' and a third identified as 'Eamonn O'Neill'. I was speechless. For a moment or two I really thought there was a matador with the same name as me. Then I realised the poster had been specially made with my name on it. I thought I was the only person in the whole world that had one of these posters. I imagined her going to a very old, extremely dusty shop in a side-street in Madrid to meet the painter of this poster. Oil paints would have been lying all over the shop, half-finished paintings that he wasn't satisfied with would be strewn everywhere and empty bottles of wine would be stacked up against the peeling plaster on the walls. He'd been a very intelligent though humble and simple man, who was the fourth generation of his family to paint bullfighting posters. I envisaged her finally convincing him, after long deliberations and at great expense, to paint a poster just for her little brother. From that point on his life would be dedicated to producing the work of art which I now held in my hands.

In reality, of course, it hadn't happened like that. These posters were flogged outside every bullring in Spain by vendors with home-printing kits. Loads of people bought them ten-a-penny and brought them back to Scotland as cheap gifts. But to me that was beside the point. It looked exotic and my imagination was stirred. After quizzing my sister I discovered she'd even been to a real bullfight. I asked her all about it. She wasn't put off by the spectacle, at least not *too* much — in fact she'd even clapped at the end of it. She showed me a wineskin that she'd used to carry wine in when she'd gone to one of these bullfights. It smelled strange. In Scotland the only alcohol I'd smelled was stale beer and strong whisky. They had a flat, medicinal and, in my mind, menacing smell. This wineskin smelled different — more alive and sharp. The only other wine I'd smelled was the St Benedictine altar wine the priest used. A few altarboys, myself included, had taken a swig of it to see what it tasted like. I gagged and almost threw up. It reminded me of cough medicine. *Bad* cough medicine. No wonder the priest looked miserable every morning at early Mass. But the Spanish wine smelled very different and it evoked a whole other set of clichéd childish images in my mind — I thought of sunshine and mountains and beautiful women and people generally having a good time. I didn't know why, but I did.

Kate had also brought me another gift from Spain. It was a book called *Little Egret and Toro*. It had a wine-coloured hard cover and it told the story of a little bird and his friend the bull. The story made an impression on me and, like most of the books I read at a young age, it stuck in my mind. The most remarkable thing about it was the illustrations. They stayed in my mind and stirred my imagination. I loved drawing and I spent hours copying them — they showed bulls, matadors in their costumes and ancient, grand bullrings. I had never seen anything like them.

Years later I tried to find the book but someone in the family said they thought it had been thrown out when we'd moved.

A year or so later my parents announced we were going to Spain to visit Kate. I couldn't sleep for weeks with the excitement. And fear. The arrangements were all very serious and sombre. The whole trip seemed more of a risk than anything else. My folks bought a green nylon travelling bag for me and a new pair of training shoes. My travelling gear. I used to get up during the night to check that they were still at the bottom of my bed.

When we arrived at Madrid airport my mother blessed herself as the wheels touched the runway. On my way out of the airport I spoke my first words of Spanish to my sister's friends: 'I can't understand Spanish.'

I remember the heat of Madrid in April – a month I associated with windy walks across Edinburgh's North Bridge and gales blowing shoppers down Glasgow's Argyle Street. I remember the sun, brighter than anything I'd ever seen before, splashed across my parents' smiling faces. For the first time in my life I could imagine them much younger, as teenagers perhaps, free of cares and with a whole, bright future ahead of them. I remember the blaring horns in the city and labyrinth of side-streets in the small towns we visited. I remember the smooth olive skin of the women and their black hair. I remember going on a cable-car above Madrid and seeing people sunbathing on the roofs of their high-rise houses – I'd never seen real people wearing so few clothes before. It was a shock to see so much skin. I remember the colour of the sky – sapphire blue, with a black rim at the horizon at night. I remember walking down the city streets in the evening and dodging cascades of water as people above watered their window-box plants. I remember the bleached walls of castles and the cool interiors of churches in places like Toledo and Segovia. I remember a man in a restaurant showing me how to pour cider, bouncing it off the rim of his glass so that the sediment landed on the floor. Then I remember watching and listening to the dogs licking the remains of the cider and scraps of food off the tiles underneath our table.

I remember the cave next to the river where we had a picnic, eating fresh strawberries and watching lines of fat red ants march across our tablecloth. The cave was owned by the man who ran the tiny one-car ferry. He'd pulled us across, asking us where we came from. His heavy voice echoed down the deep, tree-lined avenue of the slow-moving river. Halfway across he asked me to touch his hands. They felt like chainmail. To prove how hard they were, he held his lit cigarette to one of them. It smouldered and burned but he never flinched – he just laughed a friendly, throaty laugh. Then he insisted we all visit his family in their cave. The entranceway had long strings with twisted metal bottle-caps on them. They rattled when we walked through them. We dutifully made our way inside and in the dimness found his staring, silent family sitting round a small dark bar. We drank freezing soft drinks in silence until he got up the courage to ask us for any foreign coins we had – 'My child collects them,' he muttered.

I remember the interior of a church in a tiny village somewhere high in the mountains outside Madrid. It was preserved in time. To reach it we had to walk up a very steep path. The place was cold and deserted. The sky was blue and the spring air frosty and chilled. There was not one local person to be seen in the whole village. We hauled open the doors of the church and went in, our footsteps echoing around the high, thick walls. At one end was a dripping altar, all effigies and waves of wax. My parents went off to inspect this. I was left alone. I hesitated for a moment, thinking about following them, and then I spied a large glass case at one end of a pillared corridor. It looked interesting. I approached it slowly, looking up at the green faces of the saints on the peeling walls, the flickering candles and the high, tiny stained-glass windows. I passed by the ancient, scabbed velvet kneelers which lined the walls, I stepped on the cracked tiles and spied the thick cobwebs in the high corners. As I neared the mysterious glass case, it seemed to grow bigger and bigger as I became smaller and smaller. I saw what looked like a figure inside it but I turned my head away. The case was on a high podium and the morning sun bounced off its polished glass. A large brass plaque was fixed to the side which was facing me. Standing on tiptoe I tried to read the inscription. But I couldn't. It was in Spanish. I ran my little fingers along it anyway, hoping its message would enter my brain somehow. Then I raised my head to look at the figure in the case. I knew I shouldn't have but I'd have been angry with myself if I hadn't at least stolen a quick glance at it. I gasped when I saw what it contained. I'd never seen anything remotely like it in all my life.

It held an embalmed human being.

He was probably a powerful provincial bishop, someone on the very edges of sainthood, a high holy man, preserved perfectly by some skilled neighbourhood undertaker, no doubt. Whoever he was, I didn't care. I was transfixed by his waxy profile, his luminous green hands with the polished rosary beads between the fingers and his thick, coal-black beard. I forced myself to look more closely at the figure's head. I hauled myself on to the edge of the podium and now looked directly down on the figure inside. I pressed my face against the glass. My heart thumped. My breathing became laboured. In a single still moment the man's face turned and looked straight at me. I could see his beard, his stitched mouth, his plugged nostrils and his black, dead, sightless eyes. It was probably more imagination than reality, but I didn't wait to find out.

Without a sound, I jumped off the podium, took to my heels and ran like hell without once looking back. All I could hear was the squeak of my new training shoes as I sprinted along the cold, polished marble floor.

And then I remember a place called Chinchón, somewhere outside Madrid. We went there for a day-trip. It was early afternoon when we arrived and everyone was having a siesta. We walked through the main square. A few workmen, oblivious to our presence, were banging and thumping, apparently doing some building. Anonymously, we walked around the town and peered in the little shop windows. No one was to be seen. We plodded up a back street, all shiny cobblestones of different shades of grey, until we came to a high white wall. We followed it up a steep hill at the top of which we finally reached the highest point in the town – the church. The holy place was square and solid, looking more like a cinema than a church, and its huge doors were blocked and shut. My father held me up to see over the high wall so I could look at the view back down on to the little town. The uneven roof tiles stretched out to the right and the left. A few TV aerials could be seen here and there. Little squadrons of starlings noisily swooped and dived above my head. But the most remarkable feature of the town was the place we'd just left – the tiny main square. When we'd been standing in it half an hour previously, it had looked just like a picture-postcard Spanish *plaza* with a fountain at one side of it and an old lamp-post in the middle. But from a height, from my vantage point in my father's arms in front of the church, I suddenly realised what it was the workmen were building. It was a *bullring*. The town square was being converted into a little arena by blocking up entrances and erecting walls and seats.

Later, as we were leaving the town, I saw a poster, not unlike the one I had on my bedroom wall at home, advertising a bullfight in Chinchón the following week. I was intrigued by the apparent spectacle of it all and I wished I could have stayed to see it. But I knew I'd never see the bullfight in Chinchón. A week later we'd be back home to Scotland. I'd be back at school in Lanarkshire. Back to wet bus-stops, back to sodden school uniforms, back to the early-morning clouds of cheap cigarette smoke coming from the back seat of the bus, back to carved initials on desks and back to long, freezing runs around the puddle-filled football pitch during PE classes.

But I'd left Chinchón and Spain with an unanswered question. For the duration of the whole journey home I wondered how the people of Chinchón could possibly hold a bullfight in the converted town square if it had a lamp-post in the middle. Surely that presented several problems? Perhaps the bull dodged around it, I thought. Or maybe the matador just avoided going near it. It might even be handy for the matador to use as an emergency escape route, I mused – he could climb up it if the bull became too dangerous. I pondered the question for weeks, then it slipped from my head as the schoolwork, the weather, the books, the TV and all the other realities of home in Scotland swept over my mind.

Later, like every teenager, I went through my James Dean phase. I bought the posters, watched the films, and I couldn't understand why people said he died at a young age. I thought twenty-five was *old*.

My father, himself a film fan, encouraged my interest in the actor. After I discovered the local library didn't have any books on James

Dean, Dad travelled into the city and bought me a large biography imported from the States. I read it from cover to cover in one sitting. There were some pretty amazing behind-the-scenes photographs in the book. One which caught my eye showed Dean practising passes using a real Spanish bullfighting cape. Apparently he was crazy about bullfighting – it was one of his biggest interests. The author said Dean's favourite book was Hemingway's *Death in the Afternoon*. He used to read it over and over again, underlining passages and making notes in the margins. He even had a set of bull's horns in his New York apartment and talked about the idea of dropping out of Hollywood and going to Spain to become a matador. Opposite a photograph of a dead matador Dean had written: 'God gave James Dean so many gifts to share with the world, has he the right to throw them away in the bullring?' He died a few weeks after he wrote these words.

The actor's work and his disturbed life intrigued me for a while. Then, like most phases, it ended. Quietly, and for no apparent reason, I stopped reading about him and no longer watched his movies. I found I had other things on my mind; so the books on James Dean were shoved to one side and I replaced him with my Judo phase.

Nearly a decade later I graduated from university and promptly became very ill. I couldn't look at bright lights, I had ferocious headaches and my temperature shot up. I shook a lot. I constantly had very strange and fevered dreams. Loud noises hurt my head. I lay in bed for weeks on end unable to do anything for myself. All I could do was sleep, wake up for a little while, then sleep again. Eventually I was taken into hospital. The doctors tested me for some very serious illnesses but weren't sure what was wrong with me. I asked if I could leave. 'Well, we can't really keep you in here – but we'd prefer to have you stay so we can get to the bottom of what's making you ill. And make no mistake about it, you *are* ill. It's not in your head,' said an older doctor who was doing the rounds.

I felt I would be safer in the hospital but I was too confused and sleepy to make a decision. I tried to clear my head by reading a little. On my bedside cabinet were two books. One was Ernest

Hemingway's collection of short stories, *Men Without Women*; the other was a book about Spain called *A Rose for Winter* by Laurie Lee. I had been reading Hemingway's short stories for some time. My foggy, melted-down brain appreciated his clear writing. The opening story of his collection, *The Undefeated*, was about a bullfighter called Manuel García. I was captivated by the mysterious, slightly sinister world of bullfighting which this story allowed the reader to glimpse. Laurie Lee's book on Spain was different. His soft, poetic prose lulled me and sent me to sleep. One chapter told of how he fell ill in Spain – almost dying, in fact – but something happened which caused him to make a miraculous recovery. I wished a similar spontaneous burst of energy would get me out of the bed which I seemed to be getting more used to by the hour. At the back of my mind I secretly worried that I was getting worse instead of better and feared that I would not leave the hospital alive.

The doctors asked me if I'd travelled abroad recently – especially to the Far East. They seemed concerned about tropical diseases. I said I'd only been to Ireland and had stayed in a youth hostel. They said people picked up diseases in places like that where lots of different nationalities converged. Had I kissed anyone I didn't know, they asked. I said I had met a girl and I had kissed her. They reckoned I might have an acute case of glandular fever – also known as the 'kissing disease'. Then they grew more sombre. They began ruling things out. My condition seemed to be worsening instead of improving. I wasn't responding to all the antibiotics I was taking. I had heard the word 'meningitis' whispered when a senior doctor and some students came round to examine me; I knew someone my age had died from the same condition a week earlier. He'd simply fallen ill and had gone to bed to try to sleep it off – I'd thought of doing exactly the same thing myself – but he'd never woken up. He'd been found dead a few days later, killed by the virus in his own bed. I was scared out of my wits. But whenever I tried to tell anyone about my fears, they just said that I was in the right place.

I couldn't get rid of the headaches which shattered my brain whenever I looked at bright lights. My senses seemed heightened. Even my skin felt sore to the touch. I rubbed my aching arms so much I ended up with purple bruises under the skin. The darkness of the night was better – there were no lights. But I suffered from endless panic attacks then too. Cold sweats plagued me for hours. Time froze. Some nights seemed dangerously long, as if the minutes had been stretched like elastic by God. One hour lasted four. Headlong rushes of adrenaline swamped my brain. Nothing like this had ever happened to me before. Sometimes I felt as though I was living in a speeded-up film, while at other times everything just slipped off the rails and came to a painful drowsy stop. The only reference points I had for what I was feeling were in the books I'd read before I'd fallen ill. From Hemingway's stories about bullfighters I knew that they suffered the night-time horrors as well. In the brightness of daylight, underneath a white sun, they were brave and fearless. At night, when the sun had gone down and the crowds had trailed off home, the matadors went to pieces and fell apart. Some played cards or lay on top of their beds with the lights on rather than face the spectres brought on by the dark.

The doctors asked me to pull on their arms to test my strength, and to take deep breaths so they could listen to my chest. They tested my blood. I was also given more pills – lots and lots of yellow tablets, mainly antibiotics. I felt very weak. My head ached and throbbed. I found myself asking for more and more painkillers but was usually told I'd had my limit for the day. I could hardly see straight and my ribs and back and neck were in agony. When my dad came to visit me I had to ask him to change my socks for me. I couldn't even sit up and do it myself. I could tell he was angry with the doctors for not getting to the bottom of what was wrong with me. When I saw him trying to conceal his concern I began to panic and feel sorry for myself. One of the nurses looking after me had been in my class at high school and I was embarrassed when she saw me lying in bed with no strength and tears in my eyes. But throughout the time I was under her care she acted as if I was a complete stranger. I was grateful.

Eventually I couldn't even read without my mind spinning off into an anxious spiral. But I clung on to my books, hoping one day I'd be well enough to see the places those authors had written about. Memories of that visit to Spain when I was younger and the ideas I'd had about bullfighting since I was first told the animals chased big red bathtowels floated about in my head intermingled with all the images Hemingway and Laurie Lee had conjured up. They weren't normal dreams, though. They were more vivid, the visions spurred on by illness and drugs and terror.

Then something happened . . .

In the bed next to me was a man with a very bad chest complaint. He knew my father and I'd met him once when I was a little boy. He was a very nice man and recognised me and my dad when I first arrived in the hospital. He could hardly breathe, however. His thin body convulsed and wracked every time he tried to take a breath. It was painful to watch.

The strong tablets I was taking made me slip in and out of a deep sleep. Every time I woke up this man looked worse. The nurses were very good to him . . . attending him regularly and calming him down when his oxygen mask slipped off. He panicked whenever this happened. You could see from the look on his face that he was terrified of dying. His pyjamas were too big for him and he had to try and hold them on and keep the oxygen mask up to his mouth at the same time. But he was determined not to go without putting up a fight. I felt really sorry for him. At one point he signalled to me – I thought he wanted the newspaper at the foot of his bed but no, he just wanted to know someone was near by. He grabbed my hand until his eyes were able to focus on me. I could see the whiteness of his bones and the pulsing veins in his hands when he clawed at me. His ribs looked like thin sticks of bamboo which might twist and crack at any moment. His chalk-white skin was as thin as rice-paper. The only part of him which looked healthy was his thick mop of blue-black hair.

He tried to speak to me. I couldn't make out what he was saying so I moved closer. He briefly took the mask off and, pointing to my little library on the cabinet, said: 'Books . . . great thing, eh? I . . . like . . . the . . . reading . . . myself!'

He smiled and held the mask at his face again. I nodded. Then he wheezed. It took him a good few moments to catch his breath again. He took the mask off and gestured towards the books, still determined to hold a conversation.

'Hemingway . . . some man! Healthy man!' Then he took another deep breath.

I nodded.

He relaxed somewhat and lay back down on the bed in the foetal position. I could clearly see his thin shoulders through the threadbare hospital pyjamas as his body heaved up and down trying to get a deep, satisfying breath. By this time he'd almost curled himself up into a ball at the foot of the bed. His hands pinned the mask to his mouth and his eyes rolled back in their sockets.

I watched him breathing heavily for a few minutes then I turned and looked away. I smelled something odd, a sweet, heavy, unpleasant odour. It made me feel sick. I was convinced that it came from the poor guy next to me. I tried to breathe through my mouth and not through my nose so I wouldn't have to smell it. Within a short time I'd fallen asleep again.

I thought I heard a drawer slam shut. There was a commotion. I woke up and looked at the next bed. The man was turning blue. His face was twisted and contorted. He had his hands outstretched. His eyes had rolled back again. When he blinked all you could see was white. He was in terrible, silent pain.

I shouted for a nurse.

The man clawed his way to the foot of the bed and began thrashing around. He was fighting death. He scraped at the bedclothes until the cover came loose and you could see the rubber sheet underneath. And he punched the metal railing and grabbed at his neck and his chest. He was trying to pull the breath out of his lungs with his own two hands.

'Quick! He's turning blue!' I screamed at the nurse who'd appeared.

'He's dying . . .' she said matter-of-factly as she drew a curtain around his bed.

Then I did an odd thing: I grabbed my books and pulled them into bed beside me. God knows why. Perhaps I hoped they'd keep me alive. I closed my eyes and said a prayer for the old man.

He was dead within minutes. The curtain didn't stretch far enough around the bed to cover him up, so after he died I could still see his face. His mouth was wide open, as if screaming silently, and his eyes stared straight at me. My head pounded and I wanted to bury myself under the pillow where it was dark, where the bright lights wouldn't hurt my eyes and where I could go to sleep and not wake up for years.

A short time later I heard the dead man's relatives whispering behind the curtain. They were talking to a nurse, asking her for some advice. Obviously they were in great distress. But they also faced another predicament. A benefit concert had been planned for that night by some local people to raise enough money to take him to Lourdes. The relatives now feared the show would be cancelled and that they wouldn't receive any money if people knew he was dead. The nurse shrugged sympathetically and left them to sort it out amongst themselves.

I thought about Laurie Lee sitting bolt upright in his sick-bed like a man who'd been resurrected from the dead. He'd spied the spectre of death at the foot of his bed in the form of his wife already dressed in mourning. Like a bolt from the heavens, it was enough to shock him back into life again.

Then I looked over at the face of the poor fellow in the next bed and my wits jumped. I'd just witnessed an act of God. And I didn't want to hang about to see another one.

Against the wishes of a screeching nurse who implored me not to go, I fell out of bed, dressed myself, packed my books and almost ran out of the ward. When my family arrived to visit me I was standing waiting for them with a packed bag. They told me later that I was grinning like a lunatic who'd just escaped from an asylum. My father was proud of me for walking out of the place. I didn't care what I looked like. Okay, so my head thumped and the daylight hurt my eyes, but at least my nostrils were clear of the awful odour I'd smelled in the hospital. The air outside was fresh and clean. I stared out of the car all the way home, unsettled by how green the grass looked and how amazing the wind felt on my skin. I was furious with myself for not noticing, or having the ability to notice, any of this before.

I went home and slept twenty hours a day for several months until bright lights didn't hurt me any more.

The panic and terror, however, stayed with me much, much longer. Then they too slowly subsided, like one season shading imperceptibly into the next.

Years later I met Laurie Lee for lunch in London at the Chelsea Arts Club. A lot of people came up to him to shake his hand and give him a kiss. He said he knew none of them. One man claimed they'd met in a certain bar in the Far East. Laurie listened to him patiently, even recalling the meeting with great pleasure, then waved him off: 'What a nice fellow! Never met him in my life, though. I've never been to that place he mentioned in my life either. Still, easy to get confused. There are a lot of Lees in the Far East phonebooks, I'm sure!'

His jersey was on inside out and back to front. He instructed me to order a sandwich on the menu which was named after him – a 'Laurie Special', it was called.

Sitting in the club's beer garden later, I told him about my illness, the Spanish books in the hospital bedside cabinet and my sudden, Lazarus-like recovery – similar to his own – when I saw my own spectre of death in the bed next to me. I said I felt I owed him a debt of thanks or something, hence the lunch.

He smiled and said: 'No, my book didn't cure you, any more than Hemingway's did.' Then he leaned forward and, like a retired British spy who may or may not have remained always loyal to the crown, he whispered quietly: 'It was *Spain* that did the trick. Yes! It gave you something to look forward to. If you want to thank me, then thank Spain. And when you find the time, write about it . . .'

I scratched my head and, feeling slightly confused, promised him I would. Until he suggested I go to Spain, I had seen our meeting as being a sort of full-stop to the whole thing: never for one moment did I think it would lead to a whole new chapter – a chapter which I was required to write. But from then on I started to think about it.

Naïvely, I asked him if he'd any advice for me or my writing. I suppose I was hoping he'd wave a magic wand of some sort, maybe direct me to a few literary short-cuts that only a few insiders knew even existed.

There was a pause.

Full of expectation, I watched him slowly as he collected his thoughts. His eyes twinkled and, after a few minutes, he raised an eyebrow. He'd reached a conclusion. But before any words escaped from his mouth he lifted a finger to his lips and, checking to make sure none of the bar staff were watching him, he slyly pulled a little fat bottle of ale out of a plastic bag he'd sneaked into the club.

In silence he carefully began opening it underneath the table. When he'd successfully unscrewed the top, he nodded towards my empty glass. Joining in the subterfuge, I looked around and then discreetly lifted up the tumbler so he could pour some beer into it.

He broke the silence and proposed a grand toast to Spain. We clinked glasses and gulped down our drinks.

'Advice . . .?' He pondered the word for a moment. Then he gestured for me to lean a little bit closer to him.

I shifted to the edge of my wicker seat as he warily looked around to make sure no one was listening to our conversation.

He winked and give me a deranged throaty chuckle: 'It's worth remembering just one thing . . . Writers should *always* look poor.'

THREE

A Very Spanish Gesture

After watching the young would-be matadors, John Fulton and I drove back into Seville.

The wide road into the city was packed with cars. Another afternoon's siesta had ended. Everyone had surfaced again, and the part of the day Spaniards in general and Andalucians in particular love most – evening – was just beginning. Elbows hung out of windows and puffs of cigarette smoke floated in the air. Most of the drivers – men and women – wore very stylish designer sunglasses.

John Fulton told me more about how he'd become infatuated with bullfighting as a youth in America. 'I told my parents I wanted to be a bullfighter after I saw that film – *Blood and Sand* – but they just patted me on the head and said, "Yeah, that's nice." But the idea got into my head; in bullfighting we call it "the bullfighting worm". It's a worm that enters your brain through your retina and it eats out the inside of your brain so that the only thing you can think about is fighting bulls. And that's what happened to me – it changed the course of my life.'

He went on to explain how he went to the local library to read up on bullfighting. The only book he could find on the subject was Ernest Hemingway's *Death in the Afternoon* – the same book that had intrigued and captured James Dean's imagination. A dense *magnum opus*, it guides the reader through Hemingway's very personal, though extremely comprehensive, view of the world of bullfighting as it was in the 1930s.

'When my friends were playing football and baseball in a sandlot,

I was down in my basement with an old curtain imitating the photographs, the poses of the matadors that had illustrated Hemingway's book. Later on I met and fell in love with a girl who was a flamenco dancer – I figured that in the movie *Blood and Sand* Anthony Quinn and Rita Hayworth dance a kind of Spanish *paso doble* and I figured, well, if I'm going to be a matador it would be an interesting thing to know how to do, in case I bump into a Rita Hayworth somewhere along the line. So I decided to take dancing lessons and this girl and I danced together professionally as a team. Usually we worked with records and a piano but we got into the real flamenco stuff. The first day we went to practise in the barber shop of a Spaniard who lived in south Philadelphia. He'd been an aspiring bullfighter in his youth. His shop was full of bullfight posters and photographs of famous matadors. When I walked in, I said, "This is what I want to do – I don't want to be a dancer!" So he gave me my first bullfighting lessons with a barber's cloth in 2nd and South Street in south Philadelphia.'

By this time John also had a full art scholarship. He'd studied painting and illustration for three and a half years in Philadelphia before heading down to Mexico in 1953 where, dressed as a matador for the first time, he killed his very first bull in a *plaza de toros*. Later, while doing military service and stationed close to the Mexican border, Fulton was able to escape south to fight bulls on weekend passes from his army base. He saved his military pay and in March 1956 sailed for Algeciras in Spain on a one-way ticket. He had only $400 in his pocket.

'I was determined that I was going to become a matador and live in Seville. I left my home, I left my country, my culture, my family, my girlfriend, my job, my work; I chucked it all in for one thing: to become a matador. It's a very Spanish gesture, actually; it's like Cortez riding on the coast of Mexico and unloading his troops and burning his ships – there was no turning back. I found out that this was a very, very difficult profession to break into, even for a Spanish kid. But for an American with no money it was just that much harder . . . I stayed here and started going to the *tientas* with the other Spanish boys and sat on the wall hoping to get a chance to get a few passes. And that's how I started out. It took me eight years as a *novillero* to graduate to the rank of full matador, which I did in the bullring here in Seville. In 1963 I was graduated to the rank of full matador in the Maestranza bullring in Seville, which is to bullfighting what La Scala is to opera. For an American to reach the rank of full matador in this bullring would be like having an Australian Aborigine signed to sing all of the leads in a season at La Scala. It was practically impossible but I did it.'

The bulls that John Fulton faced on the day of his graduation were enormous even by Spanish standards. The first was 503 kilos, the second a massive 576 kilos. The latter was described by one critic as a 'veritable cathedral' of a bull. A leading American bullfighting commentator later wrote: 'Soon he had the arena of 13,000 people chanting "olé" in unison as he mastered the bull's swerving attacks and made it charge straight and true time after time. Then he killed the animal with a fine sword thrust, and the crowd applauded until Fulton walked out to the centre ring and bowed in acknowledgement. He was crying with joy and fulfilment and exhaustion.'

But that afternoon of triumph, and the others which followed, simply weren't enough. John's career never got going for one simple, maddening reason: he wasn't a *Spaniard.*

John explained: 'In Spain in general I was up against a real problem. The American base programme had just started here and the social strata of the military is not always the best, so the average Spaniard on the street who perhaps as a child lived through the Civil War, the Second World War, the Isolation – you know Spain was never helped by the Marshall Plan or given much money to rebuild after the war – suddenly found that his country had American air bases in it, he felt that Spain had been invaded by a hostile military force. So when an American tried to invade the bullring it was almost more than they could handle, so the opportunities for me to fight were not very abundant . . . When you walk into a bullring and your name is on a card so-and-so and "John Fulton – the American", the public immediately conjure up an idea of what an American in the bullring is going to be like; and even if you did it well, it was a culture shock to them – they couldn't accept it. If you were brave they could recognise that, and they could recognise your technical abilities, but you would never receive the unbridled enthusiasm and the unconditional support that even the worst Spaniard stumblebum would have had.'

Most men would have cracked up. The bottle would have beckoned. Early grave time. Or buy a pub and settle into the world of telling yarns to bar-stool fantasists until the first, and probably last, big heart attack.

Others would have left Spain and never looked back – except in their private dreams riddled with doubts and nightmares of what could have been. The dreams of youth suddenly metamorphosed into the unmentionable secret of their past: The Period of Failure. But none of that seemed to have happened to John Fulton.

'I was treated the way I should have expected to be treated if I'd understood the problems involved. I felt I was treated badly. Because in bullfighting if you have a good performance that should mean that you get a repeat performance and more money – at least another fight, another opportunity to show what you can do. And it seemed in my case that every time I did well, I was never repeated, my merits were never acknowledged. And so there was no continuity in my fighting. If I had been a Spanish kid, a Spanish novice who had accomplished some of the things I'd accomplished, it would have set up a continuity and more fights and more repetition which would have meant more development. Bullfighting's like anything else – it's practice, repetition, so that you can improve. But if there's no continuity it's always like fighting your first fight every time. I've had seasons where I fought once in March and once in October. I can guarantee that if you took any of the Spanish stars of my period, the top matadors, and gave them two fights – one in March and one in October – I doubt they would have done any better than I did. But they probably wouldn't have accepted the last fight in October because they'd have known that they hadn't fought all season, so the chances of them doing well would be severely limited. But I had no choice; I had to accept whatever came down the pike, and I was often forced into a premature début, in somewhere like Madrid, and you know it had fairly disastrous results. But I was determined to do the thing and I did it.'

To survive during the lean periods, John had to do most of his eating in the little tapas bars that were (and still are) dotted around Seville and every other Spanish town you can think of. Even then, his meals were taken standing up at the bar – food is cheaper if you don't occupy a table or take up a stool.

Many who knew him thought Fulton's future was in art as opposed to bullfighting. In a sense they were right – not because John didn't have what it took to become a rich and successful matador but because, as Fulton himself had told me, he simply never got enough breaks in the bullfighting industry. Because fights were hard for him to come by, he began making a living of sorts by selling sketches of bulls and matadors to tourists. Soon he was almost as well known for his first-rate artwork as he was for his bullfighting. Thus, almost by default, he fell back on his artistic skills and in time became a respected and relatively well-off professional artist. He acquired a stunning little building on the tourist trail a few hundred yards from the cathedral in the centre of Seville and turned it into his own art gallery. His work soon appeared in collections all over the world. But he never wavered from his goal of grasping any opportunity that came along to prove himself in the bullring. And when he got the chance, that's exactly what he did. He held his own, and more, alongside the finest that the country had to offer. The legend of John Fulton, the man who came to Spain and proved a non-Spaniard could, when given the chance, fight bulls with the best of them, had begun.

'I'm something of a mini-institution now. People come to Seville to track me down and buy into the whole "John Fulton thing" . . .' he said, laughing ruefully. 'There's even a photo of me standing next to Elvis Presley on the Internet. We were snapped together when I visited him on a movie set in Hollywood. I'd forgotten all about it. I don't know who put it there. Someone sent it to me recently.'

The last time John Fulton faced a bull as a *matador de toros* was on 2 April 1994 in San Miguel de Allende in Mexico. He was sixty-two years old. His second-last bull during a series of farewell fights was a disappointment – the crowd were hostile to the ageing American matador as he tried to get the bull under control. But with his last fight he managed to turn the whole occasion around. He dedicated the bull to his adopted gypsy son Federico and then set about turning in a fine performance – one that various people I'd spoken to were still talking about years later. Friends of John's had flown in from all over the world to see his last fight – known as *la despedida*. Wearing a suit of wine and gold which he'd designed himself (John had revolutionised the matador's so-called 'suit of lights' years before when he designed lighter, more comfortable suits; the heavily embroidered outfit glistens in the sunlight, hence its name), he managed to dominate the bull and kill it cleanly. It was an afternoon of triumph which ended with John being awarded the prizes of two bull's ears and being carried out of the ring. The entire stadium rose to its feet to applaud his courage and his career. Then, in a simple, moving ceremony, John's symbolic pigtail – his *coleta*, which all bullfighters have and which they attach to their own hair with a clasp – was cut off by his son Federico. His years as a matador had officially ended.

John and I had talked for half an hour during our journey back from the hacienda where we'd seen the young matadors training. We eventually arrived in Seville and he pulled over in front of my hotel. The air outside was burning and the street was already packed with people strolling up and down. The cafés were doing brisk trade and the taxis were now revving up their engines in an effort to look more businesslike. Swarms of noisy scooters buzzed by, driven by the bronzed youth of Seville.

'Come round to my gallery tomorrow morning and we'll talk again,' said John. I thanked him for his hospitality and patience in answering all my questions.

But just before I waved him off for the evening I had to ask him: 'Have you any regrets?'

He thought for a moment. Then he shook his head. He smiled and shrugged: 'I have no regrets. I just wish that I knew then what I know now. I would have done things differently. But I have no regrets.'

We shook hands and he drove off. I watched his car melt into the sounds and smells and sights of the gathering pace of the evening city.

FOUR

Indefensible but Irresistible

'¡*Vino!* ¡*Vino!*' screamed the middle-aged woman at her crippled, rumpled old husband. 'Drink it up! All of it! It's your *vino*. Look . . . ¡*Vino!* ¡*Vino!*'

The old man was the owner of a tourist shop near Seville's cathedral. It was mid-morning and he was unwilling or unable to down his first drink of wine that day. His wife was doing her damnedest to make sure he swallowed it. Finally, after much shrieking and thumping of her podgy fist on the counter top, she gave up. She plonked the baby's bottle full of wine down on the table in front of him. 'Take it or leave it! I don't care!' Then she vanished into the back room where some mysterious cooking smells were coming from.

The very instant she left, the old man grabbed the bottle and started guzzling. Then he fixed his gaze one me. I was hovering about in the background, eyeing up old postcards whose edges curled up. I smiled at him but he didn't respond. I didn't have the patience to try and buy one of the postcards nor did I have the heart to summon the woman from the place of the odd smells, so I left as quietly and unobtrusively as I'd entered.

To avoid the morning heat, I ducked into the city's famous cathedral across the *plaza*. When my eyes had adjusted to the darkness I stared around in bewilderment. It was a testament to my religion's power and arrogance. The builders who had expressed the wish to create 'a building on so magnificent a scale that posterity will believe we were mad' had, in my mind at least, succeeded with room to spare. My guidebook said that 'the total area covered 11,520 square metres, and new calculations based on cubic measurement had now pushed it in front of St Paul's in London and St Peter's in Rome as the largest church in the world, verified by the *Guinness Book of Records*'.

Mass was being said as I entered the cathedral. I stood on the edge of the service, watching the proceedings. A hook-nosed bishop in silk robes rumbled on in a bored voice, pleading with the crowd like a bad actor. He was ensconced in a huge throne of gold which glistened in the blue light from the windows. The blank-faced worshippers, all heavy eyelids and thick black hair, stood in silence listening to him. Apart from the hum of the far-off traffic, the only other sound was the slicing of the muggy air by the fans flicked by the women in the congregation. They sounded like echoes from the flapping wings of birds as they tried to take off on a still silent summer's morning.

I left the holy man and his flock and wandered over to see the huge nineteenth-century monument to Christopher Columbus. He'd been one of my heroes when I was a child. Four figures representing the Spanish kingdoms of Leon, Castille, Aragon and Navarra held up the golden coffin containing the explorer's remains.

Columbus died in 1506 and that should have been the end of his story. But, for nearly four centuries at least, he didn't rest in what you'd call eternal peace. More like a state of perpetual motion, if the legends are to be believed. According to various sources I'd come across, Columbus's bones initially went on their own journey for three years or so – no one is exactly sure where they went or why – before returning back to Seville in roughly 1509. Thus, it seemed, he'd finally come back home – but not for long. That was only the beginning. Around 1544 his remains surfaced in what's now called the Dominican Republic. Then they were spotted in Havana, but they didn't last long there either – Cuban independence was declared seven years later and Columbus's bones were on the move again. Finally, in 1899, his remains slowly made their way back across the Atlantic to their alleged final resting-place in Seville's cathedral. What's inside the monument I examined is really anybody's guess. Someone told me the golden coffin only had an arm and a foot in it.

I left the cool of the cathedral and headed for John Fulton's gallery. It was hot. The local carriage drivers were hanging about with their horses. They made vague attempts to drum up business but they didn't seem too enthusiastic. One was fast asleep under an awning. The rest went through the motions of showing their price list to anybody who would listen. A young woman walked around trying to hand out leaflets for a flamenco show later that night. No one seemed interested and she looked fed-up.

I headed up a small side-street next to the Alcázar, the former Moorish stronghold, and entered the tiny Plaza de la Alianza where John Fulton had his studio and gallery. A painted sign outside showed a matador holding paintbrushes and a palette. The gallery itself was built of brick and plaster and was painted the twin colours of Spain, red and yellow. Two bushy orange trees stood guard outside. John had tied a few of his posters around the tree trunks to entice customers inside. I found him in a back office on the telephone. While he chatted I looked around the walls. One display in particular was all about John's bullfighting career. It comprised various articles from magazines and newspapers from over the years and from all across the world. Photographs showed John as a skinny, hungry young matador. Some were from American magazines in the '60s and '70s, while others came from British, Irish and French newspapers. A separate display depicted him two decades later during his farewell bullfight in Mexico. There he was showing a large Mexican bull his cape, the animal had its head all the way down, entranced by the cloth. John defiantly stood back with his hand on his hip, a slightly incongruous-looking grey-haired figure, but still managing to appear graceful and in control. These pictures were taken in 1994 when he was in his early sixties – an age at which most men worry more about their lack of hair or about their pension funds or the form of the Saturday-morning golf game than about whether they're in good enough shape to face and kill a bull with style and poise.

One of John's friends, a 51-year-old ex-matador called Curro Comacho, worked at the gallery. When I visited he was seeing off some tourists who had been purchasing a couple of prints. He came over and introduced himself. When he learned I was a journalist he produced a beautiful book that had been written

INDEFENSIBLE BUT IRRESISTIBLE

about him a decade or so ago. At one point he'd been something of a star in the bullfighting world. The book was illustrated with black-and-white photographs of Curro when he was a younger, fitter man. I leafed through it. All around me were works of art by John Fulton: illustrations for bullfighting posters, prints of famous now-dead matadors and sketches of bullfighters in action. The walls were filled with the colours John predominantly used – reds, pinks, blacks and greys and yellows. Curro then pointed to one painting of a matador. I recognised it immediately. It was a painting John had done of Curro himself. There he was, years before, dressed in a somewhat angelic-looking suit of lights. He was gazing up at an icon of the Virgin Mary whose back was turned to the viewer. She stood on a plinth made from the horns of a bull. A pink flower was on the table and a tall, dusty candle burned on the right of the scene. It was a sombre, serious, almost sinister work. Curro pointed to the horns at the bottom of the icon and shook his head.

Just then John Fulton emerged from his office. He saw us looking at Curro's portrait. 'Do you like it?' he asked.

'It's wonderful,' I replied.

'I painted this for Curro just before his *Alternativa* – his graduation to the rank of full matador. I didn't give it to him for a while – I wasn't happy with the composition, so I fiddled with it until I got it right. Then I showed it to him. He went nuts. "Look at it! That's how I got the goring! You gave me the goring!" he said. I asked him what he meant and he pointed out that I'd painted him praying in front of the icon but the tip of the bull's horn was touching his shoulder in my painting. It was that shoulder he was gored in during his fight!' John smiled and shrugged.

'Do you believe that?' I asked Curro.

He smiled and looked at John. 'Maybe! I'm a bit superstitious.'

'Are *you* superstitious, John?'

'No,' he said categorically. 'The one and only time I prayed to the Virgin at an altar I was injured. Never again!'

Curro was still looking at his portrait with an uncertain expression on his face.

I asked John about a couple of other paintings I'd seen in the gallery. They showed muscular leaping bulls – nothing unusual there except that they seemed to be painted in a very odd substance. I'd never seen anything like it before. 'That brown paint you used – it's strange – it looks like gravy.'

'Close. It's bull's blood,' smiled John.

'Why do you use bull's blood?'

'That's what the original Spanish cave paintings of bulls were done in. I get it from the local slaughterhouse. Lots of people buy these pictures – they're very popular.'

I spotted a small, slightly forlorn-looking ink sketch of a bull hanging high up in a corner of the gallery. I peered at it. It seemed very familiar for some reason.

'Want to see it?' asked Curro.

'Sure,' I said.

He lifted it down for me to examine.

'This reminds me of the illustrations from a book that I once had – it was one of the first things that actually intrigued me about the world of bullfighting. My sister brought it back from Spain for me.'

'What age were you when you read it?' asked John.

'I don't know, I was only a young boy. It was called *Little Egret and Toro*, that much I do recall. I lost it. Anyway, this illustration reminds me of the ones in that book.'

John smiled and asked to be excused for a moment. He had some business to attend to in his office. I chatted to Curro as he hung the little sketch back up.

'How long were you a full-time matador, Curro?'

'Seven years. Hard years. Very busy. My last bullfight was in 1982 . . .' He descended the small stepladder.

'Has it changed much since you were fighting?'

'Yes, oh yes. The kids nowadays are crazy. They fight too much – night after night all over Spain. They really risk their necks. When I was young, I was brave, too, I'd take on anything. Now when I look at what they do, I think to myself, "Boy, they must be nuts!"' He smiled and shook his head.

John reappeared and handed me a package. Both he and Curro were smiling. I opened the parcel and examined the contents. It was a copy of *Little Egret and Toro*.

'A friend of mine wrote it and I was the illustrator. That sketch on the wall you recognised is from the book.'

There was a pause while I turned the book over in my hands. I thanked him for the gift.

'Let's go and see a bullring,' said John.

The late-morning sun blazed down on us. Everything was washed in its hard white light. The air was fresh and clean. Later in the day it would become pungent, but at that hour it still smelled new and scrubbed.

We walked from John's gallery, in the most beautiful part of Seville, the Barrio de Santa Cruz, past the cathedral and along the riverfront. Ten minutes or so later we reached the Plaza de Toros de la Maestranza. From the outside, it looked nothing special. You might take it to be a medium-sized concert hall or opera house. Nothing gave away its history as one of the foremost bullrings in the world. Next to the gate, a lanky, leathery-faced man in his fifties was trying to hawk postcards to the tourists who arrived by the busload. But he was out of luck and he knew it. No one was interested. He shrugged his shoulders and leaned against the wall, saving his strength for the long day ahead.

An official tour of the bullring was being organised when we arrived. It was all a noisy commotion. Dutch, French, American and English tourists lined up behind a beautiful guide named Sylvia. She was a law student taking a summer break from her studies to show people around the bullring and the museum. John Fulton knew the man in charge of the tours and, with a nod and a wink, he was allowed to lead me through privately. It was cool inside the building. We passed along a series of tunnels until eventually we emerged into blinding sunlight. The ring itself was spectacular, although smaller than I'd imagined it would be. Nevertheless, the huge bed of golden sand was very impressive. The yellow and white stone arches swept around the entire structure making it look like a gigantic birthday cake. Behind me stood the royal box. Its balcony overlooked the entire area and gave its occupants the best view in the house.

'This is where I took my *Alternativa*, the place I became a full matador.' John leaned against the wooden wall next to the stand. 'For me, this place is like a temple, a cathedral where Mass is being said . . . or something.'

'Why do you think bullfighting is still so popular? This place is presumably packed out when the bullfights, *corridas*, are on and there are enough tourists here today – what's the attraction watching an animal being killed?' I asked John.

'It's indefensible but irresistible,' he answered. 'It's been around in Spain and other parts of Europe for centuries. If you go to the caves at Altamira you'll see ancient paintings on the walls done in bull's blood like the ones I do in my studio. Palaeolithic Man did those. There are places in France too which have similar examples. Bulls to those guys represented more than just meat – they were ferocious forces of nature which had to be dominated. Men proved themselves by killing them. And plenty of humans would have died in the process, no doubt. The respect for the beasts transformed itself into cults – men literally worshipped the bull's strength. Bull cults pop up everywhere – Crete, Egypt, France, Greece and, of course, here in Spain. The Romans had a Sun-Bull religion called Mithraism. Symbols of Mithras killing a bull have been discovered in every corner of the Roman Empire. December 25th, the great Mithraic celebration of the birth of the sun, became Christmas, the birthday of Jesus. In Spain there is an argument to be made that the two religions fused. This new Christianity and the old symbolic sacrificing of bulls co-existed. They even turned it into a Christian "Good versus Evil" thing – the first theological definition of the Devil issued in AD447 by the Council of Toledo stated that the Devil is "a large black monstrous apparition with horns on its head, cloven hoofs, fair, fiery eyes, terrible teeth, an immense phallus and a sulphurous smell". Sounds like a Spanish fighting bull to me! Add to that a dash of the Roman gladitorial arena and you've got the beginnings of bullfighting. Look at this . . .' He swept his hand around the expanse before us. 'It's a Roman arena.'

I looked around the bullring. Most of the tourists had cleared off by now. I had to agree. The *plaza de toros* did indeed resemble an empty Roman arena – Kirk Douglas could have appeared at any moment, shouting, 'I am Spartacus!' and he wouldn't have looked out of place.

'The gladiators even wore pigtails – that was their caste mark – and that's roughly what matadors still wear today. Julius Caesar, for God's sake, was the first person to introduce gladiators fighting bulls in the

Coliseum of Rome! Go and visit the ring in Ronda; it's the oldest in Spain and it was originally a Roman arena. When the Moors arrived in Spain they just kept the whole thing going. Hunted bulls in arenas on horseback. When Christianity became dominant again even the Popes, the most powerful men in the Western world, couldn't stop bullfighting. Not that they didn't try: in the sixteenth century Pope Sixtus V banned the clergy from attending bullfights. They protested angrily and the Holy Father received a written protest from the University of Salamanca and supported by the King of Spain, Philip II, which said: "The fiesta is in the Spanish blood, and we cannot take it away without serious repercussions." Those words could have been written yesterday – they're still as valid as they were 400 years ago.'

We walked over to the so-called Gate of Fear, the wooden gate out of which the bull comes running when the *corrida* begins. I looked down the darkened tunnel, trying to imagine what it looks like from both the matador's and the bull's perspective.

'In the old days they killed the bulls from horseback. Their helpers moved the bulls around the ring into position with a dragged cape – it didn't take a genius to see *this* was a more entertaining spectacle. The crowd loved it. The ordinary guy with the cape, the helper, looked braver than the nobleman on the horse. By the mid-eighteenth century it seems men on foot had picked up the art of controlling the bull with the cape and then killing it with a sword. A gentleman from Seville called Loaquin Rodriguez Costillares who worked in a slaughterhouse is credited with having invented the basic pass with the cape, called the *Veronica*, and the fast *volapié* method of killing. He may also have been the first person to wear fancy, embroidered costumes.

When you go to Ronda you'll also find out about Pedro Romero. He's regarded as the other founding father of modern-day bullfighting. When he killed he stood still – he let the bull come to him. It's called the *recibiendo* method of killing. Very dangerous and very difficult. As time progressed other matadors, *killers of the bulls*, became equally well known for how they handled the bull with the cape before they killed it. That practice also started way back in the mid-eighteenth century. So you see: this thing has been around for a long, long time. People have tried to get rid of it before. Powerful people. It ain't easy.'

'What do you say to people who perceive the whole thing as being an act of cruelty?' I asked.

'The bull is dead before it gets into the ring. It's already been sold for meat. At least in here it has a chance to go out fighting. That's what Hemingway meant when he said it isn't a sport – "it's a tragedy". Except in very rare cases, the bull never leaves the arena alive. It has a chance to tackle the man before it dies, however. And the guy's on foot. Okay, the picador slows the bull down for a brief period, but for the most part it's only the matador and his sword and cape facing the bull. If I were a bull, I know what way I'd rather go. I'd rather come battering into a ring like this and die fighting. It's better than the alternative – lining up and going meekly to the slaughter. Wouldn't you rather go out fighting? I always say the same thing to people who have any qualms about it: "If you want to ban bullfighting in Spain, *good luck to you*." They won't be the first and they won't be the last. Bullfighting was here before we were and it'll be here long after we're gone.'

We left the sunlight and walked into the bowels of the *plaza de toros*. We entered a small private chapel. It was shadowed and chilled inside. The walls were covered in row upon row of yellow and blue tiles. Tiled pictures of the Madonna were built into the wall. On the right was an alcove with a statue of the Virgin standing on a little plinth inside it. She was holding the infant Jesus in her arms. Red roses in little vases were arranged all round her feet. Directly in front of me was a large altar. On the right of it was another tiled representation of the Mother of God. On the left was a tiled figure of the suffering Christ during His Passion. Carrying the cross, His face etched with pain, He gazed down on a worn kneeler like a man desperate for a rest. The main altar had yet another figure of the Madonna in a glass case. She was dressed in red, blue and white. A gold crown was on her head. Thin candles in holders fanned the edges of the case. Two vases of flowers sat to the right and left. The figure of Mary had her eyes lifted imploringly towards the heavens. She looked sad and wistful. The whole display sat on a little dark-brown mahogany table. A simple linen tablecloth covered it. Next to the kneeler on the floor, two tired-out rubber plants stood guard.

'This is the place where you sweat the big drops of sweat before a bullfight,' said John quietly.

We stood for a moment in the hushed atmosphere. Then we walked past another door along a whitewashed corridor.

'That's the infirmary. If you're injured in the ring you're brought in here.'

The doors were barred to us but I could still detect a faint odour of bleach seeping out from the gap at the bottom of the door.

We continued onwards until we could hear the tour group again. They were chattering inside the bullring's cramped museum. It was full of stuffed bulls' heads, old paintings and matador costumes. Sylvia, the guide, seemed impatient and bored as the visitors slowly shuffled around looking less than impressed by the displays.

Only one cape at the end of the museum caught my eye. It was bright pink with distinctive drawings on it. I pointed it out to my host.

'They were done by Picasso,' said John. 'He loved bullfighting.'

We left the bullring via a very small side street.

'This is probably the shortest street in Seville, but when you are walking along it to the ring to fight a bull it feels like the longest walk in the world.' John laughed as he spoke. He checked his watch. 'We have to hurry. We have an appointment with a tailor.'

John and I took a taxi across the river. It was midday and the sun was high in the sky. Its diamond whiteness threw a sharp, slicing light down on the whole city. The back streets of Seville's Triana district escaped the direct heat, however. They were shaded and cool. Wisps of breeze floated down its alleyways.

I'd already heard the name Triana and read about this area of the city in Laurie Lee's book *A Rose for Winter*. 'Triana is Seville's Roman suburb and lies just across the water,' he wrote. '. . . And here are born many of those penniless but inspired exponents of the popular Spanish arts – incomparable guitarists and dancers, feverish poets and small-boned, hot-eyed boys who go early to the bulls, and whose hunger, valour and excesses lead them to swift, unnatural deaths.'

Lee wrote these words four decades ago. More up-to-date guidebooks told tourists to watch out for their safety. I'd heard tales of rip-off merchants at dodgy flamenco shows, idle characters dealing drugs on mobile phones at all hours of the day, and after-hours scuffles on the pavement between angry local youths and rich, thoughtless tourists naïvely searching for the 'real' Spain. Those drawbacks aside, all the books suggested it was worth checking out.

One of those 'hot-eyed boys who go early to the bulls' was the legendary Sevillian matador Juan Belmonte García. In later years he described how, as a boy from Triana, he would swim the river to the fields of Tablada where, naked after swimming, he would cape bulls by moonlight. True or not, it still presented the haunting image of a desperate boy willing to risk everything for money, fame and perceived security. He was a short, squat, thick-jowled, scowling figure who looked more comical than anything else. But Belmonte's perseverance paid off and he turned the art of bullfighting on its head. He was regarded as a genius who, because of his odd, feeble build, worked the bull closer to his body than anyone had done before him. He revolutionised the whole style of bullfighting.

Belmonte's epoch ran from 1914 until 1936. He shared a so-called Golden Age with another star of the bullring, José Gomez Ortega, known more popularly as 'Joselito'. The latter was a tall, athletic, apparently laid-back man, who had grace and intelligence. He never used any tricks in his repertoire to catch the crowd's eye such as falling to one knee, grabbing on to horns or using chairs or anything; his style was classical and unadorned. He was particularly adept at killing the bull, which is considered the most revealing and dangerous part of the *corrida*. Joselito made killing look effortless. In many ways he was considered invulnerable by critics and fans. His skill seemed to come naturally to him. On some 257 occasions the consummate Joselito shared the bill with the knock-kneed Belmonte. The latter's mad, reckless and awkward-to-watch style of fighting convinced observers that he'd eventually end up dead. Hemingway immortalised him in his novel *Fiesta, The Sun Also Rises*: 'Belmonte's great attraction is working close to the bull. In bullfighting they speak of the terrain of the bull and the terrain of the bullfighter. As long as a bullfighter stays in his own terrain he is comparatively safe. Each time he enters into the terrain of the bull he is in great danger. Belmonte, in his best days, worked always in the terrain of the bull. This way he gave the sensation of coming tragedy. People went to the *corrida* to see Belmonte, to be given tragic sensations, and perhaps to see the death of Belmonte.'

For about seven years both Belmonte and Joselito were considered, in different ways, to be the very best matadors in the whole of Spain. But their Golden Age ended on 16 May 1920 when, just eight days after his twenty-fifth birthday, Joselito – the natural, invincible one, who never seemed to dance unnecessarily with danger – was gored to death in Talavera de la Reina, a town about an hour's drive west of Toledo.

I'd seen a famous photograph of him taken shortly after his death. It showed Joselito on the slab, a crisp white sheet pulled up to his neckline. His face wears a peaceful, though slightly sardonic expression. Joselito's story bears witness to the fact that in any bullfight, no matter how great the matador, no matter how brave or talented, he only has to make one mistake for everything in his world to come crashing down. Permanently.

Belmonte's story, of the kid from the gutters of Triana, who wore his heart on his sleeve and who lived to be an old man, served up a different lesson for aspiring matadors. It suggested that wealth and fame do not necessarily mean happiness or fulfilment.

During the years of General Franco's dictatorship, Belmonte was held in high esteem by the whole nation. Indeed, it wouldn't be stretching things to suggest that many Spaniards regarded him even more highly than their overbearing leader. In 1961, however, when he heard that his best friend Ernest Hemingway had committed suicide, Belmonte's reaction was chilling. He thought for a moment before saying, slowly and deliberately: 'Well done . . .' It seemed an odd reply for a man who apparently had everything. One year later, the reasoning behind his remark revealed itself. Sitting alone in his apartment which overlooked the impoverished Triana district out of which he'd dragged himself, and only a few blocks away from the bullring where he'd had some of his greatest afternoons, Juan Belmonte, then aged seventy, put a gun to his head and blew his brains out.

Our lunchtime appointment in Triana was with a man named Pedro whose bright pink business card grandly announced that he was a Tailor to the Matadors.

Our taxi took us through some narrow streets until it finally came to a halt outside an anonymous grey building. A swarthily handsome, strong-looking man wearing a pressed plain shirt and carrying a mobile phone was waiting for us. John introduced me to him. 'This is Vicente Salamanca. He's a matador from Colombia.'

I shook hands with the man whom I judged to be in his late thirties or perhaps early forties. He looked like a boxer, compact and muscular. And he had sad eyes – like those of an earnest little boy making his first Holy Communion.

John ushered us towards a doorway and pressed the intercom buzzer. The door gave a heavy click, John pushed it and we entered. The foyer was full of plants of various shades of green. We sidestepped them and were greeted by a beautiful, full-faced young woman who showed us into the tailor's shop. She wore elegant silk clothes and very soft leather shoes. The air smelled of heavy, intoxicating perfume.

'Ah, Pedro, Pedro!' John went forward to shake hands and kiss the tailor on both cheeks.

Pedro was a dapper, businesslike man in his forties, well built, wealthy looking and eager to please. The shop was small inside, smaller than I'd imagined it would be, and much more modern. I'd thought it would be all oak-panelled walls, cobwebs and ancient, sepia-tinted photographs – much like the establishment I'd envisaged my childhood bullfighting-poster artist might have lived and worked in. But it wasn't. It was modern and expensive-looking. All that gave away its function were the mannequins which displayed the matador's suit of lights and traditional Andalucian riding outfits.

Vicente immediately got down to business with Pedro. He wanted to try on a new suit of lights – a *traje de luces*. While he was in the changing-room Pedro showed me several different examples of the jackets he made. I lifted one up and felt its weight. I was shocked by how heavy it was. It was pink silk with gold and green and silver embroidery on it. Parts were raised and encrusted with sewn details. It looked spectacular, although when seen up close was perhaps slightly over-theatrical. I immediately thought how difficult it must be to wear such a jacket on a hot day.

'You sweat pounds,' John Fulton told me flatly as I examined it. 'And that's before you've even walked out on to the sand. I'm *serious*.'

Both he and Pedro explained the matador's costume. Underneath the suit of lights the matador wears stockings which are always salmon-pink in colour. They look almost like ladies' tights and are thin and transparent. Then there are skin-tight breeches that extend from the mid-belly down to the top of the calf. A starched shirt with a ruffle is worn on top, with a matching thin tie. A sash 46 inches long and seven inches wide is worn around the top of the breeches. On his feet a matador wears thin black flat-soled slippers called *zapatillas*. To his head is attached the *coleta*, a small traditional pigtail. The short jacket, the *chaquetilla*, is worn on top of the shirt. It's the heaviest part of the whole outfit. The sleeves are laced on to the jacket at the shoulders, which allows for more movement during a bullfight. Finally there's the traditional, easily identifiable hat, the *montera*, which is made of velour and silk. I picked one up and, like the jacket, was surprised to feel how much it weighed.

'People are superstitious about the colours matadors choose for their suits of lights. For example, I wore a pale lemon colour once and managed to get myself heavily criticised by a newspaperman who thought I was daring to break convention and wear yellow which is seen as bad luck,' said John. 'Then there are others who simply don't and won't ever wear a red suit of lights – they think the bull will go for them instead of the red cape.

I told John my story about running away from a bull when I was a kid. 'I was scared because I was wearing a red jersey at the time,' I laughed.

'Oh, you were safe enough. Bulls are completely colour-blind. But the myth of bulls going after anything that's red continues. God knows why!' said John.

Pedro then showed me a stunning cape which the matadors wear over one shoulder during the opening parade into the ring. It was made of the same fine silk as the jacket and breeches and again felt surprisingly sumptuous and heavy. It looked almost like a religious vestment.

'They say the suit was originally designed by the artist Goya, but no one is entirely sure. What is fact, however, is that its design has hardly changed since it was first worn in the sixteenth century. So we're a walking history lesson,' John laughed.

Vicente reappeared wearing his new outfit. It was a stunning silvery white with gold trim. He seemed sombre trying it on. Wearing his new outfit he took a few private moments shaping up in front of a large floor-to-ceiling mirror that ran along one entire wall of the shop, making careful, slow passes to an imaginary bull.

I asked Pedro's assistant how much an entire bullfighter's outfit would cost. I'd noticed the shop also sold swords, capes and *banderillas*, the wooden sticks that have a barbed point at the end of them, which are placed in the bull's shoulders during the bullfight. She obligingly pulled out a calculator and began adding up figures. Allowing for some rough calculations and varying exchange rates, the total came to about £4,000. It was a lot of money for a young matador starting out with only hopes and dreams for company.

John, Vicente and I left the tailor and walked a few blocks to a Chinese restaurant for lunch. During the meal I asked Vicente about his career as a professional matador.

'I've been in Spain now for years. I'm 38 years old and I've been a bullfighter for 22 of those. My home was Bogotá in Colombia and now I board with John Fulton here in Seville. I'm actually half-Spanish. In Colombia I'm regarded as half-Spanish, which doesn't help . . . here I'm half-Colombian, which isn't too good either.'

'How far has your career gone?' I asked him.

'I started off very well in Spain. But lately it's not so good. But I have been *sobresaliente* or substitute matador on a number of occasions on some very good *cartels* – bills or posters – which have featured some top-rate matadors. Bullfighting is a very difficult profession in which to make a living. To be a bullfighter is a marvellous thing but to make a living is extremely hard. But I've never considered doing anything else. I'm beginning to feel a bit desperate, though. If things don't work out soon I may have to think about my future in the business.'

'Would you really give up?'

'Well, I'm just not getting the opportunities to fight. I may have left it a little too late. I'm used as a substitute so often – this means I'm not really going anywhere on my own. I haven't made much money from being a bullfighter – but I have made many, many good friends.'

'Is it a hard business to crack?' I enquired.

Vicente furrowed his eyebrows thinking. He said something I didn't understand.

John translated. 'He said that the business is a very disagreeable labyrinth because of the internal politics of it . . .'

Vicente looked sad. He shrugged and threw up his hands. 'For the bullfighter's art to have any substance he must have sacrificed a lot. He must gain through merit rather than through financial backing. The people who work hard for it enjoy it more than those who are handed it on a silver platter. What can a guy who has everything feel he's accomplished? He *starts* with a million bucks . . . but what's he achieved?'

I agreed. I'd heard of certain bullfighting dynasties who produced sons who thought it was their God-given right to become matadors. They had the best private rings, the best teachers, the best equipment, the best bulls to practise with. Sometimes things worked out. Other times all they lacked was talent and courage. For guys like Vicente who struggled for decades, it must be galling to watch. I asked him what he thought of John Fulton.

'John means everything to me: brother, father, friend – everything. I would like to accomplish a little bit of what John Fulton has. I would like to have a career and retire from bullfighting like John Fulton. John's example should serve others.'

John looked embarrassed and moved by the show of loyalty. He sat in silence.

'Have you any work in the pipeline?' I asked Vicente.

'Yes, I'm hoping to act as substitute on a very good *cartel* in a week or two in Burgos,' He sounded pleased at the prospect and smiled.

'You should try and get up to Burgos to see him on the night in question . . . if you can get a ticket,' said John. 'The fiesta is on that week, and the town goes crazy. It should be good fun. I'm acting as Vicente's manager, his *apoderado*, on the day.'

'What are the chances of a substitute getting an opportunity in the ring?' I enquired.

'The *corrida* in question is a *mano-a-mano* which means "hand to hand". That's where two matadors fight three bulls each – usually it's three matadors and two bulls each. Vicente might be allowed a few passes with the cape during the *corrida* itself. Otherwise he's there to finish off the bulls if the other two matadors are injured or out of action . . . And, well, let's face it, the chances of that happening are fairly remote.' John raised his eyebrows in an expression of hopelessness.

Vicente shrugged.

'But it is good for him to at least appear on the same bill as the top men and be seen in the company, and the two matadors he's appearing with – Joselito and Enrique Ponce – are currently reckoned to be among the big names, if not *the* biggest names, in Spanish bullfighting at the moment. It won't do him any harm at all,' added John seriously.

Vicente nodded in agreement. But I could tell from his demeanour he'd rather have been guaranteed a proper appearance somewhere else as a full matador instead of being a substitute again.

'It's very frustrating for him . . . I know exactly how he feels too,' said John. He shook his head and blew out his cheeks.

Suddenly Vicente started giggling like a teenager. 'Look!'

He pointed to the small liqueur glasses we'd each been given at the end of our meal. We peered into them. A poor reproduction of a soft-porn picture was at the bottom of each one. Without liquid in the glass they were out of focus. With booze in the glass they became clear. We all laughed.

I thought for a moment and then asked John why people kept trying to break into the bullfighting business if it was so difficult.

'Lots of answers to that. Every man has his own reason. It's in Vicente's family, so for him it's tradition. On the other hand I saw Tyrone Power and Rita Hayworth in *Blood and Sand* – that's where my beginnings can be traced to. Everybody has their own tale. Most want big money and fame and honour. Others have their own private goals. Who knows? But they keep coming.'

'Do foreigners like you often try and make it over here?' I asked.

'Not often. Rarely, in fact. But it happens. I was involved in the career of a very talented young man recently who came from Tokyo of all places . . .'

'A Japanese bullfighter?' I said. It sounded improbable but somehow strangely fitting.

'Yes. His name is Atsuhiro Shimoyama. An ex-gymnast and dancer. On the day I left for Mexico for my retirement from bullfighting I was reading a paper on the plane. There, staring me in the face, was a photograph of this Japanese boy who was in training and who said he wanted to be a bullfighter. I thought this was fascinating and I thought I'd like to meet this guy and see how he'd become interested in bullfighting. When I returned to Seville I called a friend of mine who works with a news agency and who'd written up my retirement fight story. He invited me to an interview he was doing with this Japanese boy. So I went along and was amazed to find this Japanese *novillero* – trainee matador – who was as tall as I am and very athletic, very good looking, not at all what you would expect of a Japanese male, and I asked him how he got interested in bullfighting. He told me he'd seen a Sharon Stone film about bullfighting, a remake of an old Hollywood movie called *Blood and Sand.*'

'That's some coincidence,' I said. I thought about John also being the illustrator of the book I'd read as a kid.

'I know, I know . . .' The moment he told me he'd come to Spain because of a film called *Blood and Sand*, I thought, "Oh no . . . here we go again . . ." It takes a special kind of madness, whatever it is. That's why I have such an affinity, such a rapport with him, because he'd done exactly the same thing I did. Chucked it all in – his culture, his family, his job – to become a matador. So I felt I had something he needed, which was 47 years of experience, which I was very willing to give for no reason other than the fun of doing it. Because I can remember how resistant they were to an American matador and I thought it would be wonderful for a Japanese guy to succeed. And it turned out that he had tremendous talent.'

John's voice trailed off slightly. He shook his head.

'Anyway, you'll meet Atsuhiro tonight,' he went on. His voice suddenly sounded different but I didn't remark upon it. Neither, if he'd heard it, did Vicente. He just folded his arms, looked at the remains of our meal on the table and said nothing.

I decided to let it pass.

In a few hours I knew I'd be seeing John again, along with Atsuhiro, 'The Rising Sun Kid'. They were guests of honour at a *novillada*, a small bullfight specifically organised for young, up-and-coming local matadors.

The streets outside the restaurant were empty. Even the men digging up the roads had disappeared. It was siesta time. After we'd said our goodbyes John and Vicente took off in the opposite direction to me. Minutes later I saw them sweep by in a taxi. They were both smiling again, sharing a joke.

I headed back towards the centre of the city, leaving the haunted spaces of the Triana district behind me. I felt a hollowness inside me. It had been there since I heard John Fulton speaking about Atsuhiro. It was a creeping feeling of uneasiness and it stayed with me for the rest of the afternoon. It was like having a sad, second shadow I couldn't get rid of.

FIVE

A Very Disagreeable Labyrinth

I slept for a few hours in my hotel room in an attempt to clear my head. My balcony overlooked a narrow street near the cathedral. There were lots of bars in the area. At all hours of the day and night I could hear the gruff voices of customers inside shouting and laughing, the barman cracking down thick-bottomed glasses on the counter's varnished surface, football match commentaries and tinny music from radios. Opposite my hotel room was a block of apartments. I could see straight into all of them. Everyday life was going on all around me: teenagers lying on sofas, old ladies peeling vegetables, bicycles being repaired in living-rooms, men asleep in chairs in front of flickering television screens.

I'd made arrangements with John Fulton to meet him at the bullring in a little place called Alcalá de Guadaira. I found it on a huge map of Andalucia. It was only a short distance from Seville – I reckoned about a half-hour's drive at the most. I checked my watch. I still had plenty of time to spare and I was hungry so I decided to go out and get something to eat.

Before I left the room I leaned out on the balcony. I spotted a white cat in an apartment across the way. It was sitting very still, occasionally moving only its head from side to side. Clearly it was concentrating all its energies watching something on the roof of my hotel. I leaned out as far as I could from my balcony to see what it was looking at. I finally glimpsed what had gripped the cat's attention. Three fat, white doves were perched on the edge of the crumbling gutter. They, in turn, were staring straight back at the cat.

Neither side moved for five minutes. Each was transfixed by the other. But I was too hungry to keep watching.

At a nearby restaurant I ate some tortillas. The owner of the establishment, a fat old man, sat watching a crime re-enactment on a TV he had installed behind the reception desk. A bank robber wearing a crash-helmet brandished a gun at a woman, grabbed some cash and ran off. A photofit picture of him flashed on the screen. I noticed with a smirk that he looked a bit like me – in fact we had more than a passing resemblance to each other. A split-second later I caught the old man's eye. He slowly looked me up and down, then glanced cautiously back at the screen. I knew what he was thinking. I ate up, paid my bill and left quietly. I tried not to look back but the urge was too great. Sure enough, as I'd suspected, the owner and a bored-looking middle-aged waitress were watching me as I crossed the street towards my car.

The road to Alcalá de Guadaira was completely deserted. Industrial estates and the occasional petrol station were all that broke the monotony. My mind turned to the words of the Colombian matador Vicente when I'd asked him about the business of bullfighting: 'It's a very disagreeable labyrinth,' he'd said.

I had an inkling about what he meant. Before leaving for Spain I'd tried to do some research into bullfighting. This had proved to be an almost impossible task. Like John Fulton half a century before, the only book I could find on the subject was Hemingway's knowledgeable but ancient *Death in the Afternoon*.

I called the Spanish Tourist Board for help. A polite woman said they weren't allowed to assist anyone who wanted to know about bullfights. She acted as if she'd never heard of bullfighting or matadors in her life. Then she more or less hung up on me.

I tried the Spanish Embassy. No one could help me there either.

There were plenty of places that would give me information about why bullfighting should be banned. But I couldn't speak to anyone who could tell me where to see a bullfight first before I could make up my own mind on the subject.

Eventually I was told by someone that a bullfighting club existed in London. I called the number I'd been given. A man called Steve answered. He was very hesitant and nervous but we eventually chatted for about an hour.

A few weeks later a parcel arrived from Steve. It contained some pamphlets, books and videos about bullfighting. I read this material. It told me when and where the various bullfights were on throughout Spain and advised me on how much I should expect to pay for tickets. The videos had been taped straight off Spanish TV. They contained half a dozen bullfights, packaged and edited like British football matches. Each began with introductions from silk-suited ringside commentators before cutting to interviews and background films about the matadors themselves.

One of the clips showed a bullfighter going to his opulent mansion in the mountains. Viewers saw him drive up to the gates on a Harley Davidson. His family were all hanging about when he arrived at the front door. They looked poor and awkward. The matador tried to appear relaxed and nonchalant about his wealth but you could see he was just as uncomfortable as the rest of his family. Inside the house there were photos of him everywhere. One of the sofas was still covered in thick, transparent plastic wrapping.

After the short film had been screened, the video showed another matador, dressed in his suit of lights. He had a microphone clipped to his chest. He breathed heavily and chatted to his hangers-on. They watched as a big bull thundered into the ring. The crowd gasped and applauded. The matador went out and gave it a few passes. Then a fat picador entered the ring on a horse and stuck his pole into the bull's thick neck muscle. Blood spurted out of it like a fountain. The matador asked for mineral water at the side of the ring and spoke to his men about the state of the bull. The *banderillos* moved in and planted their sticks in the bull's back. Then the matador went out with a little cape and made the bull almost wrap itself around him as it charged at the red material. The animal looked tired and hypnotised. The crowd cheered and shouted, '¡Olé! ¡Olé!' The bullfighter responded rather theatrically. He made faces and took the applause like a conquering general. Sometimes he looked like a very bad actor. Then, quite suddenly, he produced a sword. By now the bull was panting and still. The matador lined the animal up and, with a very twisted expression on his face, he stepped forward just as the bull moved, plunging the sword between the animal's shoulder-blades. The bull kept going for a little while. It charged at capes other men waved in front of it. Then, after coughing up some blood, it collapsed and died. The matador smiled and walked around the ring, taking the applause from the crowd. I could hear him breathing heavily through the little radio-mike which was still attached to his suit of lights.

The video then cut to a series of edited highlights of the bull's best moments during the fight. It charged, ran after the cape, then died at the end. The whole thing looked rather silly in slow motion with the commentator chattering on in the background.

I sat on the floor in front of the TV screen and watched five more fights like that one. They were easy enough to follow. Three matadors each fought two bulls. They took it in turns to face the animals. Each fight was divided into a prologue, followed by three acts, and an epilogue.

The prologue starts with the bull charging out of the so-called Gate of Fear on to the sand. After a few moments the matador emerges from behind the fence and plays the bull using a big heavy cape and a series of long, slow passes. The first act which follows this consists of the picadors, mounted on heavily padded horses, sticking their steel-tipped lances into the bull's thick neck muscle. The second act sees the *banderillos* putting their barbed 27-inch sticks into the bull's shoulders. The third act is made up of what's referred to in Spanish as the *faena*: using a small red cape the matador does a series of fancy passes with the tiring, almost defeated, bull. This is when the crowd seem to come alive. They cheer and applaud the matadors who do the intricate passes well, and appreciate the skill of those who seem to put themselves in harm's way. The epilogue sees the matador lining up the bull for the kill – which is known as the Moment of Truth. The bullfight ends when the matador plunges his sword high up between the bull's shoulder-blades – the aim being to sever or penetrate the aorta, the largest artery leaving the heart.

None of the bullfights I watched lasted any longer than 20 minutes. In most cases the bulls didn't die instantly. Some staggered around looking confused. One wet itself and looked pathetic. A few turned in circles by *banderillos* waving capes until, gasping and choking on the blood running out of their mouths, they fell to the sand. I'd read that they vomited blood when their lungs were punctured if the sword had been badly, or just incorrectly, placed. Others were finished off by the matador with either a long sword with a small crosspiece near the end or with a short, very sharp dagger.

When it was over the matadors were sometimes allowed to complete a lap of honour. White hankies being waved by the crowd meant the bullfighters were given prizes – one or both ears and sometimes a tail. People in the audience threw cigars and wineskins into the ring. The matadors even kissed young women and children.

Some of the men had been brave all right and deserved the applause. Some of the bulls had surprised me with their sheer ferocity. But I also felt sorry for a few that had started out so bravely and then had ended up drenched in their own blood, hardly able to move. That had been sickening to watch and I could quite understand how people would be appalled and angered by such a sight. But I'd seen bulls die in a slaughterhouse and I knew that that wasn't any better. Death is never very pretty, especially where the meat industry is concerned. A guy who worked in one abbatoir told me the slaughtermen often played with the bulls, kneecapping them with bolt-guns and such like, before they killed them. He said the bulls lining up to be killed sensed their imminent demise as soon as they arrived and sniffed death in the air. If I'd been a bull bound for the butcher's shop, I'd rather have gone out fighting in a *corrida*. At least in a bullfight they have half a chance to gore their killers before they are finished off themselves.

At the end of watching the video for the first time I felt strange – a bit like a teenager who'd just watched a porn film they'd found after poking around in their parents' bedroom. But with each successive viewing of the tape this uneasy feeling became less and less pronounced, until eventually I had forgotten it had ever been there at all.

Apart from Steve's material, I had also gathered some press clippings to help with my research. They were very confusing. No two reports agreed on facts or figures about bullfighting in the 1990s. One newspaper said that Spaniards spent, on average, about £800 million on bullfighting tickets. But the writer didn't know how many tickets that worked out at. Another article claimed there were about two million tickets sold for the top thousand bullfights every year. But another said that, for all the bullfights across the country, some 61 million tickets had been bought. One author stated with great authority that about 16,500 bullfights were held annually, while another wrote with equal certainty that the figure was much lower, no more than a thousand. Yet another article reported there were 324 bullrings in Spain and that 37,000 bulls had died in them the previous year. A different source quoted figures that were much, much lower. One journalist said there were only about a hundred professional matadors in the whole of Spain and that hardly any of them managed to get booked into bullrings for real fights on anything like a regular basis. Most bummed around the country looking for breaks whilst others supported themselves with part-time jobs and dreams. The only statistic that any two articles agreed on was that about 200,000 people were employed in the Spanish bullfighting industry, representing about one per cent of the nation's entire workforce.

Many of the clippings alluded to the fact that bullfighting in the 1990s was enjoying a resurgence in popularity. One author wrote: 'It is enough to make the bullfight's many critics, inside and outside Spain, despair; in defiance of every expectation and prediction, bullfighting in the enlightened Spain of today is more popular and fashionable than it has been since the 1960s.'

One piece described the new bullrings being built in Spain which had shopping centres attached to them and multistorey carparks. Some had retractable roofs. Others were completely enclosed, like American football stadiums, and bullfights could be watched under floodlights. The bullfighting industry apparently saw a profitable future ahead for itself in the twenty-first century. Some of the articles suggested reasons why this might be so. Following is the gist of what they said.

Franco and his policy of Isolationism had come and gone. Thus, in the broadest of terms, things had *changed*. Spain's economy was unrecognisable: its political institutions had developed, its social fabric had been altered – indeed, it was alleged that the nation's very mindset had been transformed. The country's leaders no longer encouraged the people to perceive outsiders as a threat to Spain or its culture. It was now acceptable, even encouraged, to think of oneself as a European as well as a Spaniard. These changes were underlined by the staging of the Olympic Games in Barcelona, the

Expo'92 event in Seville and the fact that Madrid had its own stint as the European Community's Capital of Culture.

But, according to a number of commentators, for some this change was a case of too much, too fast. Bullfighting became one of the symbols of the past that traditionally minded Spaniards decided they wanted to cling on to. Whether deliberate or unconscious, they did it, and at a time when Europe was becoming increasingly homogenous. Instead of embracing this sameness, many in Spain decided to be different. They kept going to bullfights. It might not have been politically correct but that didn't matter too much. What *was* important was that this activity was part of their tradition, their culture and their identity and, by buying more tickets in greater numbers, their future.

Bullfighting was one of the things in their lives that made them Spaniards. And in an era when everyone appeared to be eating the same burgers, wearing the same jeans, sporting the same designer sunglasses and smoking the same imported cigarettes, defining your national identity felt very important. Bullfighting was something which seemed to bring the Spanish classes together in one place and at one time. Even the King and his mother attended the fights in Madrid. Press reviews appeared in the arts – not sports – section. A government review of bullfighting in 1992 defined it as a 'cultural tradition'. That was the year Europe came to Spain. If ever there was a time one would have expected the government to bow to international opinion and either ban or heavily reconstruct bullfighting, this would have been it. But it simply didn't happen. Apart from a few cosmetic changes – which even some *aficionados* felt were overdue – the *corrida* stayed pretty much the way it had always been. In fact, the report was interpreted as a nod from central government that it recognised the role and standing of the industry. So, in its own way, bullfighting, like other areas of Spanish life, had arguably been modernised. It was, to the annoyance of many and to the joy of a significant number, part of a process rather than a victim of it.

Some people who'd visited Spain told me I was in for a shock when I saw just how popular bullfighting really was amongst the ordinary Spaniards. Not everyone liked it but those who did, *really* did. Bullfighting was good for business, they said. Spanish and international companies happily lent their name and money to the industry. Even British car companies with royal crests invested money in big bullfights as a way of promoting their vehicles.

The current crop of matadors were treated like movie-stars. They were always in the tabloid press and were hounded by the paparazzi. Many were millionaires, I read. They lived in castles that had swimming-pools and they dated all the top super-models.

'Not a bad way to live for killing half-drugged stupid animals that have had their horns shaved,' someone told me.

The articles and books I'd read confirmed such stories. Bullfighters did live in luxury – but only the top ones. In the 1960s a matador with very long arms, extremely white teeth and an unruly mop of thick hair called El Cordobés had cleaned up. He was a kind of bullfighting rock-star and he became a millionaire. I heard that he blew it and was periodically forced to come out of retirement in the '90s to support his lifestyle and his extended family.

Some reports suggested the latest line-up of top matadors were earning huge amounts of money for their afternoon's performance – figures ranging from £20,000 to £100,000 had been mentioned in articles I'd read. Some of the top half-dozen or so matadors were reputedly in the million-pounds-a-year bracket. They had bodyguards, sports cars and scandals. Many fought bulls almost every day during the season, which runs from March until October. Then they hopped on a plane and went to South America for the winter season there. For months they fought regularly in places like Mexico and Colombia before returning to Spain in the spring to start all over again. It sounded like a hard schedule to me.

Some said this led to burn-out, just like young actors or high-flying yuppies. Most also had huge entourages to keep happy. Family members tagged along, as well as managers, drivers, cooks, publicity people – they all had to be paid. As soon as the money came in, it would go straight back out again.

I also came across a couple of expensive American magazines which said that bullfighters liked to give the press the runaround. They were petulant and cheeky. They flaunted their money like poor boys who'd never had any. Some, like Jesulín de Ubrique, were mini-industries. I saw a picture of him. He had bad acne and his jaws looked sunken like those of people who'd lost their teeth at a young age. But apparently this guy was a superstar in Spain. Women sent him their underwear. The singer Madonna had even wanted him to star in one of her videos but he'd refused because he'd better things to do. I read that Jesulín liked to jump on the bull's back during a fight, that he'd organised bullfights for women only and that he'd dropped his trousers on TV to show off his scars from gorings.

Young Spaniards were apparently attending bullfights in greater numbers than ever before. Some commentators claimed it was like the fad for smoking fine cigars or drinking expensive malt whisky. Rich young professionals were embracing and affecting a taste for the vices and the symbols of the old, staid, comfortable and unhealthy lifestyle their parents once enjoyed. It could just be a passing craze, said some, a way of kicking against the smothering effects of political correctness; on the other hand, it might be an indication of a genuine resurgence in popularity for a part of Spanish culture whose death had long been forecast.

I also heard that some bullfights were fixed. I wasn't too surprised. A boxing trainer once explained to me how professional bouts in the UK were fixed. One fighter on the way up needs a workout; another boxer who's not so hot needs some cash. They agree to a good, hard bout that'll give the fans their money's worth. At the end it'll be declared a draw. The referee will be in on the whole thing. Everybody goes home happy. Nobody loses out and both boxers end up with some money in their pockets. The trainer told me this was called a 'smudger' fight.

Various people suggested the same thing happened in bullfighting. Some said it was really corrupt. Shaving the bull's horns was an old trick. I read that a bull with shaved or blunted horns was in terrible pain. It hated charging at anything. A Madrid-based journalist told me that shaving horns made 'a goring less likely; the horn tip can slide off in many cases if it hits the leg: if it does go in, it's usually less severe than if it were sharp . . . [and that] it certainly does some psychological damage to the bull as well as being physically weakening to have the animal penned up while they're doing this operation'.

But another source told me this was all nonsense. According to him, bulls with shaven horns would charge at a tank – he said most bulls, even the unfit, poor-looking specimens everybody complained about, were able to charge, head-first, straight into the wooden fence around the ring when they first hit the sand. But I'd read that, regardless of the pain factor, shaven horns often subsequently threw the bull off balance and that the animal's natural ferocity and range of attacking skills fell apart during the fight because of this. That was a difficult accusation to prove. Indeed, I was told it was extremely difficult to actually see if a bull had shaven horns. Some men were very good at disguising their handiwork. Everything from a file to a blow-torch could be used in the process. To prove anything, the authorities would literally require the use of a microscope – a piece of equipment not often found at the average Spanish bullring, by all accounts.

Some articles complained about the general physical condition of the bulls being fought in Spain. A poor-quality bull meant the matadors simply weren't in as much danger. That's why they could fight so frequently and become so rich; they knew the animals they were facing were weaker than in years gone by. The bulls I'd seen in the video appeared dangerous enough, although a couple did look fat and out of shape. One fell over. It looked sad and scared.

Another way a fight could be fixed was by having the picador really go to town on the bulls with his steel-tipped *pica*. This would weaken it, soften it up, take the fighting spirit out of it and make it easier to kill. In days gone by, the bull had regularly gutted the picador's horse. The arena used to be strewn with dead horses with their entrails hanging out. In 1928 a mattress-like covering was introduced to stop this happening. Some picadors also used really large horses to make their job easier, a number even going as far as riding carthorses. New rules in 1992 restricted the size of the horses. The rules were later reviewed when the bullfighting industry complained the bulls were causing havoc with the lighter, more vulnerable horses. So the heavier horses came back.

I saw the picadors doing their job in the videos I'd watched. The crowd booed and jeered when they stuck the pike into the bull. Nobody seemed to like the picador or what he did. Often the matador would dramatically wave the picador away from the bull. When he did this the crowd would cheer and clap. I heard later that matadors often do this for show and to curry favour with the crowd. Before the fight they'd agree with the picador what the moves would be. Anything they did during the fight, I was assured, was just for public consumption.

It all sounded shady – and interesting.

My journey from Seville to Alcalá de Guadaira didn't take too long. I'd hardly seen another car during the entire drive. Towards the end of it the only thing that had roused me from my thoughts had been the sight of a huge factory on the horizon going up in flames. A couple of people stood idly next to the blazing fire; one seemed to be chatting on a mobile phone when I drove by. Neither looked too concerned. A few moments later a posse of fire engines went screaming by me in the opposite direction. They looked much more worried.

The town I was heading for was famous for two things: its bread and its sand. In terms of trivia I suppose it was the sand that interested me more. Apparently Alcalá sand was to be found in bullrings all over Spain. It was the golden, glistening stuff which looked almost unreal – like a scrubbed-sand version of emerald-green Astro-turf or something. *Too* yellow, *too* clean. It was only found in Alcalá de Guadaira. And, sure enough, there it was, a quarry full of the stuff, as I took the turn-off into town. It glowed in the early-evening light like silted treasure.

A shabby poster tied to a lamppost with a filthy piece of string announced the event I was on my way to see: the *novillada* bullfight which was being held in the local bullring. It was for the professional hopefuls, the boys who were one step up from the kids I'd seen at the training ranch. Tonight's event was for those who had sweated and practised in private with imaginary bulls. Tonight they would wear the matador's costume and face a live bull for the first time. It was due to begin at 7.30 p.m.

The sky was patched with heavy, low clouds. The air, which had been still most of the day, now contained the first wisps of a breeze and the temperature had dropped. Sunlight occasionally pierced the gloom. Without it, the *novillada* would feel strangely incomplete. And the *novilleros'* suits of lights would not, as if by some kind of alchemy, sparkle and glisten into life as they went about the serious business of spilling blood.

SIX

The Novilleros

There was a thick, bumper-to-bumper traffic jam outside Alcalá de Guadaira's bullring. Engines were revved, horns were honked and people walking by on the pavement shouted and waved at the stranded drivers. A man wearing a flat black cap, the sole indication of his dubious official status, spent a minute or so chatting to the driver of each car he had to guide into parking spaces. Everyone seemed to know him. They all gossiped and laughed. I saw him shaking hands with several people. I thought I was going to be late for the *novillada* but nobody seemed in much of a hurry.

The queue of traffic slithered forward. Through the cool, comfortable evening air I sniffed the aroma of cooking. Just above the noise of the car engines, I could hear people talking. The low hum of conversation and laughter drifted into the air.

I parked my car and headed for the sounds and smells. The bullring in Alcalá de Guadaira was a low, compact structure just five minutes from the main Seville highway. Across the road were a few small grocery shops and video rental stores. Blocks of flats were dotted around. Messy-looking families hung out of the windows, gesturing and waving to unseen figures behind them. I could see some small birds swooping and dive-bombing above the bullring, their shadows circling over its whitewashed walls.

I walked around the side of the *plaza de toros*, kicking up curling clouds of brown dust, past a thick-set, smiling man who was standing all by himself underneath a large poster announcing the week's events in the bullring.

The bullfights were sponsored by a national bank. As I passed him the man grunted at me. He seemed distracted by the lump of burning ash which had just fallen from his cigarette on to his Jack Daniels T-shirt.

I found myself at the edge of a surging crowd. Two men were on duty at the gate. A policeman stood nearby, half-asleep and disinterested in the entire proceedings. The men at the gate waved me through into a small courtyard. I was hardly noticed; they were busy talking to each other about something which seemed very important.

I slipped in amongst the shifting mass of people. To my right was a shed-cum-bar. On one side drinks were being served to a thick wedge of people who were crowded around the counter. To the right was a seated area, filled with people watching football on a large-screen TV. You had to shout to make yourself heard above the din. Green tables and chairs spilled out onto the courtyard where I stood. Little children ran around playing tag and pulling at their parents' clothes. The adults ignored them and drank and smoked and talked. Heads were thrown back with laughter whenever anyone said something funny.

I spotted some stables on the other side of the courtyard. As I slowly made my way through the throng I caught snatches of different conversations. The words floated and melted in the air like snowflakes on a sunlit winter's morning.

Young men in starched blue overalls stood at the entrance to the stables. A couple of dappled grey horses were behind them. Their attention was focused on the brown horses which were hitched to a harness with bells on the back. This would be used later to drag the dead bulls from the ring. The boys smiled and chatted to each other. They passed a cigarette round and drank beer from little fat brown bottles.

Large sections of the crowd started shifting towards the tunnelled entrance into the bullring itself. Old hunchbacked ladies dressed in black, children in white shirts and men wearing flat caps all disappeared noisily into the blackness of the passageway. I moved in behind them, following everyone else.

A man with a trombone sprinted past me, full of apologies and smiles. The instrument gleamed under his arm as he pushed his way through the crowd and up the thick white concrete stairs.

Suddenly I was surrounded by young *novilleros*. They swarmed into the tunnel in their red, black, green, gold, pink and white suits of lights, looking like extras from an opera chorus. Some local photographers snapped their pictures. They puffed out their chests, holding their capes over their arms. Some older men also wore suits of lights. They looked fat and out of condition. These were the retired matadors who had trained the boys. Their bellies bulged beneath their outfits. They walked awkwardly in their black slippers, like men who'd been rejected from the army because of flat feet.

The *novilleros* in contrast looked shiny and polished and light on their feet. Their hair was slicked into place, parted severely to show the greeny whiteness of their scalps. They had the concentrated expression of seminarians. Some spoke to each other out of the corner of their mouths. Others smiled and shook hands. Every minute or so, a look of worried detachment would flit across their faces.

I noticed one young man who was facing the ring. He had given up doing what the rest of his companions were doing – which was either ignoring completely or merely glancing every so often at the yellow bed of sand behind them. Instead, this *novillero* had succumbed to the temptation; he had decided to try and stare the sand out. So he stood there, his chest muscles straining, his legs and buttocks clenched tight like a cat ready to pounce and his shoulders square and tense. His jaw tightened and relaxed and tightened and relaxed again. He rubbed his chin. Then his jaw muscles began working again.

Another *novillero* watched him staring at the sand. He too stared at the yellow sea for a moment but then stopped himself. He couldn't look at his staring colleague any longer. He turned his back on both the sand and the other *novillero* and searched for someone to smile at or chat to. His face was the deathly pale of a reluctant, nightmare-plagued sailor who had to leave port in a storm.

One of the photographers came up to me. 'Are you American?' he asked in flawless English. I told him I was living in New York but that I wasn't from there.

He introduced himself and told me his name was Juan. He was tall and thin, with the build of a long-distance runner, and looked as if he needed a good shave. I told him why I was in Alcalá de Guadaira.

'That's very good. Most journalists only come to Spain to see the very big bullfights – you know, all the money and the glamour and the women. You need to see this . . .' he said, waving a long arm in the direction of the bullring. 'Yes, you need to see the small, cheap, local *corridas* and the *novilleros*. When you watch them you'll see them thinking, you can see them trying to solve problems.'

'What do you mean?' I asked.

'The bullfighter, in theory, has to tackle and win the bull with his technique, his training, his science – his art. The top matadors can do that, or at least give the appearance of doing it, very well. They also know a few shortcuts too, which can be annoying. But these young men are still learning – they make mistakes. So you actually see them perform right up to the top of their ability. You see them learning. They are still a work in progress.' He smiled and hunched himself down to my height.

I told him I was waiting for John Fulton and Atsuhiro.

'Ah, yes, the "Rising Sun Kid" . . .' He said the nickname in Spanish. 'Everyone knows him! And Mr Fulton too. It was such a shame about the boy's accident.'

'What happened?'

'He was caught by a bull, suffered some sort of seizure the next day and ended up almost dying. He is now paralysed down one side of his body. I don't know if he can even walk any more,' said Juan with a shrug.

I thought of the change in John Fulton's voice when he talked of Atsuhiro. And I recalled the feeling of sadness I'd been aware of after lunch.

'Was he good?'

'I heard he was very good . . . and the crowds liked him too. But from what I hear I don't think he'll ever fight again. Such a shame, eh?'

I muttered a reply. My mind was wandering. The air was filled with dust and the broken sunlight kept coming and going, lifting and lowering, like a swinging lightbulb in a darkened room.

The crowd around us continued to buzz excitedly in the minutes leading up to the beginning of the *novillada*. All the *novilleros* were fixed in place by the river of old men in oily flat caps and sunglasses, knowing expressions on their craggy, crumpled faces. They hung about, washing themselves in the glow of youth. A few heads turned. A section of the crowd lurched awkwardly towards someone who'd arrived. I stood on my tiptoes to see who it was.

Juan spotted them first. It was John Fulton and Atsuhiro Shimoyama. Both were much taller than the Spaniards around them and stood out among the mob. People shook their hands and John smiled, receiving pats on the back. Atsuhiro was about the same height as him. He wore a white T-shirt and faded tan jeans. At first glance he looked incredibly fit.

Then he moved.

He walked like a man I once knew who'd suffered a very bad stroke. I used to see him bravely battling up the street, one pace at a time, his face displaying his resolve to get to where he was going no matter how long it took. Even in the worst weather he battled his way along the road. In the wind and rain and snow he fought his physical and mental obstacles out on the pavement, in full public view, one step at a time.

Atsuhiro had the gait of someone dragging heavy limbs that no longer worked or felt anything. He had to roll his body very slowly, forcing himself forward, a delicate balancing act between determination and limited physical resources. His left side was groggy and limp. His hand, curled and empty, hung at his side. But his face looked young and alive and capable. He smiled hopefully as he moved a few inches at a time down the slope. Nobody put out a hand to help him and he was grateful. At first he spoke to a few familiar faces, smiling, cracking some jokes and thanking some friends for their encouragement. But as he neared the bottom he grew more detached, more still. I realised his eyes were completely focused on the sand. He was soaking up the atmosphere and doing what he'd always done before his accident. He was preparing himself to fight. He was still acting like a *novillero* about to face a bull.

In front of Atsuhiro the floor of the bullring was being hosed down. The silver sheets of water glistened until they were slowly absorbed by the golden sand. If a wind blew across the arena the damp sand would not be disturbed as easily as fine, dry sand would. Wind annoys matadors because it upsets bulls and blows capes. The workmen with the hoses moved around amongst puddles which shone briefly like newly minted pennies.

I went over to John and shook his hand. He whispered into my ear: 'It's Atsuhiro's first time appearing in public since the accident.'

'I heard a bit about what happened. He looks well,' I said. I meant it. Apart from the obvious effects of the paralysis there was still an umistakable air of strength about Atsuhiro.

'He's nervous about tonight but I think he'll be okay. Lay off questioning him, though – it's a tough time for him,' said John. I nodded and went forward to Atsuhiro. John introduced me to him and his Japanese girlfriend. We all slowly made our way to our seats in the stands.

Some people began clapping and waving at Atsuhiro. He nodded gracefully, acknowledging the recognition before sitting down.

A trumpet sounded.

I heard horses' hooves, saw the young *novilleros* gather in a group next to the red gate and watched as they fixed their ornate, glittering capes around their shoulders. Someone nodded to a man at the gates who heaved the doors open. Two bailiffs (men on horseback who control the proceedings in the arena), wearing black velvet capes and breeches and ruffled lace collars, trotted into the ring on high mounts.

In their wake, the assembled *novilleros* lifted their heads, blessed themselves and took a step forward. Their feet left the cool hardness of the grey concrete and then, in one step, felt the soft, forgiving punch of the sand on their soles. They had left behind one world and entered another. Some looked comfortable in the moment. Others seemed to be acting – trying to remember how they thought a matador should look.

That was how it began.

They lined up in front of some photographers and stood there for a few moments. Then they moved off as one, heading for the other side of the ring. The crowd clapped and whistled and shouted.

We were sitting on the shady side of the ring. The sun, which came and went every few seconds, briefly illuminated the six suits of lights that crossed the sand. The costumes instantly lit up, as if someone had just turned on little bulbs which had been secretly sewn into their fabric.

'Atsuhiro knows many of those boys,' said John. 'He trained with quite a few of them.'

The *novilleros* unfurled their large capes and began making slow, graceful passes with them. The capes were bright pink and yellow and they glowed in the evening light. From the other side of the ring they looked like a flock of exotic birds.

Another trumpet sounded.

The ring cleared and, after a brief pause, a bull came battering out of the Gate of Fear. It wasn't as big as the bulls I had seen in Steve's video, but it did look very lively and spirited. The main criterion for the bulls in *novilladas* without picadors is that they must be less than three years old.

The first *novillero* to face the bull was a solemn fellow dressed in red. He was awkward and stiff, but he seemed very keen to impress. His long face gave nothing away, showing neither fear nor pleasure. The crowd responded when he made the bull pass him close and well. He got carried away and suddenly, in an instant, the bull was on top of him. It thumped him clumsily with the side of its horns. He lay still until other men with capes lured it away from him. Then, when he knew the coast was clear, he jumped to his feet and dramatically threw his arm up in a 'Look, I'm fine!' gesture. Only his limbs did the gesturing, however: his face never changed. Everyone applauded. John shook his head and looked at his feet.

And that was the pattern for the rest of the first *novillada*.

In some *novilladas*, like this one, there aren't any picadors. So, after the big capes, it was time for the *banderillas* to be placed by the older men who'd trained the hopefuls. Although at first sight they'd appeared plump and bad on their feet, some of the most out-of-shape men surprised everyone by running the fastest. When the bulls thundered towards them they scuttled out of the way like pedestrians trying to avoid a skidding car.

When it came time for the first boy to kill the bull he looked sweaty and nervous. He'd been on the floor twice and his suit was peppered with sand. You could tell he just wanted it to finish as quickly as possible. His feet twitched every time he had to make a pass with the small cape, the *muleta*. Then, for the first time, his face registered emotion: fear. His thigh muscle shook and went into spasm when the bull came too close. But he eventually pulled himself together enough to face the animal squarely. Then, an instant too late, he lunged with his sword at the bull's shoulders.

The blade hit bone and bounced out.

The bull had almost caught him in the thigh with its right horn. When they realised what had happened, the crowd gasped.

A few moments later the *novillero* faced the panting beast again. He sighted it along the blade of the short sword, crooked his leg and launched himself at it. This time the sword went deep into the bull and it only managed to trot around for a few paces before, unwillingly, it fell over. Blood pumped out its shoulders where the sword had penetrated and on to the damp sand. I felt pleased for the boy but, in a way, sorry for the bull. I consoled myself with the thought that it had been a brave enough bull and that, in some ways, made me feel better.

The crowd were desperate for a chance to applaud and now they had it. They clapped and cheered. John Fulton smiled at the ecstatic reaction going on around him. 'I think this guy's entire family must be here tonight!' he laughed.

Hankies were waved. An ear was awarded and the boy did a lap of honour flanked by two older matadors while everyone gave him a standing ovation. Flowers and wineskins were thrown into the ring. It was more a ritual than anything else. A bit over the top. He had survived rather than triumphed. But it didn't matter. We could see the utter relief on his face as he walked by. His hair, previously locked into place, was now dishevelled. The detachment on his face was gone. He was now living the moment. He was taking it all in and enjoying it. And he looked drained of every last drop of his strength.

We sat down and waited. Another, heavier bull trotted into the ring. It was the colour of peat, all sweating and angry. It ran at some capes that were waved at it, showing a fierce ability to use both horns well. It also turned very quickly, highly sensitive to the slightest noise or sight.

Then it spied the young *novillero*, who warily spread out his cape like a man setting out a stall of wares. In an instant, with the speed of a racehorse, the bull went for the space between the boy and his cape. The *novillero* was not expecting this. In the blink of an eye, he was on the ground underneath the animal. The bull's horns ploughed and drilled at the sand inches from his head. So eager was it to open the boy's skull with its horns that it missed its target and managed only to kiss him with its snout instead. When it realised what it was doing it backed up and bashed its horns down on the *novillero*'s shoulders, but he managed to squirm away. The bull spied some other capes and, remembering what had caught its attention in the first place, went charging after them. The boy sat up like a man on the operating table who'd awakened halfway through surgery. He jumped to his feet, ran a few paces, realised he'd lost his cape, grabbed it, then backed off.

The crowd was silent.

The boy realised he'd shown fear. He hesitated, clearly thinking about his next move. He had to control his instinct to run in the opposite direction to a dangerous animal before he could ever hope to control the bull itself with the cape. He forced himself back towards it. It stopped charging the other capes and stood for a moment looking at its opponent.

It was then, with the bull looking at him, that the *novillero* realised he was no longer wearing his slippers. They'd come off during the initial tussle and were lying, like discarded toys, on the other side of the ring. He could have panicked, feeling like a fraud in an incomplete disguise, but, to his credit, he didn't. Instead, furrowing his brow, he faced the bull. It responded quickly, charging in a very straight line which allowed the *novillero* to begin some very good passes. And, when he found his form, he kept going. And the bull kept charging straight and turning well – just fast enough to look dramatic, but not so fast as to scare the boy or throw him off his stride. After a series of passes he finished with a little flourish and turned his back on the bull. It stood there, watching him walk away.

After the *banderillos* had stuck their barbed sticks into its back, the bull seemed subdued. I'd read that the most dangerous part of a fight is towards the end and not, as I'd thought, at the beginning. At the beginning it's all strength, muscle and energy, but towards the end when it's panting and tired it instinctively conserves energy and strength. It is then, when a matador might drop his guard or bring the bull too close for a fancy pass, that it can kill him with one flick of its head and horns. For the longer a *corrida* goes on, the more knowledgeable a bull becomes. Sometimes it realises that it's not the billowing cape which is the threat but rather the man holding it.

The boy shouted at the bull to charge. The soles of his sheer pink stockings were covered in sand.

But the bull wouldn't move.

He shouted again. His thin, desperate voice echoed around the arena.

This time it charged straight at him, not the cape. It was learning. The *novillero* instantly repositioned himself and gave it a good pass. The bull was confused. It turned like a small, nimble dog and charged again, and again he passed it well. The crowd cheered, '¡*Olé! ¡Olé!*' The band played. The bull kept charging straight and the boy kept passing it. He arched his back, leaned into the bull and, with the sword in his right hand, passed the bull several times in a row. Then he snapped his series of passes shut and, folding the cape under his arm, faced the crowd and basked in their applause. The bull stood behind him, breathing heavily, looking very angry and confused.

Finally, the *novillero* lined up the bull for the kill. The sword in his right hand was aimed between the shoulders, the *muleta* in his left tantalising the beast with its movement. There was a moment of silence. The crowd hushed itself. Then the boy ran at the animal. It saw him coming. As he neared the bull, it glanced towards the cloth of the cape, changed its mind, and went for the boy instead. This was its last chance. The bull tossed the *novillero* over its back. The boy's sword went in one direction while he went in the other, but he landed on his feet, battered but not bloodied, and quickly got out of reach while the bull attacked the shroud of red that lay on the sand before it.

A solitary *banderilla* which had fallen out of the animal's back during the tossing lay on the sand.

A few moments later, close to where I was sitting, the *novillero* repeated the same process of lining the bull up and preparing himself to kill it.

A few seconds passed.

Then, throwing discipline and style to the wind, the boy hopped towards it. The bull simultaneously pounced at the cape like a cat going after a bird it had patiently stalked. The sword went in at a high, awkward angle, but it went in nonetheless.

The *novillero* backed off with relief and stayed away until the bull staggered around and then fell over.

The boy looked scared even when the bull was dying. His eyes were fixed on it, half expecting it to jump up and charge after him again. But it didn't. It lay down on the sand like an exhausted man in need of a rest. It blinked a few times, licked itself, and died. It had been an intelligent animal and had put up a hell of a fight.

The *novillero* waited for the crowd's reaction.

Slowly it came, muted rather than ecstatic applause. No hankies, No ears. But he did get to walk around the ring for a half-hearted lap of honour.

'I think he's getting that just for showing up and going home in one piece!' said John, laughing. Atsuhiro grinned when he heard this, shook his head and tried to stuff a peanut up John's nose.

Then the crowd rose to their feet as one and applauded. The *novillero* stood to the side of the ring, clapping too. The bull was being dragged around the ring on its own lap of honour. The horsemen slapped their mounts and shouted and whistled as they ran the bull quickly around the *plaza de toros*. The horses' bells echoed and jangled. It sounded like something you should only hear at Christmas-time. The sagging, heavy beast ploughed a trench in the sand as it lurched and battered and bounced around the arena. A small, limping man appeared out of nowhere, hurrying round the ring, filling in and smoothing out the furrows and waves with a long wooden rake. Every so often he stopped to wipe his brow and relight the tiny cigarette which stuck to his lips. The sand seemed to engulf him and, from a distance, he looked like a dwarf in a circus.

I left John and Atsuhiro alone for a while and headed out the entrance tunnel just in time to see the brave bull from the previous fight being dragged out of the ring by the men and their sleigh-bell horses. They sprinted ahead of me, all creaking leather and hollow hooves, leaving two wet trails of blood edged with yellow sand on the dusty grey floor of the tunnel.

A few moments later I found the dead bull lying on a concrete floor of the corral next to the stables. Half a dozen men in white boilersuits and black wellington boots, most of them smoking and smiling, had got to work on it the moment it arrived. A thick-waisted grey-haired man started with the blunt end of an axe.

Another man sliced the hide off with a very sharp knife. They opened it up, the blue-white guts spilling out like gigantic stuffed worms. Four men each snapped, then sawed off its legs. A guy at the front beheaded it with exactly four blows of his axe. Then he stopped to scratch his nose. Under his feet blood streamed across the concrete and collected in deep puddles on the sand.

The only sound was the far-off cheering of the crowd. The slaughtermen worked intensively in the quietness of their corral. No one spoke; they just worked.

The slaughtermen were watched by a small gathering of boys. They stood on tiptoe for a better view. One or two whispered but mostly they just stood there quietly, lost in their own thoughts and taking it all in.

'Hey, man, where are you from?'

I turned round and spied five young men at the side of the corral. One had been video-taping the dismemberment of the bull.

'Scotland, more or less,' I answered. I noticed they were swaying unsteadily on their feet. One of them, a guy with peroxide-blond hair, could hardly even stand. They all clutched cans of beer. They had very white teeth and very clean clothes.

'Where are *you* from?' I asked the one who'd questioned me.

'America . . . the States . . . We're in the Navy . . . Man, do you know anything about this bullfighting stuff?' His eyes were wide open, and he looked concerned.

I told them a little bit about what I knew. They were confused and they swayed some more.

'I thought it was one bullfighter guy against one bull – there's three or four men running into the ring every time one of them hits the deck. What kind of a contest is that? The bull doesn't have a chance,' said the tallest guy who wore a sweatshirt that said 'WOLVERINES' on it. He had stopped taping the butchers and he held a tiny camera by his side.

'Well, it's not really a bullfight – there's no fight – the bull would win a fight. So in that sense it's not a fair contest. It's not a sport. It's a performance where, nearly always, the bull will die. It never wins. It can't. As someone said to me, "Hey, the bull's hamburger meat from the moment it's born."' I shrugged.

'Hey, I like hamburgers . . . but that ain't fair. Not in my book. It's not very . . .' He struggled to find the right word. He swigged his beer while we waited. 'It's not very American! Yeah, not very American!'

Everyone grunted in agreement. Suddenly something landed at our feet. One of them glanced down, focused for a second, then jumped back. His eyes were bulging.

The freshly skinned and boned head of the bull lay on the ground. Its raw flesh was slimy and red. Its round eyes glistened like two half-sucked boiled sweets.

'What happens to the . . . the . . . thing back there now?' asked one of them.

'You mean the bull?'

'Yeah, sure, the bull, the bull . . . What'll they do with it now?'

'It goes on sale. People will buy it, then they'll eat it. It's meat.'

'Oh God! This country is something else . . .' said the youngest of the sailors. 'I'm really looking forward to going home.' He gulped and swayed.

His friends looked at him, looked at the bull's head on the ground and then looked at me. They shook their heads. They blinked a lot. Then they, too, gulped and swayed.

I rejoined John and Atsuhiro. Another *novillero* fight had just ended.

'You missed a spectacular tossing,' said John. 'One kid was knocked all over the place. Every time he got up, the bull just knocked him straight back down. He was up in the air more often than he was down on the ground. Still, he managed to kill the bull well enough.'

'Did he get an award or a lap of honour?' I enquired.

'No, he didn't have time really,' said John, eating a handful of peanuts which Atsuhiro was dishing out to everyone sitting nearby.

'Why not?'

'Oh, I think he was carted straight off to an ambulance,' said John, carefully brushing some crumbs off his clean shirt.

From the other side of the sand a young blond *novillero* in a silver suit of lights approached where we were sitting. He walked right across the arena and took off his hat. Everyone fell silent. He addressed the crowd. This was the first time this evening that anything like this had happened.

The *novillero* proceeded to make a short speech of dedication to Atsuhiro. He was a former classmate and they both clearly knew each other. Then he threw his hat to where we were seated. John caught it and gave it to Atsuhiro. He stood up, holding the hat in his right hand, and took the salute from the boy. The entire stadium rose to its feet and applauded Atsuhiro. He gracefully bowed, holding the hat at arm's length, acknowledging the cheering. As he slowly gazed around the *plaza de toros* in Alcalá de Guadaira, he looked just like a matador who'd made the finest kill of the evening, instead of a young man who'd almost been killed himself. I looked at John Fulton. He shook his head. His eyes were full of tears.

A minute or so later Atsuhiro's friend was digging a deep hole for himself.

All night the *novilleros* had been taking crazier and crazier risks, trying things they weren't yet skilled enough to do. This had been in an attempt to impress the crowd, their peers and any managers who might be doing some local talent-spotting. Now, this young boy fell to his knees in front of the gate from which the bull would emerge. He slowly spread out his cape. Then he dramatically blessed himself with big wide hand movements so that everyone could see what a risk he was taking. The crowd went 'Ooooh!' and applauded for a second or two.

Then everyone fell silent.

I quickly left John and Atsuhiro and hurried down to the edge of the ring where I met Juan, the photographer I'd been speaking to earlier. I wanted a better view of what was about to happen. When he saw me, Juan put his hand on my shoulder and pointed to the almost prostrate *novillero*. He pronounced every word very clearly and very deliberately so I understood him: 'He . . . is . . . a . . . madman . . .'

Then he nodded. Then he shook his head.

The boy was attempting to do a variation of the *Farol de Rodillas* – a kind of very spectacular kneeling pass. Usually this is a somewhat desperate attempt to get the crowd behind the matador right from the outset of a fight. Sometimes it's done when the bull had already rushed into the ring, other times it is done just as the bull enters from the Gate of Fear, the *toril*. This was where the boy was doing it. When the pass is done here it's known as a *Porta Gayola*. In a way this can be more risky. The bull's been in a pen for a while, usually in the shade, so when it enters the bright sunlight of the ring it's temporarily blinded. The theory is that it'll follow the cape which is whirled over and to the side of the matador's head. In practice, however, it often does neither and smashes straight into them both.

The boy spread the cape out. The bull couldn't be seen. Then the gate was opened. The boy blessed himself again, more nervously and privately this time. Then he started sort of shuffling on his knees. He couldn't keep still. His position shifted one way then the other. Suddenly he started to wobble and hop around on his knees. Clearly he'd seen the bull before we had.

Then it appeared.

The bull, black and powerful, headed straight for him. Just at the point when he should have used the cape to lure the bull away, the *novillero* saw something he didn't like and changed his mind. Instead of using the cape properly he decided to use it to aid his escape from a very tricky predicament. He stopped being a *novillero* and became a nervous young man. His training went out the window. He flung the cape over the bull's head, and dived like a swimmer in the opposite direction. The bull, draped and blinded in the cape, jumped straight over his head like a horse clearing a hurdle. The boy landed in the sand, looked up quickly, and jumped to his feet.

The people in the crowd gasped. Then they found themselves applauding the *novillero*'s recklessness.

'A guy in Seville did that a while ago . . . the bull's hoof caught his chin and ripped his entire face off,' said Juan, shaking his head.

'Good God,' I muttered

'Oh, they took him to the hospital and sewed it all back on. He's okay. Looks a little funny . . . but on the whole okay . . .' he shrugged.

I glanced at John Fulton. He rolled his eyes back in his head, shook his head and stared at his feet. Atsuhiro was grinning and enjoying himself.

Ten minutes later things has improved.

The next *novillero* was the best of the night. Javier, a slightly built 16-year-old, tackled his bull calmly and with style.

'Now, *he* seems to know what he's doing,' said John when I rejoined him in the stands. 'Look, no theatrics, just classical bullfighting. He's assured, careful and is remembering his training.'

The boy took it very slowly, always wearing the same cool, detached, very serious expression on his face. When the bull did speed up he was ready for it. He had a solution to every problem the bull presented. It therefore stopped being a threat and instead became an accomplice. He killed it on his first attempt. The bull died instantly. When the *novillero* finished the crowd petitioned for an award. He was carried around the ring on his friends' shoulders and was given an ear. But even at the very end, when people threw flowers to him, the boy still looked serious. It was as if he couldn't stop himself concentrating. He was young and fresh, but his face was like that of an old, careful man.

At the end of the series of fights the *novilleros* were all paraded around the ring. They looked happy and relieved. Only the boy who had been taken to hospital was missing.

As we were about to leave the arena a crowd of local girls in their late teens came swarming all over Atsuhiro. John produced little cards with his friend's photo on them for him to sign. The girls shook Atsuhiro's hand, put their arms around him and smiled for pictures with him. He grinned and signed autographs like a professional as the flashbulbs went off. It lasted for ten minutes or so until the crowd of young women finally and reluctantly moved away.

I stood back watching all this alongside John Fulton.

'It was like handling Elvis Presley.' His voice was full of irony.

After the *novillada* we were invited by one of the organisers to join him for a drink. In the shed-cum-bar behind the bullring he placed a pile of food and drinks on the table, insisted I take photographs of everyone and went around shaking hands. He bowed and scraped like a butler every time he came within arm's length of either John or Atsuhiro.

Outside in the courtyard half a dozen filthy kids ran by waving bull's horns at each other. One was using his T-shirt as a cape and shouting '¡*Olé!* . . .' while another charged at him like a bull.

As we ate and drank the darkness fell. The whitewashed walls of the bullring became grey shadows. Time passed easily. Someone turned on the huge TV and flicked through the channels until they found a football match. The crowd cheered and shouted. The local team from Seville were playing an important fixture in Madrid and everyone immediately began whistling and screaming at the proceedings.

Rows upon rows of photographs were hung around the walls. Some showed *novilleros*, remarkably similar to the boys I'd just seen. Other shots were of older men, looking serious and mature. It was hard to know exactly when the pictures had been taken – the suits of lights stayed exactly the same no matter what the period. Only the hair seemed to alter. Fringes came and went, sideburns were long then short, hair was blown-dry then greased back again. That was the only way you could possibly hope to tell when the photos were taken. Some were shot right here, at the very table where we were sitting. Other young and old faces stared out of pictures. Some had clearly had a good time, but others looked battered and bruised.

I wondered how many good times this little makeshift bar had seen; how many old memories were hauled out and shined up for young ears; how many dreams had been nursed over a bottle of cheap beer after a *novillada*; how many cracked ribs, how many trips to the toilet where blood had been pissed; how many disasters which had led to the borrowed suits of lights never being worn again. This was where a professional career in bullfighting could begin and end in a single evening.

Suddenly, we were all plunged into pitch darkness. The electricity had cut out. It happened at the worst possible time for the football fans – a penalty was about to be taken – so I knew they'd be furious. For a split second there was silence. In that instant I heard a dog barking somewhere off in the distance. And I heard a voice.

'Aw, good grief . . .'

It was John Fulton sitting next to me in the shadows. Atsuhiro laughed.

Someone shouted. Then more shouts filled the air. Lots of laughter.

Then the bar lit up, music slowly wound up to speed on a cassette-player, the lights went on above our heads, the TV spluttered into life. John shook his head in disbelief and everyone cheered.

I glimpsed our host arguing with a waiter in the corner of the shed. He'd ordered lots of extra food and drink which stood in a mound in the middle of the table. It was enough to feed the entire crowd. But he didn't seem to have the money to pay for it. There was a lot of shrugging and clapping of empty pockets going on. Eventually the waiter threw his arms up, helped himself to a bit of fried pork and left. Our host downed a beer and ran after him, offering to leave his address as a guarantee of payment.

John pretended not to notice what was happening. But I caught his eye and he blew his cheeks out as if to say 'Oh dear . . .'.

Through the haze of the beer I smiled and patted him on the shoulder. He grinned back at me. Atsuhiro nudged John and chuckled. Then we all started to giggle.

Our laughter echoed out of the bar and into the darkness, it drifted through the empty tunnel leading into the deserted, litter-strewn bullring, floated past the spot where the cropped-haired kids had been playing in the dust with the horns until, finally, it edged its way upwards into the still, cool air of the night.

SEVEN

The Rising Sun Kid

'*Niño del Sol Naciente* – that's the name we gave him . . . The Rising Sun Kid.'

I was in John Fulton's studio the following day. The late-morning sunlight flooded through the glass ceiling of his stunning penthouse art studio. John was showing me around the place.

The walls were lined with personal photographs, postcards and assorted bric-à-brac. Shelves were filled with large art books and books about bullfighting. Many of them contained shots of John himself. There he was as a skinny youth, looking out of a grainy black-and-white photograph like a young, much lankier Frank Sinatra, all hollow cheeks and thin wrists. Another showed him during his graduation to the rank of full matador, his hair swept back and his skin tanned. One photo taken a few years later revealed John in Madrid, looking older and wiser but still enthusiastic. Another small snap showed him standing next to Ernest Hemingway and his wife Mary when the writer was on assignment for *Life* magazine in Spain in 1959. Then there was a shot of John and Peter O'Toole both dressed in suits of lights: John told me he was so sick of turning up on the set of *Lawrence of Arabia* every day dressed in Peter O'Toole's costume that he decided to make the actor dress up as him – just for one afternoon. Finally, there was an intriguing picture of John at a party: Bobby Moore, the English football legend, was facing John; a distinguished looking Henri Charrier – the real Papillon – was in the middle of the group while a diminutive character dressed in strange silk clothes was holding court. 'No one knew who he was. He was always throwing lavish parties in Málaga or Marbella – we just called him the "Phoney Count",' laughed John.

Against another wall was a pile of boxes. Postcards and leaflets peeped out from their lids. I searched through them: they all showed Atsuhiro Shimoyama as a *novillero*. In one of the glossy flyers he was holding a bunch of red roses in his right hand and a bull's ear which he'd just cut off in his left. His face glistened with sweat, but he was happy and pleased with himself. His green-and-gold suit of lights looked fantastic. Beneath it was another shot of Atsuhiro using his *muleta* to give passes to a three-year-old bull. The bull's head was lowered as Atsuhiro leaned way out, using every inch of his lithe frame to slowly lead the bull into a graceful pass. Another shot showed him being carried out of a bullring by a group of young people. One of them, an attractive young woman, was holding up a large watermelon for some reason. Everyone was smiling and laughing, like people snapped halfway through a successful birthday party, clearly having a fantastic time. The hero of the hour, The Rising Sun Kid, was on their shoulders. Wearing a pink-and-gold suit of lights, Atsuhiro held up both hands in a victory salute. A small red bloodstain was visible on his inner thigh. It had probably come from the bull he'd just killed.

'He was in perfect physical condition. He'd been a dancer and a gymnast in Japan before he became interested in bullfighting. That was good, because if you take a Spanish kid who wants to be a bullfighter, you've got to turn him into an athlete as well. Nowadays in modern bullfighting, physical conditioning is really important . . .'

John sat down and leafed through some more photos of Atsuhiro he'd pulled out of a drawer to show me.

'He was also brave, he was graceful, and had a pleasing charisma that got to the Spaniards immediately. The moment he walked into the bullring people reacted to him. And of course when he fought the bulls, he didn't just fight them: he fought them with one of the purest styles. He knocked the socks off them. They never expected it. It took everyone by surprise,' he said raising his eyebrows.

'How did you manage his career?' I asked John.

'My own plan was that it should be a very slow progression. That he should really be properly prepared in private before he ever appeared in a public bullfight. And so the plan was to train him, get him some experience on the ranches, and then buy a number of bulls – reject bulls – starting with two-year-olds and then working up to four-year-olds, so that he'd be able to handle a fully grown bull. So, when he made his début with aspiring Spanish novices, he would appear superior to all of them because of the experience he'd gained privately rather than publicly.' John laid his hands out flat on the table where we were sitting.

'Why was that so important?' I wondered.

John smiled and leaned back in his seat. 'Because a Spanish bullfighter can start out without knowing his ass from his elbow and stumble around the ring in a novice bullfight – two weeks later no one will even remember he looked like a stumblebum. But if John Fulton stumbled around or if Atsuhiro stumbled around, they would remember for the rest of their lives. No matter how good he became afterwards, they would always say, "I saw him years ago, he's no good." I was anxious to fight anywhere and that was a mistake. But I tried to avoid doing the same with Atsuhiro, for several reasons. The main one being that once he made his début as a novice he would spend the shortest time possible in the novice ranks and go right into the semi-pro ranks after the first season. Then, the following season, he would become a full matador. Because he had the ability . . .'

John went on to explain how he had managed to get some financial investment from backers interested in Atsuhiro's career. The plan was to make sure The Rising Sun Kid wasn't snapped up by bigger fish if he ever hit the big time.

'Investors insisted that I had him signed to a five-year contract or they wouldn't put up any money. And so by the time that happened, the season was well under way, he was anxious to start fighting and I made probably some bad judgements, some bad decisions, and pushed him a little too soon. And of course this accident happened . . .'

I leafed through some of the photographs of Atsuhiro which were lying on the table. 'Tell me about the accident, John,' I said.

'Well, in 1995 we had a series of six *novilladas,* starting on 8 July and going on till 16 August. That day, the 16th, was when he was injured. On 12 August he'd been tossed by a bull and it had stepped on the calf of his leg and he was in tremendous pain. By the time we got to the town in the South of France where he was supposed to fight on the 14th, he could hardly walk. And so I said, "Really, don't fight. It's ridiculous for you to fight when you're in this condition." And he said, "No, we've come a long way." Even the impresario said, "No, no – we'll substitute you and put you on later." I should have insisted, but he wanted to fight having gone all that way. It was a very windy day; his bull was – well, each time you gave him a pass, rather than turning around and attacking again it would run off. It was a huge bullring and so he was forced to really overdo it on his bad leg. But he was good and the people liked him; he was very brave, he got knocked down a couple of times, but his performance was not the success we needed. And the critics said he looked green, which was what we were trying to avoid.

'The following day we were fighting in a small town on the Med coast in Spain. Again, when we got to this town, people saw him and said this guy can't fight he's limping so bad. But Atsuhiro said, "If they give me a shot to kill the pain, I'll fight." So I talked to a doctor there and we stopped off at the hospital on the way to the bullring and they gave him a shot. He cut both ears off the bull that afternoon, he was marvellous. He couldn't do any of the fancy stuff; all he did was straight, classic bullfighting. And he was appearing with three guys who are used to fighting in small towns and they knew all the tricks. They'd stand on one finger, they'd swallow swords, they'd jump over the bulls and do somersaults – anything. But Atsuhiro went out and with straight, classic bullfighting was awarded both of the bull's ears, and the people carried him around on their shoulders for about half an hour after the fight was over. He was about another hour or so signing autographs.

'The next day we went to another town and he really couldn't walk. But he said, "I'll fight if I can get a shot." So we talked to a doctor and at the time he was supposed to get a shot before the fight . . . but the doctor never showed up. So he was not in his best physical condition and the bulls were very, very big. They never let us see them before the fight, and the guy who set this up for me said, "Ah, don't worry about it, they'll be just like they were in the other town." They were much larger. Much more difficult animals.

'During the course of the fight one of the bulls tossed its head up and cracked him on the jaw, and hit him on the side of the neck. Well, we didn't know it had hit him on the side of the neck, we saw it hit him on the jaw. It swelled up, they had to bleed it, and they suggested we get an X-ray but he seemed fine, except that he was depressed. He seemed really down. What happened was the following day he suffered a thrombosis. They rushed him to the hospital . . .'

The sun streamed down on us as we talked. John spoke very clearly and carefully, picking his way through the chronology of events and the words like someone doing a Sunday morning reading in church. I asked him to explain in more detail about the thrombosis.

'We didn't see it. If we'd seen it, if we'd been able to recognise it, he probably wouldn't be paralysed. But there was no way that anyone could have suspected; even if we'd been in a place where they could have done a test on him it wouldn't have shown up until it was too late . . . I live a hundred yards from the big social security hospital and I'd gone out for some antibiotics. When I came back, Atsuhiro said to me, "I can't talk properly, my tongue's not working and I can't feel my fingers . . ." and he raised his arm to show me that he couldn't move his fingers. He said, "Something is happening to my brain." His arm was just completely limp. He tried to stand up and his leg went. So by the time I got the car out we could hardly lift him into the car, Vicente and I, and we drove him straight over to the hospital.

'They didn't know what to do. They put him in observation, they X-rayed his neck, they thought it was a bone thing. Until they did a proper CAT scan they didn't see what the real damage was. And that was 24 hours later. By that time he had a massive thrombosis that affected a large area of his brain and particularly the motor area of his movements of the hand and the foot and the left side of his body.'

'How did he cope with that?' I asked.

'Well,' said John, 'he didn't understand what had happened to him. He was in a coma for five days. He was completely gone. We have a carotid artery on each side of our neck and just before it gets to the jawline it splits into two: one of them is the exterior one, which irrigates all of the face and scalp; the interior one irrigates the brain. The interior carotid artery was clogged and so the blood couldn't reach the brain. No oxygen got to his brain.'

John leaned back in his seat and shook his head. Then he explained how it was that Atsuhiro had managed to survive.

'The simplest way to explain it is this: we have an emergency plumbing system which goes from one side of the body to the other. That, in an emergency, can work and in Atsuhiro's case, since he was young and in such tremendous physical condition, it picked up and blood was being supplied from the right side of the brain to the left side, so the damage wasn't any more extensive. It was extensive enough but this thing functioned. We were told afterwards that it functions in only 15 per cent of cases. So he could have died. Or been totally paralysed.'

John pursed his lips, shook his head again and then stood up. He looked through some videos which were stacked behind the TV until he found the one he wanted.

'Okay, you saw Atsuhiro last night in Alcalá de Guadaira. You saw him walk by himself, chatting, laughing, signing autographs and even trying to stick a peanut up my nose. He's doing really well – right? Now watch this; this is what he was like shortly after his accident.'

He pressed the play button on the machine.

The image which flickered onto the screen showed Atsuhiro in hospital. He was wearing sky-blue pyjamas and was sitting in a wheelchair. His left arm was cradled in a thick, heavily padded sling. On the hospital wall behind him were some religious postcards, some snaps of bullfighters and a cartoon of him. A small Japanese flag was on top of a tray next to his bed.

I heard John's voice, off-camera, asking Atsuhiro a question – something simple like, 'How are you today?'

In response Atsuhiro stared straight ahead. His eyes moved slowly. He was having great difficulty forming an answer to the question. He blinked a few times. Then he slowly gave a wandering answer. He looked shell-shocked. The drugs and the accident had slowed him down beyond recognition.

John paused the image on the screen. The frozen image of Atsuhiro sitting in hospital was painful to see. He looked hollow – a young man groping, trying to grasp on to something, anything, that would help him get back to the place he'd been both physically and mentally, before the accident in the bullring.

John stopped the tape. He went through the pile of cassettes again until he found one which he put in the video machine.

The picture showed John himself at a ranch. Rays from the late spring sunshine bathed everything in a warm glow. John was playing with a young cow – a 'mosquito' he derisively called it when I asked him what it was – and it flew past him as he expertly used a small cape on it. When he finished a series of passes there was a round of applause from the small group of onlookers. At the edge of the screen, next to a fence, Atsuhiro appeared. Other men, including John and Vicente, helped him out towards the animal. He was walking slowly, the left side of his body still limp and slack. But he faced the animal alone. Other matadors stood to the side with capes, ready to distract the animal if it threatened him. But they weren't needed. The animal charged and, using his right hand, Atsuhiro gave it several good passes. Everyone cheered.

When he'd finished with the cape, Atsuhiro walked across the bullring, past whoever was shooting the tape and straight out towards a field.

'Atsuhiro! Where are you going?' called the cameraman.

No answer.

'Atsuhiro . . . what are you doing?'

Atsuhiro had stopped at the edge of a field, unzipped his flies with his right hand and shouted over his shoulder: 'What do you think I'm doing? I'm taking a piss!'

The tape clicked off.

John sat back smiling. 'That was taken a month or so ago. As you can see he's much better.'

'So how is he now?' I asked.

'Well, you saw him last night. He's recovered amazingly well. At the hospital they gave him a wheelchair and told him to get used to it, that it would be his companion for the rest of his life. Now he walks by himself, without a cane or a crutch or anything. He still doesn't have a normal gait and the worst part is his lower arm and hand. From the knee down and from the elbow down he has practically no control over his movement. But he's determined he's going to recover and return to the ring to fight again. The doctors say he's crazy, that it's impossible . . .'

'How do you feel about that?'

'I'm a romantic and I believe in miracles and I believe that people can make miracles happen. And, although I have my doubts, I have to believe that it's possible for him to overcome this thing, because he believes it so thoroughly. It's the motor behind an incredibly gruelling and boring and exhausting rehabilitation programme with exercises. You see, the Spanish doctor said: "The brain cells are dead, they never rejuvenate: get used to being a cripple – you'll never fight a bull, dance or do gymnastics again." The international neurologist said: "If you do these exercises, it's possible that you could cause enough stimulation to the healthy parts of the brain around the dead part that it might be possible for them to assume some of the jobs that those burnt-out circuits did." And so that's really the only hope we have. And all the exercises they gave him are designed to stimulate the healthy neurals to try to make new connections and take over those movements . . .'

He showed me designs for a hand exerciser which he'd manufactured himself based on photographs of a very expensive model he'd seen advertised in a medical catalogue. He'd also painted a series of Japanese-style pictures which he hoped would stimulate Atsuhiro's brain. When the young man's family visited from Japan, John looked after them, showed them around and reassured them about Atsuhiro. He said he was very grateful for their understanding about the whole affair. They knew that Atsuhiro had been doing what he wanted to do when he was injured.

John took me on a little tour of his house. Some parts were decorated in Romanesque themes, other parts were North African, and one stunning little room was all blue with a kaleidoscopic ceiling containing inlaid stained-glass stars.

'Great room,' I said, looking at the ceiling and the walls and the glass beads hanging over the door.

'I did it for a belly-dancer I once got to know . . . she liked it.'

A huge portrait of John in his suit of lights was hung on one of the walls going up the stairs.

'It was a gift – someone did it for me after seeing me fight,' said

John. It looked awesome. John, decades before, gazed down like a knight from another century.

I spied a carved Roman foot made of marble on the floor.

'I went to some Roman ruins at Itálica which is just outside Seville. An old local man was using that as a door-stop of all things. I bought it from him. I felt I had to rescue it. I couldn't believe what he was using it for. He hadn't a clue what it was or what it was worth,' John told me.

'What do you do with it?' I enquired.

'Oh, to be honest, I use it as a door-stop.'

We went back up to the studio and sat down. The air had heated up with the sunshine. John opened a window. The noise of traffic drifted in. The only thing that was louder was the sound of singing birds.

'How do you feel about bullfighting now? With Atsuhiro and everything . . . do you still love it?' I asked him.

'Yeah, bullfighting has been the most important thing in my life and it's been the most important thing in Atsuhiro's life. Of course, I'm extremely critical now of young men who have been given every opportunity to develop as bullfighters and don't – because they don't understand what they're throwing away. And, for whatever reason, it comes to them perhaps too easily nowadays. In my day you had to do well in one fight so that you could get another one. Nowadays, if you have the financial backing, it doesn't matter what you do. You may never be a great star but it's not going to interrupt your series of performances because they're all paid for. So the younger guys tend to be a bit lax. When I see that and I think of my situation, what my situation was like and what Atsuhiro's situation is like, it really angers me. To see them throwing away these opportunities . . . I often cry at bullfights because I can just imagine what Atsuhiro would have done by now if this hadn't happened to him. I mean, the young Spanish guys who were his contemporaries, some of them are leading *novilleros* now, and I was convinced that he had more talent than any of them.'

He went on to say that he was hoping to put together a big cartel for a bullfight in Seville – a benefit event with all the proceeds going to Atsuhiro to help pay for his convalescence. He said it was very difficult to pin down some of the top names in the business to give

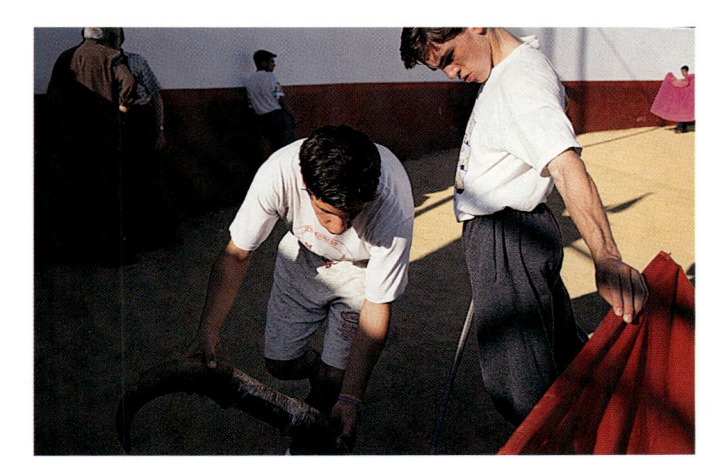

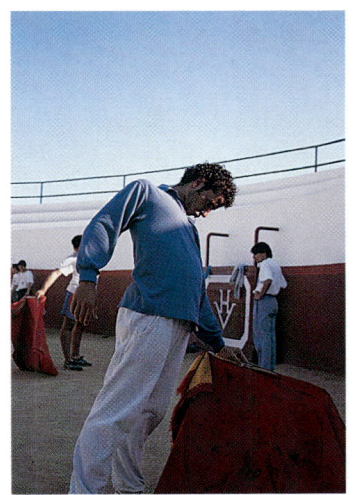

These teenagers are training in 100-degree heat under a burning Sevillian sun: their eyes are on the prize of a career in bullfighting. Potential managers watch from the side, hoping to spot a prospect

ABOVE: John Fulton, early 1950s, skinny, hungry and dreaming; TOP RIGHT: John Fulton with Peter O'Toole during the filming of *Lawrence of Arabia*. Fulton was O'Toole's stand-in during the shooting and the actor agreed to dress up as John for one day – as a matador; BELOW RIGHT: San Miguel de Allende, Mexico, 1994: at the age of 62, John Fulton faced a bull for the last time as a professional *matador de toros*. His first fight had taken place in this very bullring four decades before

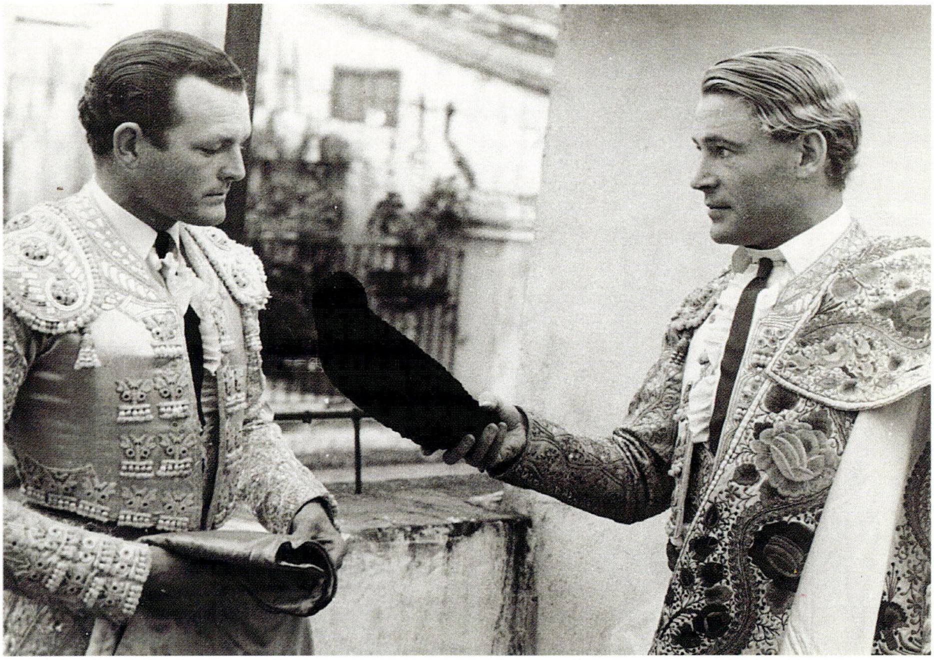

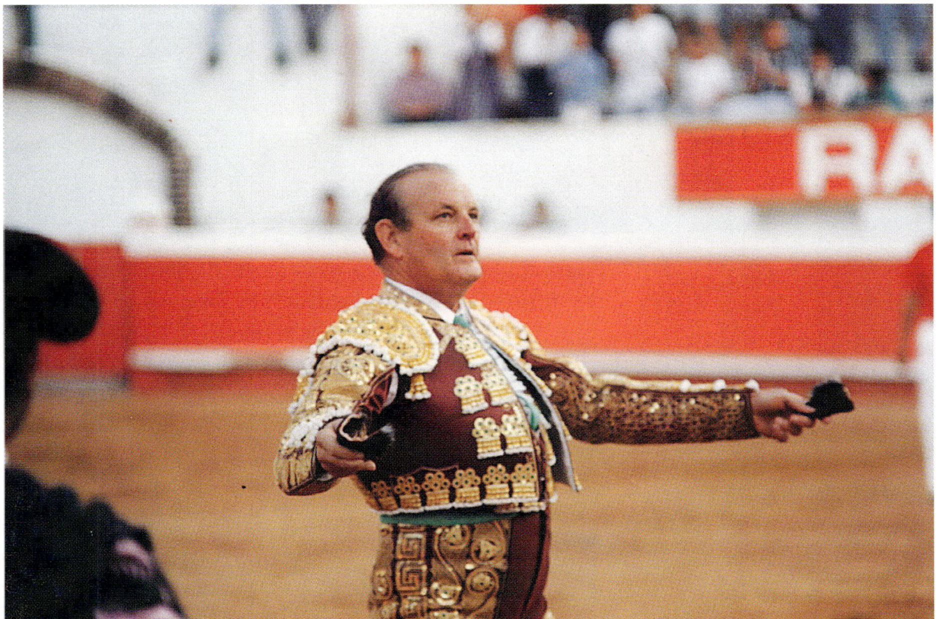
RA

ABOVE: Northern Spain, 1994: A triumphant Atsuhiro Shimoyama, the 'Rising Sun Kid', is held aloft by local *aficionados* after a successful bullfight (photo © Damaio Miron);
TOP RIGHT: Seville, 1995: Atsuhiro in the aftermath of the almost fatal illness which struck him after he'd been hit by a bull's horns. He's lucky to be alive;
BELOW RIGHT: Atsuhiro takes a bow after a bull is dedicated to him following a *novillada*

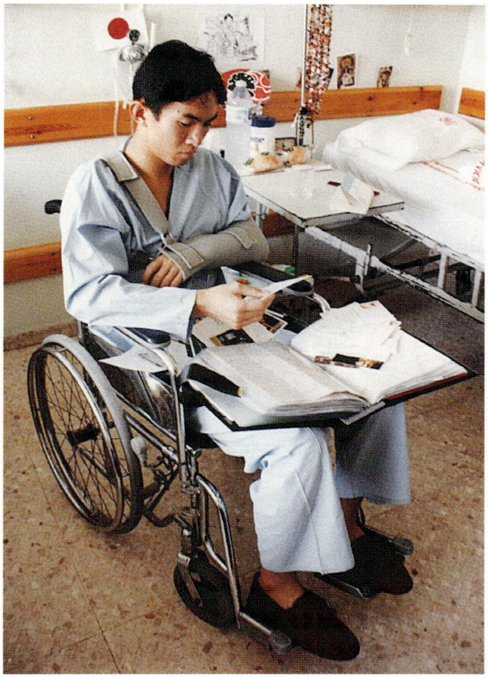

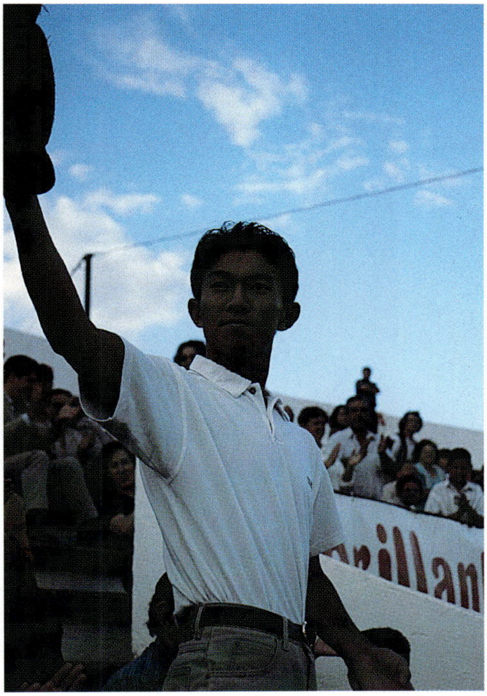

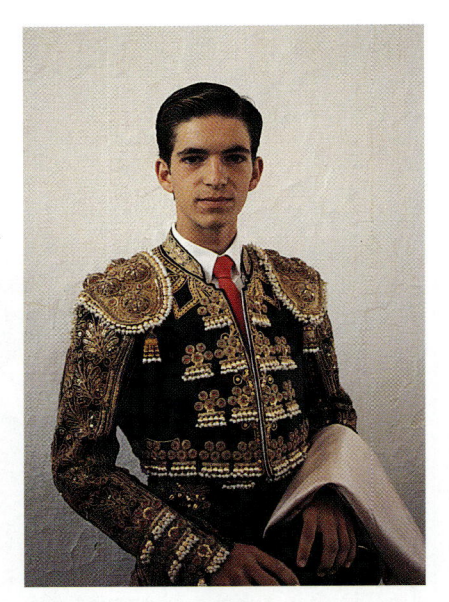

The *novilleros*: almost ready and not quite willing, nervously awaiting the signal that tells them they can face a bull in public for the first time. Most will make it through the evening in one piece – albeit with bruised ribs and dented pride

TOP LEFT: This *novillero* shows more guts than style as he lines the bull up for the kill – this is the point known as the 'moment of truth';
TOP RIGHT: this hopeful has lost his cape and his shoes; he's seriously thinking about running but he can't – his family is watching and so is half the town.
So he stays and faces the bull and eventually kills it;
ABOVE: this young man almost got beheaded trying to do a fancy move with the cape as the bull entered the ring

FROM THE TOP: The bull is due: locals lean over the entrance to the bullring waiting to catch the first glimpse of the beast; a second later it appears, battering towards the so-called 'gate of fear'; after a lap of honour once the matador has killed it, the bull is unceremoniously dragged from the ring; the butchers from the local slaughterhouse go to work on the dead bull. The meat will be sold in local shops in less than 24 hours him a cast-iron guarantee they would show up on the night, but he said he wouldn't give up. 'In fact I'm off down the Med coast tonight to Algeciras to see a top matador and his manager and then, if you're going up to Burgos, I'll probably see you when I'm there too, because I'm planning to approach two top names there during the *feria*. I have to. We need to raise some money for him. I really don't want to let Atsuhiro down. Anyway, matadors are usually good at helping out one another in hard times. Some of them had it difficult themselves and lots of them have heard about Atsuhiro's predicament. He knew plenty of them personally.'

In one of the videos I'd seen earlier there was a clip of Atsuhiro at a training ranch working alongside some of the richest and most sought-after names in the Spanish bullfighting world. They genuinely seemed to like him and he chatted and moved amongst them very easily. If he hadn't had the accident, he might, just might, have been a star himself.

'What would you say to people who suggest that maybe you're living your dream through him? How would you respond to a comment like that?'

John thought for a moment. The sun streamed through the transparent ceiling, making everything look like an old sepia-coloured photograph.

'I don't know . . . there might be some of that there. He's Japanese, I'm an American, we're from two different cultures. His acceptance is night and day to mine. Mine was negative, totally negative, except on the very high level by other professionals, people on ranches and things like that. But Atsuhiro had spontaneous mass acceptance; nobody gave a damn if John Fulton became a bullfighter, and everybody wanted Atsuhiro to become a bullfighter. We were mobbed everywhere we went. I enjoyed that because he enjoyed it. I enjoyed watching him. If I gave him a tip or a technique and he used it, and seemed excited and pleased with it, well, that excited and pleased me. I mean, shit, 42 years of your life dedicated to the bull-fighting profession, in which you gain experience, to simply go to the tomb with that in your head seems like a terrible waste of time to me. And here I had somebody who needed what I had, what I could give him. And I gave it to him, for the fun of giving it. Nothing would have made me happier than seeing Atsuhiro become the first Japanese matador in the history of bullfighting . . .

'And it had nothing to do with the money that he could have made, which would have been incredible, not only from the bulls but from sponsorship, from Japanese corporations. But that was secondary; the important thing for me was to see the way he assimilated the 24-carat information that I was able to give him, assimilate it, perform it, watch the reaction of the Spaniards to it . . . that was what excited me.'

John then reached for a scrap of paper and a pen and turned to me.

'When I first met Atsuhiro, I told him the bullfighting industry was like no other in the world. But he was determined to try. We were in a bar somewhere or a café, I can't remember where, and I grabbed a napkin and wrote this down on it . . .'

John scribbled on the piece of paper.

'I wrote that in normal life, "One plus one equals two". Always. Then underneath it I wrote: "One plus one can equal 11, two or even 96." That's bullfighting. I was trying to show Atsuhiro how corrupt and difficult a world it is to try and break into. What did he do? Well, he took the pen and paper off me and wrote: "John plus Atsuhiro equals . . ."'

John paused, holding the pen above the paper.

'Equals what?' I asked.

He said nothing. He just drew something on the paper. Then he turned it around so I could see what it was. I read: 'John plus Atsuhiro equals ∞.'

And he pointed to the mathematical symbol for infinity.

'That's what he said the two of us equalled, what we had the potential for: *infinity*. Can you believe that? Because I did . . .'

EIGHT

Where it all Started

The endless fields of sunflowers must have been beautiful a few weeks before I saw them, but by the time I drove past they looked sad and diseased. Their heads were pockmarked and drooping, and their bright yellow colour had faded to a mottled shade of copper.

I was heading south from Seville towards the white mountain town of Ronda – the place where, I'd been assured by numerous people I'd met and by the countless guidebooks I'd leafed through, the modern bullfight was born.

I'd spent most of the previous day with John Fulton talking about Atsuhiro. Then, in the evening, I'd returned to Alcalá de Guadaira to see some professional bullfights.

The second set of *corridas* was billed as one of the highlights of the town's fiesta. After the young *novilleros* had finished their guts-and-glory performances, this professional bullfight featuring three full matadors was regarded as the big attraction. So I decided to go along and see it for myself.

To my surprise, the crowd which turned up at the pro-night in Alcalá was much smaller than the one attending *novilladas* the night before. In fact, the bullring looked two-thirds empty. I asked one of the locals why this was. 'I don't know,' he said absent-mindedly, 'the *novilladas* are better fun, I suppose. They're always on their arses . . .'

It was a windier night than the evening before. The men with the hoses were out spraying the sand more regularly than they had been 24 hours previously. The matadors used jugs of water on their capes to keep the material from being blown everywhere. The heavy fabric looked blotched and stained when they'd finished soaking it.

The sun bounced off the empty bleached-white stone seats. A dog wandered around, sniffing at empty peanut packets and cocking its leg every so often. The men who looked after the bullring seemed fed up. The excitement from the young *novilleros* who'd been performing all week had worn off. The organisers leaned on the barriers, the skin on their faces pushed into folds by their resting hands. I saw them glancing at their watches several times and yawning. They were clearly keen for the night to be over and done with.

The three matadors were uninspiring. I sat quietly in the stands watching them. Initially they seemed competent enough but the bulls they were given, which were slow and fat, made them look awkward and bland. A journalist in Madrid had told me that the average Spanish fighting bulls of the 1990s were dreadful. 'They've got to do something about these weak bulls,' he commented, sighing in exasperation. He said the problem could be traced back to the late 1960s when the industry ruled that matadors had to face four-year-old bulls instead of three-year-olds. This decision didn't please many bullfighters, who believed that the older the bull the more dangerous and wily it'll be. According to the journalist, breeders had colluded with managers to produce a generation of bulls which were 'less fierce: more of a collaborator than an enemy'.

The matadors I saw in Alcalá de Guadaira tried their best to add some flair to their performances but ended up looking like circus acts. You could tell the bulls had either been tampered with or were just very sad, nervous and unhealthy animals that should never have been allowed near a cape. But that didn't stop the matadors from pulling out all the stops in an effort to generate some excitement. One of them threw away his sword and cape at one point and held his jacket open to show the bull his chest. His gesture of defiance and bravery seemed rehearsed and out of place. The spectators in the almost empty bullring barely reacted. Several of the bulls fell over, their tongues flopping around in their mouths and the blood pouring down their backs. The matadors attempted to dispatch them with their short swords. Sometimes they died, other times they just refused to go. People started talking, lit cigarettes or drank rather than watch the bull cling on to life.

The whole thing, from beginning to end, was a sad sight.

Each time a bull was due to enter the ring groups of kids hung over the side of the wall to watch. The organisers shouted at them and shooed them away, but they did the same thing every time anyway. Some threw the wrapping-paper from sweets or half-finished ice-creams at the bulls when they came running out.

Because it was a professional *corrida*, picadors were included in each fight. They were older men, fat and padded, on huge horses, who entered the bullring like pantomime villains. Their huge bellies were held in place by wide, straining silk sashes. One of them, younger than the others, looked like a fat trainee opera singer. Few were greeted with anything other than silence and most were sent on their way with jeers and boos. Their long poles with the *pic* at the end could really damage a bull's muscles. It was a different animal after it had encountered the picador – and the crowd knew this. Given that the animals were in fairly poor shape anyway, the spectators weren't inclined to see the bulls' condition reduced further just so the matador could have an easy time of it. This increased their hostility to the picador, who looked like an embalmed Dr Frankenstein creation on his mount. One of the bulls, the fifth of the evening, collapsed when the picador jabbed it with his lance. The crowd became lively for a moment, shouting at the picador and screaming about the unhealthy state of the fat bull. The organisers looked at each other sideways and blew out their cheeks hard.

Even when the matadors started working the bulls with their *muletas* the crowd never really warmed to them. A few self-conscious '¡Olés!' were heard but they echoed around the deserted spaces and blew away on the breeze. An uneasy silence settled on the crowd. The whole affair was lacklustre. Everyone was just going through the motions.

A photographer from the local newspaper, a thin, dapper man dressed in fine Italian clothes and wearing a very sweet aftershave, caught my eye. He turned his back on the proceedings, took a sip from a can of beer, narrowed his eyes, and shook his head looking at the ground.

At the end of each fight, some half-hearted awards were given to the bullfighters, before each matador went on a tour of the bullring.

They conspicuously avoided going near the vast empty areas. To be fair, I think they had tried to give the locals a half-decent show. But they were second-raters, perhaps even third-raters, and everyone knew it. Even the kids just stared at them. No one asked for autographs. A couple of them did, however, have their little followings. Some glamorous women sat in the front seats beside smartly dressed men in blazers and straw hats. The rest of the crowd looked as if they had come straight from work, but this group of bullfighter-groupies looked as if they'd taken all day to choose their clothes. They seemed out of place – which was exactly their intention. When their favourite bullfighter walked around the ring on his lap of honour they threw him a bunch of flowers. It wasn't a spontaneous gesture. The matador, dressed in 'celestial blue' according to the programme, slowed down when he came near them because he knew the flowers were about to be thrown. It was all staged and, in a way, sad.

The following morning, before I checked out of my hotel to drive to Ronda, I read the early editions of the local newspapers to see if they'd reported the previous evening's *corrida* accurately. I'd heard the papers were often guilty of writing glowing reviews of very bad bullfights. But the articles I skimmed through seemed fair enough: the headlines called the bulls 'mediocre' and the matadors 'modest'. They went on to say the *plaza de toros* had only been a quarter full and it mentioned the troublesome wind. One even said the fans 'had lost interest' in the proceedings and that they hadn't responded to the three matadors as they had earlier in the week to the young *novilleros*.

One reviewer also noted that the high point of the last fight – in fact the high point of the whole evening – had been when a gigantic rat had scurried across the sand of the bullring. It suddenly appeared, bringing everything to a standstill, and was greeted with whistling and clapping. From that point on, the matador never looked really in charge of anything. It had been humiliating. He knew, and so did everyone else including the reporter, that he'd been upstaged by a rodent.

The writer noted that, like all the bulls, the rat had been 'a bit overweight'.

WHERE IT ALL STARTED

The landscape changed as the sun shifted. One moment the sky looked benign and peaceful; the next it was brooding and threatening. The clouds looked like pillows of mud in murky pond water.

Ronda lies in the heart of the Serrania de Ronda mountains, on a plateau about 2,300 feet above sea level. The tourist books talk of the town as one of the finest places in the whole of Spain. But the road I took there was winding and disappointing. I felt as though I was entering by the back door. A housing estate greeted me, the graffiti on its walls complaining about the government. The wide nondescript highway which followed narrowed into a long street with trees along one side. Then I turned a corner and suddenly I was in the centre of town. It felt like a place under siege. Hundreds of tourists were wandering around. Their faces had that dazed, lethargic expression you see on tourists throughout the world. They filed in and out of tiny shops which all sold the same things: ceramic plates, matador dolls, wind-up bulls and postcards of pigs smoking cigarettes.

A very modern carpark was situated underneath an apparently ancient cobbled town square. I emerged from its cool blackness and, half-blinded by the sun, went off to find a hotel for the night.

Ten minutes later I opened the shutters of my top-floor window and looked across the rooftops of the town. The grey mountains in the distance were striped by lines of broken clouds. Beneath them were bleached green hills, dappled with clumps of trees and crops. The sun was beginning to lower and a strong wind was blowing. Below me on the street an old lady walked along with an arthritic dog following her. Every few paces she stopped and shouted at it. Then she pulled a shapeless wine-coloured woollen cardigan about her bony shoulders.

I went out and wandered around the back streets. Bits of newspaper, swirls of dust and empty cans rattled and rustled through the darkened chilled passages. Everyone from the Romans to the Arabs to the Greeks had been here at one time or another. The buildings and the houses and the places of worship all reflected their diverse influences: Moorish symbols invoking North Africa ('There's no conqueror but Allah' said one carved doorway) jostled for position next to dying Christs and sorrowful Virgins. The people who lived in this town were descended from some of the oldest civilisations in the Western world. I'd read that traders came and went from this area of Spain thousands of years before Jesus was born.

I walked through the alleyway. Some long, interesting-looking, grand and imposing passageways led nowhere. Other bland entranceways, dark and unwelcoming, opened up to reveal secret mini-palaces. Green plants and red and yellow and blue flowers hung from windows which were gilded with iron façades. Houses seemed to be built one on top of another. Layer upon layer of rooms and doors and stairs. In tunnels of sunlight everything was bleached and whitewashed. But in the concealed places, in the shadows thrown up by the tall buildings, they looked dark and grey and the early-evening breeze felt cold.

I eventually emerged into the main square. A few diehard tourists straggled around its perimeter. They were mostly couples huddled close together keeping each other warm. The edges of the square were studded with numerous dark little shop doorways. I entered one to see if anything interesting was on offer. An old woman swaddled in dark woollens, her head covered with a blue scarf, jumped to her feet when I went in.

'Round-a-Square! Round-a-Square!' She waved her stumpy little arms in the direction of rows of linen tablecloths. Some were square shaped, others were for round tables. 'Nice for Mama! Nice for Mama!'

I felt the quality with my fingers. The linen was soft and cool and clean.

'Price cheap! Price cheap!' She had the voice of a jackdaw. When I gently demurred she instantly stopped talking, her thin mouth snapping shut like the worn brass clasp on an old leather purse.

At the far end of the square was the famous Tajo Bridge. The gorge beneath it dropped for 500 feet on either side. Children played around on it, standing close to the edge and looking over the side to have their photo taken. Their parents didn't seem to mind. They hugged themselves to keep out the cold.

I walked across the bridge into the old part of Ronda, the Moorish and aristocratic quarter. It was old all right, but cleaned-up old. The road was being recobbled and every dark stone looked like a polished 1,000-year-old oriental egg. It was impossible to walk anywhere.

The drop from the pavement to the surface of the road was about two feet. Two old women had to help each other down the step, one hanging onto a piece of the other's dress. They looked like exhausted climbers roped together in the Himalayas.

I visited a little antique shop. A grey-haired man hovered around while I leafed through some old photographs. Stoic, pious faces stared back at me from the sepia-tinted images. The women wore mourning black, heavy silver brooches and stiff collars and high combs in their hair. The men's eyes were coal black; they were determined to look respectable. An old broken-down chest of drawers lay at one end of the shop. It wasn't for sale but when the proprietor left me alone for a moment, I couldn't resist poking around inside. I opened some of the drawers and thrust my hand into their darkness, feeling around for the contents: I found an old whalebone corset in the top drawer and the bottom half of a set of salmon-pink false teeth in the lowest. When I closed the drawer with a thud, I heard the teeth rattle and skid around like a hockey puck in the hollow space.

After leaving the shop I walked back towards the bridge and descended a steep set of steps into the gorge. Grey and copper walls of stone surrounded me. From the ground I realised why Ronda was so important to its past invaders and inhabitants. Its sheer height, position and inaccessibility made it the perfect place to conquer and defend. Anyone approaching it would be visible for miles. It was an ideal defensive stronghold: difficult to get into and even more difficult to get shifted out of by force.

The Gadalevín river – which means 'deep river' – was hardly visible. The summer heat had almost completely dried it up. The stones which should have been buried below deep, fast-flowing water poked out, exposed and cracked, like faces beneath crumpled and threadbare shrouds.

I retraced my way back up the steep steps. These had been built by local Christian slaves when the town had been conquered by the Arabs. They were then forced to draw water from the river and carry it back up into the centre of Ronda. It gave rise to a local proverb which says: 'In Ronda you will die heaving up water skins.'

I walked back across the bridge in the cool evening light. It was here, allegedly, that the peasants of Ronda had committed one of the most barbaric acts of the Spanish Civil War. Hemingway described the incident in *For Whom the Bell Tolls*. The people had taken matters into their own hands one day and, encouraged by armed Republicans, formed a sickle-waving gauntlet through which they forced local fascist sympathisers to run. Some ran straight off the edge of the gorge to their deaths, others were battered and thrown off. He wrote:

> He placed them in two lines as you would place men for a rope-pulling contest, or as they stand in a city to watch the ending of a bicycle road race with just room for the cyclists to pass between, or as men stood to allow the passage of a holy image in a procession. Two metres was left between the lines and they extended from the door of the *Ayuntamiento* [Town Hall] clear across the *plaza* to the edge of the cliff. So that, from the doorway of the *Ayuntamiento*, looking across the *plaza*, one coming out would see two solid lines of people waiting. They were armed with flails such as are used to beat out the grain, and they were a good flail's length apart . . . I heard a voice shout, 'Here comes the first one,' and it was Don Benito García, the mayor . . . Then I saw a man three men down from where I was standing and his face was working and he was biting his lips and his hands were white on his flail. I saw him looking towards Don Benito, watching him come on. And still nothing happened. Then, just before Don Benito came abreast of this man, the man raised his flail high so that it struck the man beside him and smashed a blow at Don Benito that hit him on the side of the head and Don Benito looked at him and the man struck him again and shouted, 'That's for you, *Cabron* [bastard],' and the blow hit Don Benito in the face and he raised his hands to his face and they beat him until he fell and the man who had struck him first called to others to help him and he pulled on the collar of Don Benito's shirt and others took hold of his arms and with his face in the dust of the *plaza*, they dragged him over the walk to the edge of the cliff and threw him over and into the river. And the man who hit him first was kneeling by the edge of the cliff looking over after him and saying,

'The *Cabron*! The *Cabron*! Oh, the *Cabron*!' He was a tenant of Don Benito and they had never gotten along together . . .

I stared over the edge of the cliff imagining I could still see blood on the rock face. I remembered the first time I'd read that passage, how horrified I was and how difficult it had been to sleep that night without dreaming of a chanting, out-of-control, hate-filled mob killing men and enjoying it.

I walked around for a while, letting the fresh air and the dying sun wash the uneasiness out of my mind. Finally, I headed for a cheap restaurant down one of the town's side streets. It smelled of strong coffee and wine. As I was reading the menu outside the restaurant I looked in the window of a tiny barber shop next door.

Men sat in cramped chairs, impassively watching news reports on the TV about a boat which had sunk. Their expressions never once changed, not even when a weeping woman appeared on the screen, being supported by relatives. When another report about a bombing came on, the barber stopped cutting his customer's hair, excused himself, then switched the channel to a bullfight. The men immediately shifted in their seats, sat up and shrugged off their glazed expressions.

After I'd eaten I left the restaurant and walked back through the darkness to my hotel. Deserted shops and empty bars echoed to the sounds of radios and TVs. I heard the odd voice shouting or screech of a chair shifting suddenly on a hard wooden floor.

Every so often a low whistle would sound around the edges of buildings, across rooftops and down tight little streets. It was the wind from the mountains, still blowing and filled with the coldness of the spring which it never seemed to shrug off; still searching and whining like a banshee, even on a summer's night.

The following morning four stray dogs followed me across town in the pale sunlight. I threw them a piece of my croissant as I walked towards the bullring. One of them, a black dog, swallowed it in one bite. A drooling, coffee-coloured Corgi, so old it could hardly walk, waddled along behind the other three. Its eyes were red and weeping, and it had the bearing of a Calcutta beggar.

The bullring was empty when I arrived. I looked around at the thousands of seats, and the countless arches, high columns and dark tunnels which led into the ring. Although it was beginning to warm up a little in the direct sunlight, it was still as cold as night in the dark places. When I sat down on a seat to gaze around the bullring I immediately felt the cold slap of the stone through my trousers.

In the quiet of the moment I absorbed the atmosphere. My guidebooks told me the ring was built in 1781 and was probably the oldest *plaza de toros* in the world. It also had – at 66 metres – reputedly the widest bullring to be found anywhere. The structure was for the most part made of wood and it looked and felt just like the Roman arena it had once been. One writer claimed that the horses which used to be routinely gored to death by the bulls – in the days before they wore protective padding – were dragged out of the arena at the end of the bullfights and thrown over the edge of the cliffs into the gorge. Then the hungry buzzards ate them.

By the time I'd picked my way down through the seats and hopped on to the sand, more tourists had begun arriving. I walked across to the little white-walled museum which was located at one side of the ring. Inside I learned the details of Ronda's most famous bullfighting son – Pedro Romero, the man John Fulton had told me about. He was born in 1755 and started working with bulls when he was only eight years old. His grandfather Francesco invented the killing sword and the small cape, the *muleta*. His father Juan Romero was the first person to organise properly the matador's crew, the team of men known as the *cuadrilla*. Pedro stopped fighting bulls when he was 72 years old and he died at the age of 90 without once having been gored. It was reported that he managed to kill about 6,000 bulls during his career, most of them by the very difficult stationary *recibiendo* method.

Tourists of various nationalities were filtering in. Old candyfloss-haired ladies clutching handbags and peering through horn-rimmed spectacles, teenage girls drinking cans of Cola and wide-eyed *aficionados* filming everything with video cameras. They all filed through the little museum, looking at the first ancient examples of posters for bullfights, seeing the early suits of lights, examining paintings of the Romero family and poking at the stuffed bulls' heads.

John Fulton's suit of lights was also on display. Designed by the man himself, the cape showed an intricate embroidered representation of the crucified Christ. Photographs of John and some examples of his artwork were also hanging up. Near by was a smaller section showing Atsuhiro. In the photograph he was smiling and waving after a successful *novillada*. I looked at both displays for a few minutes: John's and Atsuhiro's faces and fates were permanently intertwined. Their brief brilliant moments of triumph were recorded and sealed behind glass cases, safe from the ravages of time and the pain of bulls.

Outside, wind blew the sand around in snapping waves. People walked across the bullring shielding their eyes. A woman waved a jacket around and shouted '*¡Olé!*' while her friends took photographs of her.

On my way out I met a middle-aged English couple from Kent. The man had a talent for spotting and identifying accents, he said. He accurately pinpointed mine to within a few miles of my home town in less than two or three sentences. I asked him what the trick was.

'I used to sell travel insurance . . . one of the biggest in the country, actually. I was always on the road – you get to know towns and accents, you know,' he told me.

I asked him why he'd visited Ronda's bullring. He thought for a moment.

'Well, it's historical, isn't it? It's the home of bullfighting. I'm no fan but I know that Spanish people do like it. Love it or loathe it, they say this is where it all started. That must be worth something.' He sniffed the air and brushed some fluff off his trousers.

His wife sat impassively beside him, fiddling with a camera. He looked like an insurance man all right: bland and trustworthy. What my parents might have called 'well-to-do'. His wife looked like the runner-up in a village flower show.

'Do you like bullfights?' I asked her.

'Oh, God, no!' she said. She was shocked I'd even asked. 'I like watching the running of the bulls in Pamplona, though – at least they get to kill a few people for a change. That's nice!' She suddenly sounded perky.

They went on to tell me they'd been travelling the length and breadth of Spain for about a month. They pulled their coats around them as they spoke. I noticed the man was wearing sandals without any socks on his weather-beaten feet. His toes were purple with the cold and his yellowing nails needed cutting.

'Córdoba was nice,' he said.

'Oh yes! Lovely . . . lovely . . .' muttered his wife.

'Segovia wasn't bad either . . .' he said, gazing heavenwards.

'Very nice. . . very nice,' she chirped.

'Stayed away from the Costas, though.' He wrinkled his nose up.

'Don't like the Costas! Don't like the Costas!' His wife shook her head in agreement. She turned her nose up in disgust and shivered at the thought of the Costas.

'Did Turkey last year . . . Very nice, very nice . . .'

'Oh, very nice, very nice . . .' She smiled and let her shoulders relax at the thought of Turkey.

'Nice breakfasts in Turkey . . . Nice bit of breakfast . . .' He looked sombre and serious, his eyes glazed over and staring into the middle-distance.

'Yes, they did a nice breakfast . . .' his wife agreed.

I said I had to go. They wished me all the best. They said they were already planning their holiday for the following year. Italy was a possibility.

I left the *plaza de toros* as more tourists were arriving on buses. The weather was warm one minute, then cold the instant the wind blew. But the mountain air was fresh and pure. The stray dogs were where I'd left them. They'd found a place in a sickle of sunlight and lay close together for extra warmth.

Near by were life-size statues of two famous matadors. The first was of Cayetano Ordoñez, also known as Niño de la Palma. The other was of his son Antonio Ordoñez. Ernest Hemingway, just as he had with their home town of Ronda, had a hand in immortalising both of them. He wrote about Cayetano in *Fiesta, The Sun Also Rises*. Then, in 1959, he wrote about Antonio for his *Life* magazine 'Dangerous Summer' article and subsequent book of the same name.

At his peak, Cayetano was regarded as a near genius in Spanish bullfighting. When he'd first arrived on the scene, a Madrid-based bullfighting critic wrote: 'He is from Ronda . . . and they call him Cayetano.' It was intended to be what it was: a simple, dramatic announcement. It worked. He was instantly hailed as the saviour of modern bullfighting. And Antonio was considered by many to be as great as his father, if not greater. The fact that he hailed from Ronda, the spiritual birthplace of the *corrida*, didn't do him any harm either.

I left the proud, strutting statues of the Ordeñez father and son behind and walked off to find a shop where I was told I could obtain photographs of the two matadors in their heyday.

After a few wrong turns up side streets I eventually found the place I was looking for. The photographs were in the window. One showed a shady-looking Hemingway standing between Cayetano and Antonio in 1959, the year he visited Ronda and called it a 'strange and lovely town'. Another pictured a younger, moodier Antonio, a year earlier, casually leaning on the wall around the Ronda bullring. A third had an uncertain, heavier Antonio standing next to another well-known American bullfighting fan, the jocular, replete Orson Welles.

I entered the shop and a little bell rang. A thin young man asked me if he could be of any assistance. When I expressed an interest in the pictures I was invited into the back office for an audience with Mr Miguel, the original photographer. I was gravely informed that Mr Miguel was 81 years old and the most famous photographer in Ronda.

Moments later, in a dingy little cave of an office, the leaning walls completely covered with old photographs and grand calendars, I shook hands with Mr Miguel as he slowly hoisted himself out of a chair. He looked like an ageing, unconcerned pope. His assistant showed him the photographs I was interested in. He peered at them with such care you might have sworn he'd never clapped his eyes on them before.

'I took these photographs when you weren't even born! Ha!'

He seemed surprised by my choice. Most foreign visitors were interested in snaps of Ronda at sunset or shots of the deep gorge in all its glory, he told me, not old bullfighters with dead writers and directors.

'You have an eye for the bulls, eh? Ha!' He tapped the side of his temple when he spoke, closing one eye like a poker player sizing up his hand.

I asked him how long he'd been taking photographs. He sniffed and assumed an air of importance.

'I started when I was only 14! Ha! – 14! I've taken 45,000 portraits for First Communions and 22,000 weddings right here in Ronda. My family are the people who live here.'

'Did you know who some of the famous people were when you took their pictures?' I asked.

'Yes, of course. Orson Welles – a big man, a big star! Hollywood!' He waved his arms as if he were trying singlehandedly to lift up the famous Hollywood sign.

'I am like him and his films. People saw what he saw. Now they see what I see. Because of these photographs, my eyes are famous all over the world . . . you understand?' he asked. I nodded.

'Ha! I do not like leaving Ronda. Whenever I did I always felt like returning!' He gave a rumbling little dismissive laugh, then he shuffled away from me.

He collapsed with a sigh on top of a regal red velvet cushion which lay in a cheap white metal chair and once gain took up residence behind a small oak desk. Underneath his throne he kept a large pile of important documents that only he got to look at. The most valuable were at the bottom, covered by a gold embroidered cloth.

I started to chat with him but in response to my questions about his career and his photographs he raised a finger and said: 'Wait!'

He slowly stood up, all aching joints and bent limbs, to his full height of four and a half feet. Then, with watery eyes and shaky hands, he reached under the cloth and probed around until, by touch alone, he found what he was looking for. He produced a large press-clipping about himself and handed it to me as though it was a royal proclamation. Then he bowed and sat down again. His fingers played over a long, very sharp pair of lead-coloured scissors which lay in front of him.

His assistant, a quiet, humble young man who had to shout at Mr Miguel to be heard, gave him the photographs which I'd purchased and he set about signing them for me. He wrote slowly and carefully in a very ornate hand.

'He works all day long, every day in the laboratory upstairs. He's the best in the business. Just look at his handwriting.' the assistant whispered.

'I thought he was deaf,' I said.

'Only sometimes . . .' he murmured.

Carefully and with a touch of reluctance Mr Miguel handed me the prints when he'd signed them.

I thanked him profusely. Then I pointed out a photograph on the wall which showed him between two very busty blonde models. He smiled a toothless grin, wagged an old crooked finger at me and muttered something under his breath.

I asked him about the Hemingway photograph. I mentioned the Spanish Civil War and the fact that he'd written about it in *For Whom the Bell Tolls*. I said it was alleged some of the action took place in Ronda, that the gorge had been mentioned and that people had been thrown off. I asked him if he remembered that time. There was a pause for a few seconds. He stared impassively into space. Then he looked up at me. He grunted something and shrugged. The conversation moved on.

'Ernesto Hemingway knew his bulls. He was a great *aficionado*,' he said.

I asked why he thought this was.

'He knew about Ronda and the Ordoñez men, didn't he? He must have known something to write about them! I sometimes still see Antonio Ordoñez – he visits me in my office here. We talk about the old times . . . We have had a long mutual friendship. When he sees me with my camera he readily follows my posing advice – he doesn't respect all photographers like that!'

His eyes wandered off towards the back of the office. He blinked and scratched the side of his head. I looked at the press article he'd given me. A cough broke the momentary silence. I looked up. Then with another clearing of his throat, he decided it was time for me to go.

Our meeting had ended. I stood up, shook hands with him and collected my photographs.

He smiled and laughed before waving me on my way.

'I sang in light opera when I was young! I had a pleasant voice, too! I could even play the piano . . .' he cackled without looking up.

I quietly made my way to the grease-stained door. I glanced back at him as I left the shop. He was already hard at work. His bald head and highly polished leather shoes were sparkling by the yellow light of his little desk lamp. He was leaning over the desk, his tongue licking his lips and his eyes screwed up in concentration, as he carefully cut up some prints with his long scissors. He looked like a child working on a school project.

In the space of a few seconds I had become a thing of the remote past for him. A faded comma in the story of his life.

NINE

Hemingway and Nirvana

'The President of the Hemingway Association is an American named Allen Josephs. He has a summer home outside Málaga. He's expecting you.'

I was talking on the telephone to John Fulton from my hotel room in Ronda and he'd already made the introductions on my behalf. The President of the Hemingway Association was in the south of Spain on holiday so John was only too happy to put us in touch with each other. Our paths had already crossed during the briefest of handshakes one day in John's gallery in Seville, and now, after leaving Ronda, it was going to be possible to talk to Allen Josephs properly about Hemingway, Spain and bullfighting. It seemed too good an opportunity to pass up.

Allen Josephs was staying in a town on the Mediterranean coast called Nerja. Before I left Ronda I consulted my guidebook; it warned me to book ahead when going near the coastline. I telephoned the number of a hostel in Nerja which called itself Nirvana. A cockney accent answered. I asked if they had a room to spare for the night. There was a pause, the sound of a hand being clapped over the receiver, and then I heard the person who'd answered the phone shouting: 'This bloke wants a room for tonight – what'll I say?'

In the distance a shrill woman's voice answered: 'Where's he from, then?'

'He's a Scottish geezer – I think.'

Another pause. Then the woman said: 'Yeah, s'pose we'll have a room for 'im.'

The hand was removed from the receiver. 'No problem, mate. What time do you expect to arrive at Nirvana then, eh?'

The fields on the outskirts of Ronda were lush and fertile. Then the landscape changed from green and plentiful to rocky and bare. It reminded me of the Burren in the west of Ireland and the rocky wastelands of Wyoming in the USA – at first they appear inhospitable places until you probe below the surface and find families who've lived in the area for centuries. From the road, however, it seemed an other-worldly place of bleached white and cold grey rocks, with the odd desperate, persevering splash of deep green reaching outwards towards the rain and sun. It highlighted one of the many contradictions of Spain: that a nation so renowned for the clichéd images of endless beaches of yellow ochre and continuous blazing sunshine is also known to many of its inhabitants as a mountainous country, with snow and rain falling during every month of the year. One coastal town I'd read about merited a single mention in one little guidebook for once having a very high suicide rate because of the constant blasting it took from the winds. Its inhabitants went crazy and killed themselves when the gusts took hold of their town and shook it every year. Nowadays they just windsurf instead.

The road from the mountainous region of Ronda to the coastline of the Spanish Mediterranean was almost empty. The odd goatherdsman loped by in the fields, oblivious to everything except the jangling of the beasts' bells. A few black BMWs or Mercedes flashed by me, the drivers taking hairpin bends at 80 m.p.h. with one hand on the steering wheel, the other holding a mobile phone. They were braver than I was: three or four times I drove around a high mountain bend to discover a massive hole where part of the road should have been. The road had subsided and there was a 300-foot drop to the valley floor below.

The air heated up as I neared the coastline and the road descended slowly. I convinced myself I could taste the sharp tang of salt in the wind. Finally I turned a corner and spied the Rock of Gibraltar way off in the distance. Beyond that, in the mist of the horizon, lay North Africa.

Marbella went by in a blur of fast-food restaurants, topless beaches and women with dyed blonde hair. A wide road took me towards Málaga, past cement factories and marinas. Little patches of beach clung on to the coastline here and there. Families holding hands stood at the edge of the road like athletes, ready to sprint across at the slightest opportunity. Double-parked cars gave the whole route a racing-track feel. Everyone broke the speed limit.

I took a bypass motorway around Málaga. It looked like a Hollywood film set that had spun out of control, or a valley that someone had poured millions upon millions of tons of yellow and grey concrete into, which had all slithered towards the sea, forming itself into little square caves in the process. On the outskirts of the city I passed through a rundown district which had hundreds and hundreds of cheap holiday apartments to rent. They looked just like the sort of place you might see in any major city anywhere in the world. If they'd have been grey they'd have fitted in well in Moscow or Glasgow or New York. Here they were painted yellow. Brown stains the colour of strong tea ran down the walls next to rusting drainpipes. Inflatable beach toys lay on the stairs. T-shirts and towels sprinkled with sand flapped on makeshift drying ropes. The apartments had names like 'The Sands', 'Med Dream' or 'Sunset Villas'. One was simply called 'Paradise'; it looked more like hell. Some seemed as if they'd swallowed up entire villages. The shops advertised English newspapers – 'Get Your *Sun* and *Daily Star* Here – We Have Bingo Cards Too!' – and British food: 'Bangers and Mash', 'Meat and Veg' and 'Bacon and Eggs' said the signs.

I passed whole groups of people walking one behind the other as I drove further along the coast. They looked like ordinary families, teenagers and their friends and older people with bad feet. They were walking towards the beach they'd been promised in the brochures. They carried beach balls and magazines and six-packs of beer. When I passed them they were miles from anywhere. They looked like the lines of refugees I'd seen in black-and-white footage from the Second World War.

Nerja lay along the coast outside Málaga. The guidebook said it had once been a fishing village. The author sounded wistful. Obviously there wasn't much fishing done in Nerja any more. I arrived late in the afternoon and found myself stuck in a noisy traffic jam. Horns blared and deafening little motorbikes which sounded like mosquitoes on steroids zipped by.

Suddenly, out of the middle of the traffic, an elephant appeared. It was led by a man in a sequined metallic blue suit. He approached my car and handed me a leaflet advertising the circus he and the elephant were part of. A second or two after he'd moved on, the elephant plodded by. It looked old and ill. Two young guys walked behind it. They also wore sequined suits although they didn't seem to fit them very well. They looked like a poor man's Elvis impersonator.

A few minutes later I found my hotel. It lay about ten minutes' drive outside the town of Nerja. If the owners were aiming for Nirvana when they named their establishment, they still had a long way to go from what I saw. 'Purgatory' would have been more apt.

'Bleedin' Spanish plumbers – don't know their arse from their elbows!'

The owner was a scorched-face man in his early fifties who wore a very bright T-shirt. When I arrived he was arguing with a couple of Spanish workmen who seemed to be having some problem with a toilet in the room adjoining the one I'd been allocated.

'Spanish job fuckin' creation if you ask me – you hire one bloke to do a repair for you and he tells you he needs to hire another four to finish it. Probably all his brothers too . . . fuckin' con artists!'

I half-nodded and, with much shoving and pushing, finally opened the ill-fitting door to my room.

'There's fresh towels in there, mate!' shouted the owner after me. Then I heard him stomping about in the next room while the workmen got on with fixing the plumbing in silence.

A stunning range of mountains lay across the valley from the hostel. At one time they must have looked down on the rich fields which led right down to the edge of the Mediterranean; now they had a jumbled collection of holiday homes and winding roads in their foothills. It looked like a suburb of Málaga. A couple of rooms down from me I saw a fat man with grey hair and very long sideburns at his window. I waved to him and smiled. He ignored me and stared out towards the sea which lay across the road. He looked very unhappy.

The owner's son served dinner. It was a hot night, yet he wore big thick boots which were in fashion back in the UK. They were the sort of boots American workmen wear when they're digging up roads. This young guy clumped around in them like Boris Karloff with the laces undone. He had an earring through his nose and a skinhead haircut.

My fellow guests in the Nirvana hostel were mostly British. I could hear accents from lots of different cities during the meal. Most had put on their best clothes for dinner. They tucked into their food with gusto, hunched over the table, looking at each other discreetly. Everybody seemed very tense. Most of the children were dressed in the latest high street fashions. They seemed annoyed that there wasn't more for them to do. The hostel was right at the edge of a busy main road. The beach was opposite but it was hard to get to. If you walked down the short sloping driveway at the wrong time of the day you were liable to get run over. Apart from the constant background noise of the traffic and the odd snatch of conversation, all you could hear was the cleaning of plates as people swept up every last morsel of their food.

One woman at the table next to mine wore what my mother would have called a cocktail dress. She was with the fat guy with the grey sideburns. She drank pale-pink sparkling wine and stared silently into space throughout the meal while he drank endless pints of beer. They only spoke when the young waiter asked them if they'd finished. The fat man smoked a big cigar at the end of his dessert. When he stood up to go to the toilet I noticed a couple of his shirt buttons had come undone. As he passed by I caught a glimpse of a dark-blue and red tattoo on his vast hairy belly.

In the distance I could hear a karaoke sing-song. It seemed to be coming from a small bar up the road from the hostel. The music sounded electronic and fake. I could see people moving about in the shadows. A woman's voice inside the pub was singing 'The Wild Rover'. A muffled cheer went up when she finished. Then a man started singing the Abba song 'Dancing Queen'. Everyone sitting around me could hear this too but no one said a word.

They kept eating and drinking and staring into space, pretending it wasn't happening.

*

'Spain has changed a lot . . .' Allen Josephs, an American academic from Florida and the President of the Hemingway Association, sat on a low wall at the foot of the garden of his summer home in an area of Nerja called the Balcony of Europe. Beneath him the Mediterranean lapped against the rocks.

'I've been coming here since 1962, so that's about 35 years. I was attracted to automobile racing and I thought the bullfights might be interesting. I wanted to see one to find out whether I liked it or not. I had to come all the way through Spain, it was in wintertime, November, in fact, and the only place I could find a *corrida* – actually, it wasn't even a real *corrida*, it was a festival where they don't wear suits of lights – was near Gibraltar. It was fantastic and I loved it right from the beginning. It was the greatest thing I'd ever seen. I'd been a theatre major and this was like theatre only it was real. I met John Fulton in 1963 in Málaga, and back then Orson Welles was around. Those were the days when the bullfighters had these great old Rolls-Royces that they drove around in on the terrible Spanish roads; you can't imagine how bad the roads were in those days – just dreadful. The *feria* in Málaga was a big deal . . . and that's when I met John. By this time I'd seen 60 or 70 bullfights.

Allen looked just as you would imagine the President of the Hemingway Association might look; a well-built, distinguished 50-something with a thick rugged beard.

'I came to Spain when I was 19. I'd read some Hemingway before I came and I thought I would like it – but I had no idea how much I really would like it. It was like coming home to a place I'd never been to before. I was raised in the American south – North Carolina – but my family is Lebanese, and so they are not exactly Southerners. When I got to Spain I found a whole country full of people just like my family. Things are very real in Spain. It's very unlike life in the United States . . . Spanish people's passions are stronger, everything is in greater relief, things are more passionate; there's more feeling, less repression, less puritanism here in Spain.'

'What do you think about it now?' I asked.

He raised his eyebrows: 'Every day Spain is more like the United States – not that I don't like things about the United States, but I think the variety of culture is the spice of life. It worries me that we're going to have McDonald's hamburgers, just to use an example, everywhere. Spanish TV is a terrible copy of American TV. You see these stupid game shows and these talk shows that are on in the morning with these idiots telling all the worst secrets of their lives – it's embarrassing, it's horrifying. It's the antithesis about what I liked about Spain.'

I asked Allen why Spain featured in Ernest Hemingway's writing so much – what was the attraction for an American writer with the whole world to roam?

He thought for a moment, stroking his beard and looking out at the blue sea. 'Spain was the most important country for Hemingway, there's no doubt about that,' he said finally. 'He said a couple of times that Spain was his favourite country. He wrote that it was his favourite country next to his own but he never spent any time in the United States – the United States was not his favourite country. In a couple of places he talks about how we've ruined the United States – and when he got to Spain he thought it was unspoilt. And I think that almost all of us who come to Spain have this feeling that it's unspoilt, although it's *not* unspoilt any more – although the kids that come today find it unspoilt in comparison to what they have at home. But when I came to Spain it really was unspoilt, and when Hemingway came it *really* was unspoilt – it was 1923. Hemingway was always looking for something that he called "the last good country", which was about the woods up in northern Michigan where he spent time as a child, about virgin woods that had not been timbered. And the subtext of the story is that every place but this place has been ruined, and this [Spain] is the one place that hasn't been ruined.

'Hemingway came along in the 1920s when the colonial ideal – of one culture being superior to another, having a right to take over another culture – was still very much in everybody's mind. But Hemingway was not like that. He had tremendous sensitivity to the Italians, to the French and particularly to the Spaniards. He was actually an enemy of the modern world, the overly rational, sophisticated, modernised, overly civilised world.'

One of the places I hoped to visit during my summer in Spain was Pamplona. Hemingway had probably been the first non-Spaniard to write about the week-long fiesta of San Fermines which takes place every July. He was the first writer to describe the famous running of the bulls through the streets in *Fiesta, The Sun Also Rises*. I questioned Allen about the book's origins.

'He was a struggling young artist trying to write a book; you write the best book you can and you write about what's important to you and that's what he did. It's a great book. We read it with fascination 70 years later – it's an absolute classic. He hit on something – that contrast between the jaded world of Paris and its bohemians and the pristine untouched world of Pamplona. The world of ritual, the world of tradition. A lot of people in Pamplona think of him as a great writer who understood Spain and Spanish traditions, as the first and maybe the best writer ever to talk about these things. On the other hand, there are some who say that Hemingway ruined San Fermines because he brought all these foreigners here; but they are mistaken. They would argue strongly that it's Hemingway's fault – but it's not Hemingway's fault. Between the Spanish Civil War and 1953 he didn't even set foot in Spain. Television brings more foreigners than anything he ever wrote. Every year at this time CNN and other news stations from all over the world broadcast the running of the bulls . . .'

Allen had been attending the running of the bulls in Pamplona for many years. I'd heard that it was a madhouse full of Hemingway lookalikes, drop-outs and thrill-seekers. He laughed at my description.

'Pamplona has the best atmosphere in the world – it's great. We don't go to Pamplona to drink, we go to Pamplona to see our friends. I mean, there's always a lot of drinking going on but actually I think I drink less in Pamplona than I do here, because maybe you want to be a little more circumspect because there are a lot of people who are in pretty bad shape. You can never tell when someone's going to throw a garbage can at you – you have to be on your guard. But it's a fantastic fiesta – it's a brilliant fiesta. It's a town of 200,0000 people and another 200,000 people descend upon the place. The foreign *afición* is a group of a couple of hundred people who have known each other for over 30 years – in fact, some of the old-timers in Pamplona have been going as long as 40 years. You'll see thousands of people in an advanced state of inebriation, but nobody gets in fights. It's amazing – if that were to happen in the United States there would be corpses all over the place. Spain is changing: every day you pick up the paper and there are more murders and more violence and so on. But Spain is a traditional society with fiestas and since antiquity these fiestas have served as an escape valve for pressures that can build up. Psychologically, they're probably a very healthy thing.'

'What do you think about the people who want to ban bullfighting?' I asked.

'What most people haven't learned about bullfighting is that if we didn't have the bullfight there wouldn't be any Spanish fighting bull. People who say bullfighting is cruel don't understand that if there were no bullfights the animal would cease to exist and we would not have the species at all – it simply would be gone. So we have to have something like the *corrida* in order to preserve the animal. The greenies don't understand that; they don't understand that people who are really into the *corrida* love the animal and know when an animal is really good. When it's fantastic, when it's superb and perfect, they don't kill it, they save it and make it a breeder. There's always talk about abolishing the *corrida* but this comes from people who don't understand the *corrida*; they don't understand tradition; they don't understand much of anything; they are very insensitive people actually. For the most part they want to wield power and are frequently a violent sort of people – I don't much like them. They want to tell you how to live your life. They don't respect tradition, they don't respect other people's lives. They would take away your rights, theoretically or punitively, to protect the rights of an animal which would not exist if it weren't for the *corrida* in the first place ... '

The one Hemingway book which dealt exclusively with the world of Spanish bullfighting was of course *Death in the Afternoon*. It was this non-fiction book which was partly responsible for sending the young John Fulton on his way to becoming a matador and it was the book which fascinated James Dean in Hollywood. I probed Allen for his thoughts on it.

'*Death in the Afternoon* was a somewhat surprising book at that time in Hemingway's career because he suddenly spent a lot of time writing a non-fiction work. He later told Gregory, one of his sons, that it was the hardest book he ever wrote. He first mentions it in 1925 – before he wrote *The Sun Also Rises* – saying that he's thinking about doing this big bull book with lots of photographs. It took him until 1932 to finish it. Of course, he wrote *The Sun Also Rises, A Farewell to Arms* and a bunch of short stories in the meantime, but he had to get to the point where he understood bullfighting well enough, and that takes years . . .

'The relationship between *Death in the Afternoon* and *For Whom the Bell Tolls* is interesting. You remember in *Death in the Afternoon* how there's that last chapter, chapter 20, which contains all the things he didn't put in? He later wrote a letter to somebody saying, "I'm glad you liked the 20th chapter, because that's what the book was really about." Which suggests something pretty obvious if you read the book carefully, namely that the book isn't just about the *corrida* – what we erroneously call bullfighting – but it's about a whole way of life that still existed in Spain, that had been lost in the rest of the modern world . . .

'In *Death in the Afternoon* he says: "I came to Spain because I was trying to learn how to write." He was watching bullfights at the same time as he was learning to write – writing these sketches and seeing his first *corridas*. And so there's an unmistakable kind of marriage between his prose and his learning about the *corridas*. He learned about the *corridas* and writing simultaneously and one affected the other, there's no doubt about that. He was analysing, learning about the *corrida*, and analysing how to make the emotion work on the page, which specific things would make it work.

'What he was doing was freeing us from nineteenth-century rhetoric. Instead of telling us what we ought to feel, or what his characters were feeling, he simply showed what was happening and let you infer from that what you should feel and how the character should feel. *Death in the Afternoon* is his artistic creed, the book where he tells you most about his writing.'

'Is Hemingway redundant now? Has that type of writing gone? The man, the machismo, the lore surrounding him – is it a thing of the past?' I asked.

Allen shrugged, then shook his head. 'The writer never particularly showed the hair on his chest. That was a sort of public image and that's pretty misunderstood too. If you start analysing what Hemingway wrote you'll find very little machismo there. I mean, Jake Barnes in *The Sun Also Rises* had his testicles blown off; he certainly is not macho – he's anything but macho. Frederick Henry in *A Farewell to Arms* is a deserter. Nick Adams goes through a series of trials and tribulations in which he is anything but a hero. You don't really get a hero in Hemingway until *For Whom the Bell Tolls*. Robert Jordan is really his first hero. Even in stories like *Francis Macomber* and *The Snows of Kilimanjaro*, Harry is anything but a hero and Francis Macomber is a coward. He does have his one minute of glory when he changes – and of course it's that change that the story is about; it's not about machismo at all, it's about self-realisation.

Hemingway's last trip to Spain, in 1959, was certainly all about self-realisation. *Life* magazine in New York paid for him to go to Spain that summer to write an article for them on bullfighting. It sounded like a surefire winning combination – the successful, older and wiser writer returning to the place where for him, in many ways, it had all begun.

Hemingway mulled the prospect over and agreed to it. His plan was to focus on two famous matadors, Luis Miguel Dominguin and Ronda's famous son, Antonio Ordoñez, the son of Cayetano Ordoñez, Hemingway's model for the fictional Pedro Romero in *Fiesta, The Sun Also Rises*. Both had been in the news for several reasons and had come to be regarded as rivals by critics and fans. Kenneth Tynan, for example, wrote in early 1959:

> In the years after Manolete's death [one of Spain's greatest matadors] there were many who thought Luis Miguel Dominguin might qualify [as a great]; and, certainly, no one alive knows more about the handling of fighting bulls than this tall, contemptuously handsome Castillian. But with his knowledge there went an academic coldness and a style that was a rubber stamp rather than a signature. Something was missing: and Luis Miguel, the self-proclaimed Numero Uno, did not help matters by taking a long holiday when it was officially decided to enforce the old taurine code which barred chipping and blunting bulls' horns, a repulsive modern safety measure that had become prevalent. Last summer, gambling a fortune on publicity, he made a fully-fledged comeback. And very impressive it was: there were afternoons of textbook classicism. And it was also too late.

> For last summer the word had gone around. The drums of the *aficion*, not only in Spain but wherever bull fever rages, were all beating in unison for the first time in 11 years. They were beating not for Luis Miguel but for the young Andalusian named Antonio Ordoñez, who revealed himself during the Spanish season of 1958, as the first undisputed *torero de epoch* since the death of Manolete.

Hemingway, living in far-off Cuba, had heard those drums. He knew their sound only too well. He kept in touch with the world of bullfighting through magazines and journals his Spanish friends regularly sent him in Havana. He saw some mileage in playing up the rivalry between Dominguin and Ordoñez and went out of his way to heighten the sense of drama, tension and intrigue surrounding the 1959 bullfighting season. To him they were the only two bullfighters in Spain that mattered.

It had all the necessary ingredients but it didn't turn out the way anyone, least of all *Life* or Hemingway himself expected. In fact it became, in some ways, a shameful débâcle.

The ageing writer was in bad physical and mental shape when he returned to Spain, and the photographs from that summer of '59 often show a painfully ill, usually drunken man who looked much older than his years. His conduct during the summer — getting into loud arguments in Pamplona; allowing young female groupies to fawn over him; worrying about his baldness and taking offence if anyone touched his carefully sculpted swept-over hair; drinking too much and being rude to his wife in public — suggested a man veering out of control rather than a disciplined Nobel prize-winning writer at the height of his powers. Instead of being a repeat performance of his younger, more virile days, the Spanish trip descended into an endless stream of parties organised by hangers-on; these attracted half of Pamplona, who beat a path to wherever Hemingway happened to be sitting. He wasn't the observer any more, he was the observed. But he still instinctively needed to be around and part of it. The Spanish writer José Luis Castillo-Puche who accompanied 'Papa', as the American now liked to be called, said in his book *Hemingway in Spain*:

Spain had become something more than a drug or strong spirits to Ernesto. Spain was more than a healthy stimulus, a delightful support to lean on. It was also a spiritual handhold for a shipwrecked man who had been floundering about for years in a valiant, vain attempt to fight off the terror of death.

I asked Allen Josephs for his take on *The Dangerous Summer*. He frowned at the painful thought of it: 'Well, it's a pretty sad book after *Death in the Afternoon* – it's Hemingway's last book and his worst book. He was very ill when he wrote it and very depressed. The problem is he was theoretically writing a non-fiction book, and he makes some big mistakes. In theory he's objective – and yet he's clearly *not* objective . . .'

The article/book that Hemingway produced was, like the trip itself, uneven and far from being objective. From the outset he made it clear that he favoured the younger Antonio Ordoñez over the older and wiser Dominguin. Ironically, decades before, when he'd written about Antonio's father in *Death in the Afternoon*, he'd been deeply scathing of Cayetano's diminished skill and bravery:

> Cayetano Ordoñez looked like a bullfighter, he acted like a bullfighter and for one season he was a bullfighter. I saw him in most of his fights and in all his best ones. At the end of the season he was gored severely and painfully in the thigh. That was the end of him . . . If you see Niño de la Palma [Cayetano], the chances are you will see cowardice in its least attractive form; its fat, rumpled, prematurely bald from using hair fixatives, prematurely senile form.

In *The Dangerous Summer* he favourably compared Antonio to what his father once had been before his downfall:

> Watching Antonio with the bull I saw that he had everything his father had in his great days. Cayetano had absolute technical perfection . . . Antonio was very much better . . .

Privately he was even more effusive. To the Spanish writer Castillo-Puche he remarked: 'Antonio's almost a god.'

Hemingway called the article *The Dangerous Summer* because he managed to convince himself — and presumably the *Life* magazine editors who commissioned him in the first place — that one, or both, of the matadors was going to end up dead before the season was out. They fought *mano a mano* three times in Valencia, Málaga and Ciudad Real. They both received serious gorings during the summer. Neither was laid low for long, however, and their recovery times were remarkably short. Curiously, these two supposedly deadly rivals were in fact brothers-in-law. Ordoñez was married to Dominguin's sister and his manager was Dominguin's father. But this didn't stop Hemingway from hyping up the whole scenario into something it probably wasn't:

> Bullfighting is worthless without rivalry. But with two great bullfighters it becomes a deadly rivalry. Because when one does something, and can do it regularly, that no one else can do and it is not a trick but a deadly dangerous performance only made possible by perfect nerves, judgement, courage and art and this one increases its deadliness steadily, then the other, if has temporary failure of nerves or judgement, will be gravely wounded or killed when he tries to equal or surpass it. He will have to resort to tricks and when the public learns to tell the tricks from the true thing he will be beaten in rivalry and he will be very lucky if he is still alive or in business.

I probed Allen for his thoughts about the supposed competition between the two men — how intense had it really been?

'This whole idea of this blood rivalry between them and so on — they were brothers-in-law and friends . . . yeah, there was a rivalry because there's always rivalry between *toreros*. The *corrida* itself is not a competition between the man and the animal or between the man and another man, but there is always competitiveness, there is always the competitive spirit to be the one who has the greatest triumph. But when you put together a *mano a mano* between two bullfighters with three bulls each instead of three bullfighters with two bulls each, then what you do is accentuate that competitiveness. And so they did that: they had that *mano a manos*. It was important because

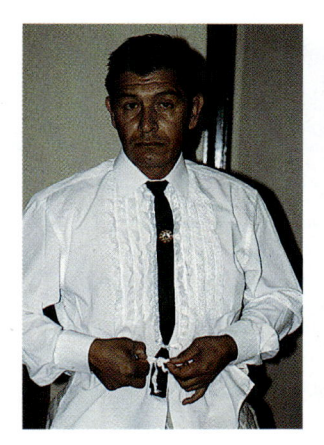

John Fulton and Vicente Salamanca size up a new *traje de luces* (suit of lights) in a Sevillian tailor's; Vicente then gets dressed for his role as *sobresaliente* or understudy, before saying a brief prayer at his little wooden altar and heading off to the *plaza de toros*

Francisco Rivera Ordoñez, the latest member of the famous dynasty of bullfighters; BELOW: Ordoñez in action in Burgos

José Miguel Arroya Delgado, 'Joselito', a millionaire matador who is probably one of the top three bullfighters in the world; he said he'd rather be back in his hotel room with a good book than facing a bull

Fiesta time in Pamplona. ABOVE: *(back row)* Ed Perez from Florida, Mike from New York, Yousef from New York, *(front row)* Frosty from France and Lord Rex, the English Master of Ceremonies; RIGHT: Joe Distler, a New York businessman and academic, has been coming to Pamplona for 30 years. He hasn't missed a single running of the bulls in that entire time

LEFT: A typical scene in the streets of Pamplona as dawn breaks; this reveller probably won't be running with the bulls in a few hours' time. Then again . . .
BELOW: And suddenly the bulls are here. Terror and madness and panic and stupidity take over for a few minutes as the bulls thunder by, through and over the crowd. Few participants realise that their inspiration, Ernest Hemingway, never actually *ran* with the bulls. He may have played tag with them in the *plaza*, but he never did *this*

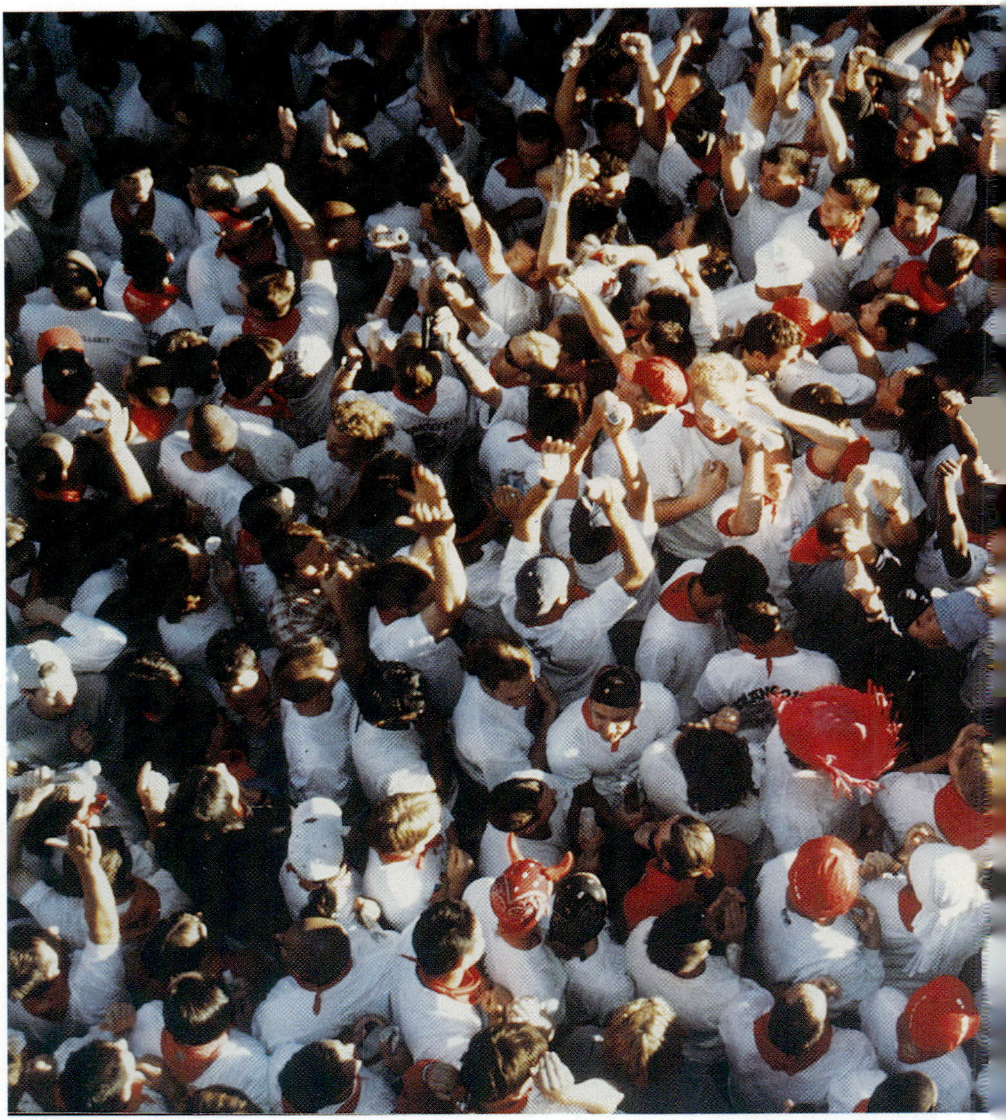

IN PICTURE: 7.50 a.m. on the first day of San Fermines. This crowd of 10,000 await their own
ent of truth; the wine has been drunk, the courage has been summoned and all that's lacking are
 bulls. Most people will run the course without even glimpsing a bull, but a mad few will wait
until they see the tips of the horns before setting off . . .
VE RIGHT: A huge bull tramples a young British tourist who inexplicably wandered into its path;
ies battered and motionless on the cobblestones; an American in the crowd hauls him to safety,
later telling me: 'I swear to God I thought the kid was dead.' The injured man lived

Ronda, 1959: Ernest Hemingway stands between two legendary figures of bullfighting, whose mythic status he helped create: on the left is Cayetano Ordoñez (who became 'Pedro Romero' in *The Sun Also Rises*) and his son, Antonio Ordoñez (who featured in *The Dangerous Summer*), is on Hemingway's right. The writer committed suicide in Idaho in 1961 on the first day of that year's San Fermines (photo © Miguel Martin)

they were the two best bullfighters – the rising young star in Ordoñez and the old maestro in Dominguin. There had been a similar situation between Dominguin and Manolete a few years before. But Hemingway exaggerated it all out of proportion and made Luis Miguel look worse than he was and made Ordoñez look better than he was. Hemingway was never very objective, but even his pretence at objectivity was not very good there. And his standards about the *corrida* had slipped . . . You could just see that he wasn't the master any more – well, he is the maestro but he's the ailing maestro. So it's kind of sad as a swansong.'

Life magazine originally commissioned Hemingway to write a neat 10,000-word piece on this alleged 'rivalry' between the 33-year-old Dominguin and his 27-year-old brother-in-law. It was due to be published in three parts. Hemingway's first draft ran to a massive 120,000 words. The *Life* editors in New York were shocked when they saw the size of the manuscript. The quality was also suspect – it was long and rambling and full of details few but the most diehard bullfighting enthusiast would be interested in. The manuscript was cut down to 70,000 words by Hemingway and his friend A.E. Hotchner. The *Life* editors were sill uncertain about its length and worth, but they went ahead and published it in three long sections. (The eventual book which came out of this manuscript – not published until 1985, almost quarter of a century after his death – ran to about 45,000 words.) In the manuscript he was overtly critical of Dominguin and excessively praising of Ordoñez. The former's response is a matter of record:

> Hemingway had no knowledge of bullfighting. His knowledge of bulls, like one's knowledge of languages or paintings, was relative. He knew more than most Americans but less than almost all Spaniards. But this is a very difficult subject to know about and I would say that only 10 per cent of matadors have any real understanding of bullfighting. I never read *Death in the Afternoon*, though I've been told about it, because there is nothing I could learn from it. It's an extremely superficial book, whose defensive tone was meant to counter Anglo-Saxon cultural hostility, and was written solely for Americans . . . I have no interest in reading

Hemingway's books. He certainly never gave me any advice or encouragement about writing. I threw away his letters and all the other letters I received because I fear papers even more than I fear bulls.

The latter, Antonio Ordoñez, had a predictably different view of the author and his abilities:

He was a fine human being: strong, sympathetic, warm and kind. He loved life . . . Hemingway's knowledge of Spanish and of Spain was very good. He knew more about the country than most educated Spaniards . . . His knowledge of bullfighting was virtually perfect . . .

The youthful John Fulton, struggling to eat a square meal and make a name for himself in Spain, also met Hemingway during that 'dangerous summer' of 1959. The writer gave him a cheque for $100 at a time when Fulton desperately needed the cash. But he failed to use his considerable influence with his friend Antonio Ordoñez to give Fulton a break in the place he really wanted it – the world of bullfighting. John had explained what happened to me when we were eating lunch in Seville.

'He asked me what he could do to help – I suggested asking Ordoñez to allow me to act as *sobresaliente* [substitute] in one of his *corridas*. Hemingway said he'd see what he could do for me. A day or two later he told me Ordoñez had said that such a position was for matadors on the way down – not up. Hemingway told me he'd vouched for my skills, said I was a good fighter. He said that was enough to convince Ordoñez and that it was all set for me to appear in Ciudad Real. I was delighted. I waited and waited but it never happened. Then I got a letter telling me A.E. Hotchner, an American and Hemingway's travelling pal, who'd never faced a bull in his life, had got the job as *sobresaliente*. I couldn't believe it. I couldn't believe this man who had shown so much respect for what bullfighting was all about would make such a mockery of the whole thing by allowing a non-matador to dress for the part. That job could have done my career some good, given me a leg up; instead . . . well, it never happened. It angered me.'

A photograph exists of the incident. I saw it in my copy of *The Dangerous Summer*. There's Antonio Ordoñez looking somewhat smug, smiling in his hotel bedroom, half dressed in his suit of lights. Hotchner, one of Hemingway's many hangers-on, is grinning and pulling on a pair of embroidered breeches. By this time Hotchner had been dubbed El Pecas, meaning 'The Freckles'. In later years he would publish a book about the author – *Papa Hemingway* – but his role and motives during the 1959 trip would be called into question. Spanish author Castillo-Puche bluntly stated in his book that he thought Hotchner was 'two-faced', 'standoffish', 'crafty', 'playing the role of the ringmaster' and that he was engaged in 'exploitation of Ernesto'. To the left of the scene in the photograph stands Hemingway, his rotund belly sticking out beneath his untucked shirt, his hair all brushed forward in an effort to conceal his baldness.

At a quick glance it's a typical locker-room scene: men together having a laugh. Significantly, however, the only person not smiling in the photograph is Hemingway himself. Later in the text of *The Dangerous Summer* – which was edited under strained circumstances with Hotchner's help – he wrote up the whole incident as some kind of farcical joke. But the photograph gives the lie to that interpretation of it. Hemingway's mind seems elsewhere. He looks hungover, adrift and apart from events.

As a younger man, Hemingway had described in the text of *Death in the Afternoon* what the atmosphere in a matador's changing-room prior to a *corrida* should be like. He wrote:

> There are some [matadors] that smile and recognise friends ... but nearly all are still-faced and detached. The matador, from living every day with death, becomes very detached, the measure of his detachment of course is the measure of his imagination and always on the days of the fight and finally, during the whole end of the season, there is a detached something in their minds that you can almost see. What is there is death and you cannot deal with it each day and know each day there is a chance of receiving it without having it make a very plain mark. It makes this mark on everyone.

He was right. And in that photograph death had made its mark on him. He may have been thinking about many things: his health, his marriage, his conduct, his failing literary powers, who knows – possibly even his broken promise to the struggling young John Fulton. But most likely he was thinking about his life and the fact that it was clearly beginning to fragment. If you look closely you can see it is he, not the matadors around him, who had the detached look of one who is about to face his own mortality.

The cracks were beginning to appear that summer but Ernest hid them well. Even close friends thought he could pull himself together. Hemingway's opinion of Spain and death were succinctly put to Castillo-Puche when he reacted to an incorrect wire-service report that had flashed around the world saying he'd passed away in Málaga:

> Me die in *Spain*? What a laugh! There have been lots of times I've fucked up and almost kicked the bucket, but not in Spain . . . Spain's not a country you *die* in, it's a country you *live* in.

But back in America it was a different story. Over the next two years Hemingway slowly fell apart both emotionally and physically. He had planned to go back to Spain in the summer of 1961 one final time for the annual running of the bulls of Pamplona, but at the last minute he wired his friends and cancelled. In the early hours of 2 July that year he loaded his favourite shotgun and blew his brains out at his home in Ketchum, Idaho. He was buried a few days later, on 7 July – the opening day of the fiesta at St Fermines.

Sitting in the shade of some knotted fruit trees, hearing the sound of the waves below us, Allen Josephs and I had spent more than two hours talking about Hemingway and Spain and bullfighting. When we finished chatting he gave me the names and addresses of various people I should look up when I got to Pamplona. He even took my notebook from me and drew me some maps of places I should seek out. John Fulton had gone to similar trouble.

'Just go to these places, ask for these people and mention John's name and you'll be fine – and welcomed,' said Allen. 'He's loved up in Pamplona – a bit of a legend, though he wouldn't admit it himself.'

I asked him where the best places were to see some more bullfights.

'Head north. You might see some *corridas* in Córdoba and around and in Madrid itself. Then everyone heads northwards towards Burgos for the *feria* – it's on for a week there prior to Pamplona. A kind of a warm-up bout for the real thing. Then, from the end of the first week in July onwards, it's San Fermines in Pamplona of course.'

I asked him for some suggestions about which matadors I should see. He gave me names and some details about their recent form. He mentioned a couple in particular. 'And you should try and catch the Ordoñez kid – he's good.'

This was Francisco Rivera Ordoñez, the 23-year-old great-grandson of Cayetano and the grandson of Antonio. I was discovering that the Ordoñez family were to bullfighting what the Kennedy family were to American politics. Francisco – dubbed 'Fran' in the tabloids – was the current rising star of the dynasty and I'd seen his face during my journey numerous times; you couldn't really miss it – he was plastered all over ten-foot-high billboards advertising various items of designer clothing.

I said I'd keep my eye out for any *corridas* which featured the latest member of the Ordoñez family, then Allen and I shook hands and said our goodbyes. It was early evening and the sun was beginning to dip towards the horizon. As he was seeing me out of his house he said: 'I'm afraid that every day one begins to sound a bit Hemingwayesque, a bit too nostalgic and "saying farewell to all that" but I'm afraid that that colourless homogeneity of the future is true and every day it's worse . . . One of the things that attracted Hemingway to Spain, and which attracts everyone to Spain is the dignity of the Spanish people, the pride and the fierceness with which they cling to their traditions and their way of life. But I think they are losing that. What will happen in the future will, I guess, depend on how much the Spaniards continue to hold to their traditions . . .'

I thought of all the tourist buses I'd seen and all the fast-food places I'd passed on my way along the coast. I knew what he meant.

'Hey . . .' he added, nudging me playfully, 'you look forward to the running of the bulls in Pamplona?'

I shuddered visibly.

He laughed. 'Some advice: never run drunk, but that doesn't mean to say you have to run completely sober either. And try to find someone you can latch on to who's done it before – and survived. But you shouldn't feel obligated to run. If you don't feel like running then don't – your instincts might be trying to tell you something.'

I left Allen's villa and headed back to my hostel on the outskirts of Nerja. On the way, I stopped to use a call-box to phone ahead to my next destination so I could book a room in advance. While I was waiting to use the telephone a teenager wearing an England football jersey staggered by wearing a Walkman and carrying a six-pack of beer. He was limping badly and kept stopping every few yards to rest his leg. I asked him if he was okay.

'Yeah, mate, no problem . . . lost the girlfriend, though. She's fucked off somewhere.' He looked about 18 years old. His face was bright red from the sun. His hair was cropped like a soldier's and streams of sweat ran down the sides of his jaws.

I asked him if he had a place to stay for the night.

'Yeah, somewhere . . .' He was very drunk.

'What happened to the leg?'

'I kicked the car the girlfriend got into. Fucking killing me ever since.'

'So where is she now?' I asked.

'Dunno . . . she'll turn up.'

He rubbed his head then tipped up the can to his mouth and drained it. He offered me one but I refused. He shrugged and popped the top on another.

An old woman was using the phone beside us. I couldn't work out who she was talking to, but she seemed to be doing some sort of shopping and she kept referring to a catalogue full of expensive vacuum cleaners. After a while the young bloke rose unsteadily to his feet.

'See you around, mate.' He began to move off. Then he stopped. 'Hey . . . where the fuck is this place?'

'What place?' I asked.

'This place! Here! Where the fuck is it?'

'You don't know where you are?'

'Yeah, I'm in fuckin' Spain. I'm not daft. But the girlfriend booked the tickets and I got on a plane in Manchester then the next thing I was *here*. So where am I? Or don't you know either?'

I smiled and nodded. He suddenly looked very young. 'You're in a place called Nerja,' I said.

'That'll do me,' he said. He gulped down some more beer. 'Stupid cow.'

The Spanish lady finished making her call and handed me the telephone. She made a great display of wiping the receiver with a handkerchief before allowing me to take it.

The young guy fixed his headphones into position, looked around for a second or two, then slowly started down the road that led to the main highway.

'Take it easy,' I shouted after him.

'Thanks,' he shouted back.

I watched him limp off, trying his best to swagger. He was still carrying his beer, cradling it in his arms like a baby.

Ten minutes later, after I'd made my calls, I drove past him. He was sitting on the grass verge at the side of the road with his head in his hands. His shoulders were heaving up and down and he appeared to be sobbing like an abandoned child.

Nirvana specialised in what it advertised as 'The Original Full English Breakfast'. I smelled sausages and bacon frying the moment I woke up. I thought I was dreaming until I peered over the balcony and spied everyone who'd eaten dinner the previous night all sitting in the same places having breakfast.

Ten minutes later I joined my fellow guests. Again, no one was speaking. The only person with anything to say was a man wearing a safari vest with lots and lots of pockets in it. As I sat down he was just starting to complain loudly to the owner about a holiday home he was due to move into. Things had gone wrong and the work hadn't been completed by the agreed date. The hostel owner seemed to be familiar with the guest and his tale.

'The bloody contractor was an alcoholic. Everybody in the place knew he was raving mad with the drink except muggins here.' He pointed at himself with his fork.

'Have another bit of bacon, mate,' said the owner. He was wearing an apron that said 'Arsenal' on it.

'We don't even have a proper floor, never mind a ceiling. I can't even take a crap if I want. Not a toilet pan in sight!' The man with the safari vest had a very red face. I couldn't work out if he was very sunburnt or just very angry. I decided it was probably a bit of both. The owner shovelled more bacon on to his plate. He nodded and thanked him, his head bobbing up and down, his mouth chewing non-stop on the mouthful of meat that was silencing him. He caught me eye. 'Wotcha!'

'Morning . . .' I said.

'Lovely, eh?' He nodded towards the sea behind us.

'Yes,' I agreed.

'Nirvana's a spot and a half, eh? Great place. Great food. Great people, Great drink. Great view. Decided to move here now that I've retired. I'll be all set when my place is fixed up. Oh, yes!' He stuffed some more sausage into his mouth.

'When will that be?' It was a stupid question but I had to ask.

'God knows,' he replied. He stared into space and absent-mindedly picked some fat out from between his front teeth. He burped. Then he leaned forward. 'These bloody Spanish workers, they're a bit slow – not like the English boys back home. I mean, God knows, they're cowboys as well but they're our cowboys if you catch my drift. This lot might be in the Common Market or whatever they're calling it these days but . . . well, you know, they're still a bit . . . backward in my opinion. I mean, for Christ's sake, I haven't clapped an eye on so much as a spirit level since I set foot in this country. Very worrying.'

He burped again and pointed at the view with his fork. 'Still, look at that . . . it's the business, eh? The business.' Then he winked and started eating again.

After packing my bags and checking out I met a couple of Spanish workmen having a break on the steep driveway outside Nirvana. They were sitting quietly by the side of the kerb sunning themselves and sipping beer from little brown dumpy bottles. I waved to them and they waved back. One was fat and middle-aged, maybe in his fifties. The other was younger, probably in his late thirties, and thinner. 'Where are you from?' he asked in perfect English.

'Scotland,' I answered.

His friend smiled and closed his eyes, leaning back in the sunshine. The man who'd spoken to me said, 'Well, what do you think of this place?'

I laughed and shrugged. 'What do you think?' I asked.

'I asked you first.'

'I like the mountains . . . but there are too many buildings – too many hotels. Like this one.'

He smiled and translated for his friend. The older man nodded and offered me a beer.

'Yeah, that's right,' said the thinner guy. 'But you know what?'

'What?' I said.

He beckoned me closer to him. 'We like their money – *mucho dinero*.' He rubbed his fingers together when he spoke and smiled a wolfish grin. His fat pal grinned and took another slug of beer. 'They can keep coming and keep doing whatever they want – as long as they bring their money.' The thin guy smiled and slowly drained his bottle. Both he and his friend were enjoying the morning sunshine.

'On holiday?' he asked. His voice was mellow and quiet.

I explained I was in Spain to find out about bullfighting. He reacted with surprise. He translated for his friend, who raised his eyebrows. I named some matadors I'd heard of and read about, and mentioned John Fulton's name as well. Their eyes widened and they shook their heads incredulously. They seemed impressed.

I threw my bags into the back of the car.

'All right, boys? Anytime soon, I 'ope?' The owner of Nirvana appeared on the balcony still wearing his Arsenal apron and waving a kitchen implement about. He spotted me and smiled.

The two workmen got to their feet. 'Enjoy the bulls,' said the workman I'd been speaking to.

'Thanks,' I replied.

'All the best, mate!' bellowed the hostel owner. I gave him a half-hearted wave. I saw him gesture with his frying-pan spatula towards the two local men who were taking their time organising their tools. 'See? What did I tell you? Never take two days to do something when you can take a week!' He shook his head and vanished back into the kitchen.

The Spanish workmen smiled at each other a little, slung their bags over their shoulders and began trudging up the hill towards the hostel. They looked like reluctant kids returning to school after the long summer holidays.

TEN

Friend, I Must Kill You

I felt as though I was doing a lunchtime drug deal.

I'd driven to Córdoba in Andalucia to see Francisco Rivera Ordoñez fighting in the city's massive *plaza de toros*. On the way I heard on the radio that it was the hottest day of the year in Spain. I arrived at the bullring just after midday. The illustrious family name, Ordoñez, headed the poster for that evening's *corrida* which was sponsored by Land Rover and Rover Cars from the UK. I wondered if Francisco and other matadors who'd made it into the top ranks still got a thrill from seeing their names advertised like that, high above the queue of people waiting to buy tickets.

It was quarter to one and the air blazed through my lungs. For nearly half an hour the queue had not budged an inch. I kept standing up on my tiptoes to try and see what was happening at the front of the line. All I could make out was a man wearing an impeccable blue shirt, who muttered every so often into a grilled opening no bigger than the size of your average postcard. This was where the tickets were being sold. The queue mostly consisted of anxious-looking businessmen types. A few well-dressed women in their forties were there too and several young couples also lined up, blank expressions on their faces. When they got too hot or bored, the girls dreamily flopped their heads on their boyfriends' shoulders and took long, deep drags on their cigarettes. They blinked like tired cats. Everyone kept staring at the brick wall hopefully. We were waiting for something to happen. It never did.

The thick shadowed heat made me drowsy and even though I was standing up I began to doze off for a few seconds at a time. I swayed and woke up with a start every time I felt myself falling forward. I must have done this ten, maybe fifteen times. At one point I crashed awake to find an old frazzled man standing in front me. For an instant I was blinded. My eyes tried to focus on the nearby sun-bleached whiteness, then they darted on to him in the gloomy darkness. He waved his arms at me. I looked around but no one was paying any attention to him. I looked back at him, my eyes focusing better by the second. A fat fly, speckled green and purple by the light, its transparent wings like fine silk, buzzed around the thumbnail cave of flesh where his right eye used to be. He was wearing a pinstriped suit and on his feet were an odd pair of frayed leather sandals. Before I could respond to him, he flapped a flat hand at me and moved on to someone else. No one paid any attention to him. He might as well have been invisible.

Forty-five minutes later I reached the front of the queue. I peered in through the grill. It was cool and dark inside and smelled of smoke and oranges. A round-faced man with drooping eyelids and a thin moustache appeared. I told him how much I wanted to pay for a seat. He stuck a cigarette in his mouth, the smoke slithering up into his eyes making him squint while he pounded a computer keyboard. Eventually he nodded and gestured to me to show him the cash. I paid up. I had a cheap seat high up in the shaded side of the stadium for that night's *corrida*.

A lengthy queue still stretched out behind me. The one-eyed beggar was asleep next to the wall. Spittle ran down one side of his mouth like foam spilling over the edges of a riverbank. His hair, such as it was, looked like a wheatfield that had been burnt to stubble. Everyone shuffled forward a few inches when I moved away from the tiny window.

I was too hot and too tired to look around the city of Córdoba. I didn't care. Just watching the lines of sagging tourists flip-flopping their way around the Moorish-built mosque, the Mezquita, made me feel weak. An ancient guidebook I had told me it was once as important to the Islamic world as Mecca and that it used to contain both an original copy of the Koran and a bone from the arm of

Mohammed himself. If those relics had still been there I might have dragged myself in, but they weren't so I stopped feeling guilty. What energy I'd had was used up trying to drive my way out of the old Jewish quarter of the city after I'd got lost in it. A police officer with high cheekbones had to give me directions. 'Follow the sun,' she said. I did. But the sun seemed to be everywhere at once. So I was lost ten minutes later.

I was a bit annoyed with myself for missing the *sorteo*, the selection process of the bulls. Apparently it had taken place while I was queuing up for my tickets and getting myself lost in the city centre. It was a simple affair but, several people had told me, worth catching if I got the chance. The process involves the representatives of the matadors who are due to fight – the bullfighters themselves rarely attend – and maybe their managers. They all turn up and look over the six bulls which are due to be killed that evening. Three of the best are selected, then they are paired off with the remaining three. Sometimes, according to John Fulton's descriptions, the discussions that take place can become somewhat robust. Everybody is trying to get an edge for their man. After much debate between the representatives on the one hand, the foreman of the bull ranch who knows each bull's form on the other, and whoever else might chip in their tuppence-worth, the names and numbers of each of the three pairs of bulls is written on a little piece of paper, rolled into a ball and chucked into a hat or cup. A draw takes place, with the most senior matador's man drawing the first ball out. Once all three have been chosen the representatives can decide which of the two bulls their man will face first; each knows his matador well and knows which type of bull he prefers and in which order he'll fight in any given set of circumstances. Once that's been done, the bulls are separated and divided into different corrals where they are kept in peace and quiet until the *corrida* begins. I managed to catch only this last part of the process and I watched the bulls as they rumbled and trotted through a series of dusty, heavy doors before disappearing into the darkness.

I returned to my car and promptly fell asleep with the air-conditioning turned up full blast. I was in a part of Spain known as the country's 'frying pan' and it was playing havoc with my Celtic blood. When I woke up I saw women and men dressed in traditional

Andalucian riding gear walking past. They looked at me quizzically. While they were basking easily in the heat, I was hugging myself in the artificially frosty atmosphere of the car's interior. They must have thought I was insane. The women who strode by had very red lips which matched their red bandanas. The men who followed them all patted one another on the back. Their hair was slicked down and looked like a crow's shiny feathers. They wore high, battered brown leather riding-boots which came right up to their knees.

A nearby bar was packed full of people drinking and chatting before the bullfight. I fought my way through it to use their bathroom. A short harassed waiter sloshed drink around with one hand and wiped the counter top with the other. When he thought no one was looking he poured Pernod into a tall glass with ice in it and gulped it down. Then he grabbed a bottle and his cloth again before taking more orders. Sweat ran down his face in thick lines like heavy glue.

Francisco Rivera Ordoñez was named after his father – Francisco Rivera – who was also a matador. Francisco Rivera was more commonly known by his fighting name, Paquirri, and it was during his heyday that he married Antonio Ordoñez's daughter Carmina, who was Francisco Rivera Ordoñez's mother. Then a scandal hit the headlines: Paquirri had had an affair with a singer named Isabel Pantoja. The details were in all the Spanish newspapers. When it broke Paquirri left his son's mother, and married the beautiful entertainer. People said it was after he took up with Isabel Pantoja that his bullfighting career started going downhill. One man told me matadors fear women's breasts more than they fear bulls' horns – 'because both can ruin their career'.

I had obtained a photograph of Paquirri in Ronda from the aged photographer Martin Miguel. It showed a handsome Francisco Rivera entering the ring in Ronda, flanked by other bullfighters including his father-in-law, an older, fuller-faced, tanned Antonio Ordoñez. The crowd behind him is cheering and clapping. Paquirri, as handsome as a Hollywood actor of the '40s, is staring off camera to the right. He looks serious – worried even. He was just 24 years old when it was taken in 1973. I'd been told that he was a good matador in his prime – an excellent killer with the sword and one of those rare bullfighters who placed his own *banderillas*.

On 26 September 1984, Paquirri was fighting in a *corrida* in the town of Pozoblanco about 50 miles outside of Córdoba. It hadn't been a good season for him and talk of retirement was in the air. During the last bullfight of the night, in what was scheduled to be the last of Paquirri's season, he was suddenly tossed and gored. For a split-second no one knew what to do . . .

Then they rushed to his aid.

He was bleeding heavily by the time he was carried out of the ring and into a waiting ambulance. His chances of survival would have been better had not the local hospital been undergoing some building work; instead, his battered, bloody and barely alive body had to endure a 50-mile run on a rough road to the nearest big city – Córdoba. They say he lived for the duration of the journey but, at the moment the ambulance arrived at the hospital, he suddenly died. He was 36 years old. The drama of the whole affair was heightened even further by the fact that Paquirri's final few moments of life were captured on video-tape by a local TV crew. A journalist in Madrid had told me what he'd seen when it was broadcast on Spanish television: 'There had been a video of him on the operating table of this poorly equipped village bullring. He was sort of telling everybody to be calm and trying to reassure the doctors . . . It was shown again and again on television after his death. He was telling the doctors the nature of his wounds. I think he said, "There are two trajectories . . ." and everyone around him was shouting. It was a big thing. He was the calmest person there. He knew he was on television, he knew someone was filming him but it was still quite an impressive document.'

His distraught wife Isabel Pantoja carried on with her singing career after the death of Paquirri. I read somewhere that she sang songs about him and frequently burst into tears at certain points during her performances when the lyrics mentioned his name or how he died.

Over a decade after Paquirri's death I was in Córdoba to see his handsome son fight. On the way into the city that day I passed the hospital where Paquirri had expired in 1984. Thirty seconds later I saw a *corrida* poster tied to a thick tree which showed his son, the young Francisco Rivera Ordoñez. He was smiling just like his grandfather Antonio. But his eyes had that distracted, uncertain look I'd seen in Paquirri's off-camera gaze in the photograph taken in Ronda. The board to which the poster was glued flapped against the tree as the rush of the city traffic sent waves of hot air sliding across the streets. It sounded like children fencing with wooden swords.

'To be fair to the guy, he performs like someone who doesn't have a dime...'

That was what Vicente Salamanca, the Colombian matador I'd met in Seville, had thought of Francisco Rivera Ordoñez. Some bullfighting families got a bad name and I thought young Ordoñez might have come in for some criticism of this nature, but he didn't. He seemed to have proved himself worthy of attention for other reasons beside his well-known family. John Fulton had nodded in agreement: 'Yeah, he's one of those exceptions to the rule; he seems to be aware of his advantages and he seems to use them well – who can blame him? The kid seems like a nice guy and, more importantly, he's good in the ring too.'

I read an article in a current Spanish magazine which echoed a similar opinion: 'With that kind of blood it is only logical Francisco Rivera Ordoñez would be mediocre – but, no, he's becoming a good bullfighter, with personality and a courage that is at times bloodcurdling.'

Another said: '[He was] the fighter of the most interest to the general public ... [His style] was an explosive mixture of classical fighting and unorthodox; as much with the cape as the *muleta* and charged with great emotion.'

Great crowds of people poured into the bullring. Men had set up stalls everywhere selling posters, cards, dolls, T-shirts, plastic wind-up bulls, mini-*banderillos*, hats, swords and videos. The police were directing the traffic. The carpark where I'd found a spot soon filled up and was eventually closed. The attendants stood around smiling and licking ice-creams.

By the time I'd queued up to get into the *plaza de toros*, bought a plastic cushion to sit on and been directed to my seat, the first fight of the evening was almost over. I could tell from the moment I entered the arena that the crowd were very hostile. Someone said the first matador had been suffering from nerves and had performed very poorly. I asked the man who was sitting next to me what had happened: 'He's a local boy . . . maybe he can't produce the goods when he's in his own back garden, who knows?'

The matador was booed as he left the ring. He shrugged, held his hands up to one of his *cuadrilla* and spat on the sand. The bull was cheered as it was dragged out the ring. The matador shook his head in bewilderment as if to say 'you win some, you lose some'.

The *plaza* was almost full, except for the seats in the sun. These were completely empty apart from one man who sat all by himself. I watched him through a pair of little binoculars that I'd brought with me. He had his arms crossed defiantly and wore a newspaper folded like a ship on top of his head.

My seat was one of the cheaper ones so I was well back from the arena itself. But I clearly recognised Francisco Rivera Ordoñez when I saw him. Compared to the other matadors and *banderillos* I'd seen walking about in the *callejon*, the passageway behind the deep red wooden fence around the ring, he looked very slim and boyish. When he appeared on the yellow sand with his large brilliant pink-and-pale-lemon-coloured cape he looked young and slight. He walked around the edges for a moment or two then retreated back into the brown darkness behind the fence again.

The gate opened.

For a moment nothing happened. There was silence in the stadium.

Suddenly the bull came flying out on to the sand. The crowd made an approving noise. The animal was blacker and bigger and more heavily muscled than any I'd ever seen before. Even at a distance I could see it was huge – although size shouldn't really matter too much since bulls can be overly fat and easily tired-out through lack of conditioning. It has been known for some unscrupulous breeders to try and pass off inflated three-year-old bulls in place of proper fully fledged four-year-olds. Three-year-olds aren't experienced enough with their horns, I'd read, and their frames simply couldn't support the extra weight which the breeders had loaded on to them through bulked-up eating habits. They looked good to begin with but tended to collapse early on, usually after the picador had gone to work on them.

Ordoñez's bull, however, seemed big, healthy *and* fast. The next thing that struck me were just how large its horns were; they were like the handlebars of a motorbike. It looked determined and angry and keen to charge.

In most cases when a bull first enters the *plaza*, the *banderillos* will wave their capes at it near the fences. When it charges they retreat quickly, often vaulting right over the wall just as the bull's horns come smashing through the woodwork behind them. They do this to test the bull's charging and running abilities. The matador who'll fight it watches from the sidelines, assessing the animal he's about to face. The better his *banderillos* perform the better he can size up what kind of bull he's up against. Does it charge straight? Does it hesitate? Is it scared? He's watching for some clues to give him the answers to all of these questions from the moment it charges at a *banderillo*.

But in the fight in Córdoba this did not happen. As the bull came running out, Francisco Ordoñez suddenly made a dash on to the bright sand. He fell to his knees, his brilliant green-and-gold suit of lights shining, and shouted at the animal. It turned, looked his way quizzically for a second then immediately charged straight at him. It ran with the speed of a fresh, well-trained, evenly conditioned racehorse. When the bull was almost on top of him, Ordoñez swung the cape to one side and over his head, holding it with both hands. The bull missed the cape and kept going. Its hooves had ploughed a neat line in the yellow-orange sand. It stopped. The crowd roared in unison. Everyone clapped and shouted – that was roughly what *should* have happened back in Alcalá de Guadaira when I'd watched the young *novillero* almost being beheaded.

Ordoñez expertly repositioned himself and shouted at the bull. It was standing gazing at the spectators which it just seemed to have noticed. It looked uncertain and angry. Then, out the corner of its eye, it spied Ordoñez. A starting-gun went off in its head and, without hesitating, it bolted straight for him. Again the matador swung the pink-and-yellow cape around, and again it missed him. And again. And again. He linked the series of passes until the bull was turning and running, and turning and running, and turning and running, like a puppy chasing after a ball. The crowd went crazy. I found myself joining in and cheering too. I knew that if I'd been facing the bull I'd have been dead by that point, so I suppose I was cheering the fact that Ordoñez had faced death and survived.

He jumped to his feet and acknowledged our approval, his white shirt looked all starched and clean, while the bull stood panting and staring at him as he walked off the sand. It was still annoyed, but also confused, trying to work out where the cape had gone.

Now it was time for Ordoñez's *banderillos* to do their work with their large capes. Dressed in deep red and silver and black and silver – *banderillos* never wear gold – they teased the bull into some charges. It was more hesitant than before, however, less certain of what it was doing. They had to be careful: if they overworked the bull at this stage of the fight it would be ruined for later. Ordoñez gazed over the *barrera* like an art lover gazing at a painting in a gallery.

A trumpet sounded.

The picadors entered the arena from the sunny side which was washed in a pale-yellow light. The senior man, his flabby arms shaking when he lanced the charging bull, went to work immediately. His less senior colleague stood at the side, watchful and poised. The bull managed to thump the picador's horse; it battered and charged and pummelled underneath and around the straw-coloured mattress-like covering. The picador's mount was blindfolded with a theatrical-looking black sash and its head strained, making it look uncharacteristically awkward and clumsy. It could have been worse: I'd read that in 1864 some 7,473 horses were killed in the course off 427 fights in Spain. In one particular fight, all the horses having been killed, it was necessary for the organiser to purchase the carriage horses which were lined up outside the arena so the *corrida* could finish.

In Córdoba, while the picador was lancing the bull, Ordoñez watched it carefully. Then, after a while, he waved his arms, his sequined suit of lights glistening, and the bull was lured away with the bright pink capes.

After the picadors had left it was time for the *banderillas* to be placed. I watched two of Ordoñez's *cuadrilla* receive their *banderillas* from some ring attendants. Some sticks were as white as snow, with blood-red ends; others were deep yellow, with flame-red tips. By now the sun had moved across the sky. Most of the *plaza* was in the stifling thick atmosphere of the shade but the blazing sunshine still sliced an arc across a third of the seats opposite me. I'd already seen this new type of *banderilla* when I was in Pedro the tailor's shop in Seville. They are 27 inches long with semi-detachable ends on them. This allows them to be more flexible and to stay attached when the bull becomes irritated with them and tries to throw them off.

This bull looked somewhat subdued and now seemed less inclined to charge. But when the *banderillos* appeared on the sand to stretch and briefly warm up, it came back to life.

They were like colourful jackals. They shouted at the bull from the edge of the ring, standing on their toes, holding their arms above their heads, the *banderillas* held aloft. Then, when the bull began to run straight at them, they cut across its line of charge at an angle. The bull was one second too slow, the *banderillos* one second too fast. When the bull lowered its head to hook and catch the man with its horns, the *banderillo* was already gone. He'd taken advantage of the bull's dropped head to lean across, like a tall, long-necked waiter picking up glasses from a low table in a packed, noisy bar, and jab the barbed sticks into the bull's thick neck muscle. Six *banderillas* were placed in total, two at a time.

The bull looked shamed. The *banderillas* were hanging from its neck, the blood was running down its back and its strength and bulk were now holding it back and weighing it down. It wasn't the lively, adept, fast and aware animal which had entered the ring fifteen minutes earlier. It was something less. A trumpet was sounded and Francisco Ordoñez returned to the fray. He was handed his sword and *muleta* by a thick-necked man in a tight-fitting blue suit. Then, after seeking and receiving ceremonial permission from the glum-faced president high up in his box to kill the bull, he began to prepare for the last part of the *corrida*.

The first thing he did was hold out his hat, dedicating the bull to the public; then he threw the *montera* over his shoulder. It landed with the bottom facing up. He left it that way. Some matadors believe the hat will fill up with their blood; others believe it's good to land bottom up so that their luck doesn't fall out of it. The bull, distracted by one of Ordoñez's *banderillos*, hung around on the other side of the ring in the sunshine. It seemed unwilling to venture back into the shade where its tormentors waited.

Ordoñez's work with the *muleta* – the *faena* – began.

At one time the purpose of this part of the bullfight was simply to line the bull up to kill it quickly. In modern bullfighting, however, it has become the main and most widely known part of the whole spectacle. As the beast charged in short bursts, Ordoñez gave it several passes, holding both the cape and the sword in his right hand. Each time it charged, the bull's head dropped lower and lower, and its attempts at hooking and chopping seemed to tire it out very quickly. Its charges suddenly became shorter and shorter, while Ordoñez did a series of natural passes which brought the beast to a complete standstill. The matador was able to turn and face it, speaking to it, using nothing but his unprotected body as bait. The bull seemed unable to move another step. It looked tired and dizzy. It didn't want to attack any more.

'¡Ai! ¡Toro! ¡Ai! . . .'

Ordoñez's shouts filled the ring. He was trying to lure the bull into some more charges.

'¡Toro!'

Then, bizarrely, a mobile phone suddenly began ringing. Its noise echoed around the *plaza*. A man in front of me shouted abuse. Other people began screaming too. The ringing continued. Ordoñez took a couple of steps back on the sand and shook his head. The bull looked at him quizzically. Then the ringing stopped as suddenly as it started and the sporadic flutter of applause which followed was shooed down in a low, intense wave of disapproval and tutting which washed throughout the entire crowd.

When the silence had settled once more, the matador fixed his position again. The bull's attention was engaged and absorbed by the shimmering movement of the *muleta* before its eyes.

'¡Toro! ¡Toro! ¡Ai, Toro!'

The bull seemed to take a breath and, after finding extra reserves, suddenly found enough strength to begin charging again. Ordoñez leaned into the passes, the bull chased the *muleta*, its entranced gaze lowered until its head was almost touching the sand. The salmon-pink stockings of the matador blurred against the red cape. In the shade the bull became a dark, heavy, almost formless shape. Only the animal's flashing horns and the gleaming, ferocious, terrified whites of its eyes pierced the blackness. As it spun around him, Ordoñez was able to slap its back, then he held on to it and let its weight carry him around like a child on a funfair ride. The bull's own strength and determination were now being used against it.

Ordoñez then held the sword and the *muleta* in his right hand and grasped the other corner of the cape with his left hand. The bull, still possessed with an urgent, unexpected burst of energy, automatically charged for the scarlet cloth of the *muleta*. Ordoñez spun around and, staring into the stands like a man waiting for a bus, calmly allowed the bull to batter past him without moving an inch. He did this several times. Then the matador finished with a snapping flick of his wrist, taking the *muleta* away from the bull and leaving it standing, forlorn and lost, literally staring into space.

Ordoñez faced the bull and taunted it. The *banderillas* hung down on the bloodied back of the animal like a ragged, slicing crown of thorns. The matador's green-and-gold suit of lights sparkled as he threw his arms open – an act known as an *Adorno* – and thrust his body out at the animal in a final, brazen gesture of defiance in the face of death.

The crowd applauded.

The bull didn't budge; it just stood there panting and looking around. It had been subdued and humiliated and seemed on the verge of destruction. It was almost time for the moment of truth. Ordoñez lined the bull up, stopped, moved it around with his cape, squared it and looked down the line of his sword. The bull was at a complete standstill. The *banderillas* hanging off its back, the blood it had lost, the aching, numbing pain it felt in its huge, bloodied neck-muscle and the increasing difficulty it had in getting its wind back were of little consequence now. Defensively, it had one option open to it: when the matador went over its right horn to place the sword it could still gore and kill him with one movement of its head. Whether it did that or not was up to the gods. No one could really say. The bull slowly brought its front hooves close together, thus opening up the space for Ordoñez to aim at high up between the bones on its shoulders. He looked down the line of his curved sword, gripping the handle tightly with his right hand, his index finger resting on top and helping with his aim. He moved the *muleta* very slightly, making sure the bull's eyes were fixed on it. His face was twisted into an almost parodied mask of intense, painful concentration. He went up on his toes like an animal ready to pounce for the kill.

There was silence in the arena. Even the small planes which had been buzzing across the sky, trailing their advertisements all afternoon, had temporarily stopped what they were doing.

Suddenly Ordoñez leapt forward.

The crowd made a collective noise: a snatched intake of breath, then a gasp. The matador's left hand with the *muleta* took the bull down, and away from him; simultaneously his right hand went in over and away from the right horn. In one single second the sword had disappeared up to its hilt between the shoulder-blade and the spinal column. From there it would penetrate or slice through the aorta, the largest artery coming out of the bull's heart.

The bull shuddered, stopped, convulsed and fell over. Its legs stuck up in the air like an upturned chair. A trickle of blood ran from its mouth.

The *banderillos* had been ready and waiting to distract the bull after the sword went in but they weren't needed. Ordoñez motioned them away and stood guard over the animal as it died. He pointed to it. It looked up at him. Then its head fell to one side, its tongue hanging out. It had been an unusually quick kill. Ordoñez touched its head, paused, then gestured to the crowd.

The place erupted. A blizzard of white hankies appeared around the stadium. A roar filled the air.

Ordoñez stood at the *barrera* drinking mineral water from a large plastic bottle which had been handed over the fence to him. The spectators applauded until Ordoñez took a lap of honour and was awarded one of the bull's ears. When he walked past the front of the area of the *plaza* where I was sitting, I was able to see the smile on his face, the bloody patches on his suit of lights from where he'd grabbed and played with the bull, and the odd trophy he held in his hands. The bull's ear was like an enlarged lucky rabbit's foot; a trickle of red blood, like watercolour paint, ran down the china-white surface of parts of its interior where the skin was white and hairless and exposed.

A man in front of me who'd been slicing a large sausage, stopped what he was doing and waved the meat at Ordoñez. Then he sat back down and resumed cutting it up, carefully placing thick slices of the sausage on a piece of fresh bread he'd just broken. He poured himself a small glass of red wine and drank it slowly as he listened through an earpiece to the radio announcer at the side of the ring giving details of the next matador and the next bull. He nodded his head silently, impressed by what he'd just seen and by what he was hearing.

Francisco Rivera Ordoñez, passing through the last shreds of sunlight on the other side of the ring, wiped the sweat off his face with a thick white towel. He waved at the only spectator who was on that side of the arena. The *aficionado*, who was still wearing his collapsed sweatstained hat made of newspaper, returned the greeting and bowed like a grateful court jester.

Everyone paused and took a deep breath. Some ran to the toilets. Others shouted for drinks. Nearly everyone smoked. The bull killed by Ordoñez had been good. The night was still fresh. Everyone seemed happy. There were four bulls still to be fought. Another couple of hours filled with possibilities beckoned.

'On the day of a bullfight, I never eat a meal after midday. I must eat early, because if I'm gored in the ring that night I have to be ready to take the anaesthetic . . .'

Francisco Rivera Ordoñez leaned back in his chair, sipped the Coke I'd bought him and smiled his boyish smile. He looked impossibly young for someone who was ranked as one of the top six matadors in Spain.

In order to meet him I'd had to drive north from Córdoba and head for a small town called Aranjuez, which was about 30 minutes by car from the centre of Madrid. We had arranged to meet in a small hotel in the middle of town. The heat indoors was unbearable even when the air-conditioning periodically spluttered into life. The whole town knew that the matadors for that evening's *corrida* were staying there. From all the activity that was going on, it looked as though the manager had been preparing for everyone's arrival all morning. He greeted me nervously at the door with a mighty handshake and an anxious grin. The foyer was decorated with posters and signed pictures of the matadors who were due to arrive. Someone had also propped up a couple of amateurish paintings by local artists which showed the matadors in extremely heroic and dramatic poses. I had to pay about £60 to a tout for a ticket to the evening's *corrida*.

As we sat together in the hotel restaurant, I asked Francisco about the attention he was attracting.

'I enjoy publicity but sometimes it's hard – the paparazzi, you know? There are always some photographers outside my house. All my friends are older than me, but I suppose that's made me mature faster. As far as women go, well, I'm interested in quality not quantity.'

'What sort of training do you do?' I asked him.

'During the winter I train on the family ranch; I train physically, fighting cows. It's hard, every day . . . train, train, train. I think all the time about why I do it. I want to be rich but it takes time to earn money.'

As I chatted to Francisco I soon became aware that every eye in the restaurant was on him. The place was heaving with his admirers. Every so often a man would interrupt us, blow thick cigar smoke towards the ceiling and mutter 'Good luck' in his ear, in the grave, knowing tones of the bullfighting insider. Several women just grabbed him by the neck and kissed him on the cheek. A couple of children with Downs Syndrome were brought over to have their photograph taken with him; he smiled and posed and asked them questions. Two young women with heavy perfume and thick make-up hung around until they could snap each other standing beside him. He smiled and asked them where they were from. They giggled and fumbled for the right words, before suddenly bursting into hysterical tears of tension and laughter. They'd met their hero at last. One old lady dressed from head to toe in black turned up, for some reason clutching what appeared to be an ancient photograph of her long-dead husband. She never explained why she had it on her person, she just held it to her bosom silently while she got Francisco to sign his name on a greasy napkin. When he'd scrawled out his signature she wrapped it up, stuck it into one of the folds of her dress and puckered her old lips to give him a kiss.

Ordoñez took it all in his stride. Wearing a starched blue shirt and pressed chino trousers, he seemed to be used to all the attention and worship. Occasionally he motioned to his sidekick, the man I'd seen wearing the dark-blue suit in Córdoba and handing Francisco his sword over the *plaza* fence before he killed the bull, to do him a favour. The man's name was Nachos and he looked like something out of the Mafia. When Francisco signalled to him, Nachos stopped talking on his mobile phone and heaved his bulk obligingly across the room towards where we were sitting. When the young matador asked him to bring us another Coke, he listened with a look of intense concentration. Then he lurched off across the room to the packed bar.

'He's my arms and legs . . .' muttered Francisco when the bull-necked Nachos was safely out of earshot.

Ordoñez began his professional career in earnest when he faced his first real bull in Ronda in 1991. He became a full matador five years later and by the time I'd met him he'd fought 101 times; he had been awarded 102 ears and five tails in the process.

'How did it begin for you?' I asked.

'My grandfather, Antonio Ordoñez, was my first teacher. I first practised at the age of four but I started to cry and ran away. But over the years I've learned a lot from him – he's my favourite matador. And of course I know all about Hemingway and the history of *The Dangerous Summer*. In fact, Hemingway is buried in Ronda or his ashes were scattered there or something – did you know that?' he asked me.

'I thought Hemingway was buried in Ketchum in Idaho,' I replied. I was certain that if the writer had been buried in Ronda then Allen Josephs would have said something to me.

'Oh, no, he's buried on our family land in Ronda,' said Francisco firmly.

'Are you sure?'

He got up to speak to his friends. I watched them all consult each other. They shook their heads and scratched their chins. The one of them whispered something in Francisco's ear. He returned to our table. 'Sorry, you're right. It's Orson Welles who's buried in the back garden.'

Some men who were gathered at the bar tried to listen to what we were saying. They wore immaculate blue blazers and silk ties. The air, such as it was, reeked of strong perfume, cigarette smoke and alcohol. I noticed a few women powder their noses and twiddle their thumbs, looking bored and rich. Waiters buzzed around in short white jackets and tight bow-ties, the sweat running down their faces. The majority of the crowd for the evening's *corrida* in Aranjuez had travelled down from Madrid for the day. They were there to see and be seen.

I asked Francisco about the bulls he fights.

'When the bull comes out, you study him – he's your friend. At the beginning of the fight you are afraid. But after you study his moves, his face, you start a conversation with his feelings. Of course I'm afraid but not too much – I'm not crazy! The bull is an animal but he can show everybody that he is a royal animal. He can immortalise himself; that animal can be a part of your life for ever . . .'

'What about when you have to kill it?' I asked.

'Well, at the moment of truth, I just think to myself: "Friend, I must kill you . . ." Afterwards, it's awesome. Standing in front of a cheering crowd, I can *feel* the people's emotion.'

He smiled and shook his head. Looking at him I thought he had a slightly academic air about him, like an earnest young student who'd look comfortable striding across an Ivy League campus carrying an armful of books.

Francisco wasn't even a teenager when his father died just as the ambulance reached the hospital in Córdoba. I asked him about it.

'I was in Seville with my mother when it happened in 1984.' His voice dropped.

'Do you remember it?'

'I remember everything,' he said, shaking his head. 'I'm sorry. I don't like talking about it.'

How did his mother feel now that her son was doing the very thing which led to her husband's early death?

He stared into space for a second or two then said flatly: 'Every time I fight my mother almost dies . . .'

I asked him what he thought of people who believe that what he did, and what his family have done for generations, is an obscene and objectionable way to make a living?

He sat up, smiled and launched into a story about a very famous American actress who'd been in Spain recently to do some filming. Apparently she'd spotted Francisco in an exclusive restaurant and wanted to meet him. All was going well with the introductions until the actress discovered he was a matador. She was shocked and repulsed: bullfighting was not politically correct enough for her Los Angeles sensibilities and so she beat a hasty retreat. Francisco said he was, to put it mildly, disappointed. He sat back, smiling and making faces, when he'd finished.

I laughed at the story and began to note down the details but Francisco pleaded with me not to mention the tale or her name, which was internationally known. Eventually we compromised: I could recount the anecdote but I agreed to forget her name. He showed his relief by slumping into his chair and fanning himself, letting out a sigh and gulping down his Coke in the process.

'This is not a job, it's a way of life,' he said, rolling his eyes. 'Life now is for bullfighting: when I'm awake, when I'm asleep – all the time is for bullfighting. Sometime in the future I'll play with my life.'

'When will that time come?' I asked him.

'Well,' he said shrugging, 'I suppose the bulls will tell me . . .'

I left Francisco midway through the afternoon. He had to go back to his room and dress for the evening's *corrida*. I walked around Aranjuez, even though it was a baking hot, windless day. I had a late lunch at a small outdoor café and ended up talking to a middle-aged couple from London. They said they went on holiday to Spain every year so that they could secretly attend as many bullfights as possible. Their friends would have been appalled, they confided, if they'd told them they liked watching matadors and bulls. They played Scrabble to kill the hours before the bullfight which was due to begin at seven that evening.

By six o'clock a small crowd had gathered outside the Hotel Isabelle II where the matadors, their managers, their *cuadrillas* and their hangers-on were staying. A white curtain hanging from a first-floor window twitched every now and then when a matador's manager warily glanced out on the scene below.

At 6.35 p.m. the fat picador emerged dressed in his embroidered suit of white and silver, hauling his heavily protected limbs along like a man who'd suffered numerous fractures. He hoisted himself into a waiting car. A few moments later the rest of the matador's team descended the red-tiled steps. They were all square-jawed, reliable and friendly-looking fellows. They looked like ushers on their way to a wedding ceremony. They dutifully packed themselves into a blue van, smiling and chatting as they waited for their absent colleague. Several quiet minutes slipped past. The small crowd that was gathered were, for the most part, silent.

For the first time in the whole day I felt a breeze in the air. A few leaves rustled in the skinny trees near the hotel entrance.

At exactly 6.42 p.m. Francisco Rivera Ordoñez emerged from the hotel. His green-and-gold suit of lights jumped alive when the sun's splintered rays caught it. Changed out of his chinos and casual shirt he looked different – older and more formal. He was no longer smiling. His face was completely set and he ignored the polite round of applause which greeted him. Some press photographers ran after him as he bolted across the carpark towards the waiting van. A few flashbulbs went off, piercing the evening light.

The old woman who'd kissed him that afternoon stood to the side. She was still holding her husband's framed photograph like a talisman. She rubbed her face, blessed herself with the sign of the cross, then muttered something. Then she scuttled off up the street, talking to herself.

The *plaza de toros* in Aranjuez was only two minutes away from the hotel by car. I drove behind the matador's van as he headed towards it. The distance, I thought, was a short one or a long one, depending on who you were and what your purpose was in going there.

Our posse of cars reached the bullring quickly. It was an ancient little arena, made of scarred stone and wood. A cloud of dust floated around Francisco's *cuadrilla* as the men piled out of the van. A few moments later the young matador himself left the vehicle. I watched him walk through billowing clouds of yellow dirt, his embroidered suit of lights with its fancy stitchwork swaying in time with his movements. He glanced neither right nor left. He paid no attention to the three paramedic ambulances he had to walk past. His stride was purposeful and certain and he seemed happy to reach the welcoming cool darkness which veiled the matadors' entrance to the *plaza*, although he'd told me that afternoon that he liked fighting in the numbing heat of the Spanish summers.

Almost four decades previously, in the same place, at the same time of day, Francisco's grandfather, Antonio, had gone through the same process and entered the same bullring for the same purpose: to fight and kill a bull. But on that occasion something had gone wrong and his second bull of the *corrida* had gored him badly. When he'd killed the animal he was bleeding heavily from a wound on his thigh. His men had tried to drag him from the Aranjuez bullring but he resisted their attempts to help, shouting at his brother angrily: 'And you call yourself an Ordoñez!' After he'd killed the bull, Antonio had collapsed. Those who were there reported he was deathly white from loss of blood and severe shock. Later he was rushed to hospital for emergency life-saving surgery. He recovered and lived to fight another day. His close friend Ernest Hemingway later wrote in *The Dangerous Summer*: 'It was a good day for bulls at Aranjuez . . .' Neither he, a seasoned *aficionado*, nor the experienced young matador Antonio, had foreseen the near-fatal tragedy which happened that day.

Inside the Aranjuez *plaza de toros*, Antonio's grandson was focused on the white light at the end of the tunnel which led him and his *cuadrilla* out on to the sand. In the distance the trumpets sounded and the parade consisting of the mounted constables, the three matadors, his *banderillos*, the mounted picadors and their helpers – known as 'wise monkeys' – and the men with the bell-wringing horses who drag the dead bulls from the ring, all moved off. I watched Francisco as he passed by me. It was only then that he seemed to relax a little. He was on sure ground, surrounded by his men and certain of his own abilities.

The appointed hour had arrived and it would soon be time for Francisco Rivera Ordoñez to perform.

From that point on, it would all be a matter of skill. And luck.

ELEVEN

A Chic Night Out

'What's your first language?'

I was eating breakfast in Aranjuez and was being accosted by a huge Peruvian man who spoke English with a thick South American accent.

'English,' I answered, buttering a piece of toast.

'Can't be!' he boomed. His belly stuck out from under the table. He poured himself some coffee and shook his head.

'It is,' I answered.

'Can't be! Not with an accent like *that* . . .'

'I have a Scottish accent, but my first language is English.'

'Nah . . . don't believe it!'

I shrugged.

'I thought you all spoke Scottish . . .'

'You mean Gaelic?'

'Yeah, Gaelic. Why can't you speak that? You'd sound more natural,' he said. 'I can hardly understand your English!'

'You speak good English, not a trace of an accent,' I lied.

'Thank you – you're so kind. But I know this already.'

I left Aranjuez and headed north. I planned to spend one evening in Madrid and then drive on to Burgos the next day where I hoped to meet John Fulton and Vicente Salamanca.

I arrived at my hotel in Madrid about an hour later and picked up my ticket for that evening's bullfight at the reception desk. A friend of someone I knew in London had organised things for me. I was told she had an acquaintance in the capital who could pull some strings at short notice. I showered, changed my clothes, caught a cab and hurried along the Gran Via to Las Ventas, the legendary *plaza de toros* in Madrid, to meet this friend of a friend.

From the outside, Madrid's biggest bullring looked impressive. Stalls, like others I'd seen before, were set out selling postcards, hankies, lighters, T-shirts, videos, hats, mugs, children's capes and swords, water and peanuts. Thousands of people hung around the square in front of the entrance. Others patiently lined up in long queues and touts, in full view of the authorities, tried to sell tickets at inflated rates. The *plaza*'s huge arched entranceway, almost Moorish in design, was guarded by a couple of armed policemen. I joined a line of people and shuffled to the front. A guard took my ticket and pointed me in the right direction. My skin prickled with the heat even when I reached the shade inside.

Madrid, in the world of bullfighting, has always been one of those places – like Seville or Mexico City – where matadors must prove themselves in front of some of the most critical crowds in the world. It can't be avoided. Forty years previously, even the legendary Manuel Benítez, El Cordobés, had left Andalucia behind and headed north to Madrid and Las Ventas, as though being pulled by someone or something. He went there with little more to his name than the clothes he stood up in and the impossible dream of one day making it big as a matador. A former employer recalled how he'd met the future bullfighter in Madrid before he became famous:

> Every man who works for me I know him. I know all their faces. I don't let anything get away from me. So one day in the spring of 1957 . . . I saw a new face. Right away, I noticed him and I'll tell you why. He had long arms. He was mixing mortar in a tub and heaving it up to a mason on the second floor with one fling of his shovel. You don't get many who can do that. I asked my son who'd hired him who he was. 'Some bum who just came up from Andalucia,' he said.
>
> A few days later I saw him again. I came around a corner and there he was playing *torero* with an empty cement sack. Just because I'm an *aficionado* I'm not going to let every kid

who wants to be a *torero* play bullfighter on my time . . . For something like that I usually fired a kid right away . . . Him, I decided to give a second chance. I remembered those long arms of his.

'Listen kid,' I said, 'you want to be a bullfighter, you go down there to Las Ventas. You want to be a mason, go back to your mortar. I'm not paying you to wave those empty sacks in the air.' He understood. He went back to work.

Well, a little while later, a couple of weeks maybe, I went to the bullfight at Las Ventas. I have my regular place there . . . As the fifth bull came out of the *toril*, an *espotaneo* [a spontaneous one] jumped into the ring. The kid didn't have any luck. As he jumped, a Guardia Civil grabbed his foot . . . The Guardia picked him up and marched him off to jail.

I forgot about it until the next day when I saw a picture of the *espotaneo* in the papers. It was the kid with the long arms . . . What a picture it was. You ought to see it. He has a snarl on his face, a defiance for the world like an animal in a cage. That kid, I told myself, he'd sell his mother to a Moorish whoremaster to become a bullfighter.

El Cordobés's jump into the ring landed him on the front pages of the Madrid newspapers as well as in the cells. I'd seen that particular photograph in a book I'd read and it was exactly as the man described it: there was Manuel Benítez, El Cordobés, his hair flying, a scowl on his face, trying to hold up a threadbare pair of trousers as two Guardia Civil officers frogmarched him out of Las Ventas. His desperation paid off and someone eventually gave him a break, allowing him to appear on a *novillada* cartel. He was so relieved he broke down and wept the first time he tried on a faded second-hand suit of lights. When he was dressing he told his manager that he was prepared to 'walk over my own guts if I have to, to kill my bulls'. With El Cordobés, from day one, it was all or nothing. Many thought he was half mad. When asked why he so badly wanted to be a bullfighter, he snapped: 'Because I'm fed up being hungry.' Then he told his crying sister as he was leaving for his first proper bullfight: 'Don't worry, Angelita, tonight, either I'll buy you a house or I'll dress you in mourning.'

He proved himself and, true to his word, he did buy that house. And more houses. And a ranch. And cars. And have parties and women and fame and fortune. And have his photograph taken in a shirt and tie standing next to Franco – even though his father had died in one of the dictator's civil war prison camps. The illiterate 'bum from Andalucia' who'd once been spotted with a scrap of newspaper trying to get a mangy stray dog to charge at it like a bull when he was living rough on the streets, had come a long way. His heyday was in the 1960s when, for a time, he ruled the world of bullfighting like Joselito, Belmonte or Manolete. He was to bullfighting what the Rolling Stones or the Beatles were to rock music in the early '60s. Audiences had been sceptical of both. At first they laughed; then they paid to laugh; then they paid to stay; finally they paid, stayed and screamed for more. Manuel Benítez, the man from Córdoba, turned the whole damn industry on its head. Apart from his determination to prove his point and be a great matador and make himself a pile of money in the process, it was tellingly noted by one journalist after interviewing him that, although he lacked a formal education, El Cordobés was, in his view, quite simply 'super-intelligent'. He also noted that he was a 'nice fella' into the bargain.

Since those great days he'd 'retired' numerous times and made countless comebacks. Flying to Spain, for example, I'd seen his picture grinning out of a glossy magazine. There he was, stripped to the waist, suntanned and healthy-looking in his early sixties. A crowd of young people, most of whom weren't even born when he was in his prime, were carrying him shoulder-high around a bullring in some tenth-rate little town where he'd just fought in a *corrida*. He looked slightly unhinged and hungry despite his years. But he was still smiling that big bright, improbably white, death-defying smile of his.

Now, in the mid-1990s, another bullfighter, claiming to be his illegitimate son, used the name 'El Cordobés'. He smiled like his alleged father and sometimes fought like him too, they said. I'd already seen him grinning like a naughty schoolboy from the pages of a fashion spread, all cheeky smiles and dirty-blond tousled hair, in a trendy Spanish magazine. The accompanying article was written by a knowledgeable Madrid-based American named Bill Lyons who'd been covering bullfighting in Spain for a wide range of American publications for over three decades. He had a serious reputation for knowing his matadors and his bulls. He told me over the phone that El Cordobés Jnr was a 'hot dogger – people don't take him seriously'. I also heard that El Cordobés Snr had tried to sue this 'son' on the grounds that he shouldn't be using his name: the judge ruled against him and the younger man was allowed to continue calling himself El Cordobés. But people said he couldn't make his mind up whether he wanted to be a brilliant showman like his supposed father, or a classical young matador in his own right in the more traditional mould of rising stars like Francisco Rivera Ordoñez.

El Cordobés Jnr's main rival in the showman stakes was Jesulín de Ubrique, the flash character from the mountains of Andalucia. He was the reason I was in Madrid and it was him that I was going to see fighting in Las Ventas.

Apparently the Madrid *aficionados* weren't particularly fond of Jesulín de Ubrique. He clowned around a bit too much, they said, and worried more about his media image, his women, his fast cars and his bank account, than he did about his bulls. He was also supposedly something of an avowed old-fashioned male chauvinist, once holding a free women-only bullfight which ended with the large crowd chucking their underwear on to the sand at the end of the fight. In public he went out of his way on more than one occasion to declare his belief that Spain's few female matadors should not be allowed into the same ring as men. It was a short-sighted stance to take, in my opinion. Cristina Sánchez, for example, Spain's number one and very first fully fledged female matador, was highly regarded by many seasoned critics. I was desperately keen to see her in action and if I'd had unlimited time and resources I'd have driven halfway across Spain to find her. She had a notorious reputation for being very difficult to pin down for interviews, however, especially with foreign journalists whom she always treated warily. As luck would have it, I kept missing her: when my schedule took me to one end of Spain, fate had her appearing the same night in some town at the other end. But, from what I read, she was regarded as being very good. She certainly earned plenty of money and generated a mountain of slightly sexist profiles which recounted her every gesture, pout and item of clothing. More usefully, she also served as a (somewhat reluctant it has to be said) role model for young girls who flocked to matador training schools in various parts of Spain once she'd become a success and broken down a few outdated barriers in the process. After reading some very positive articles on Christina and seeing a clip of her fighting, I began to think that Jesulín de Ubrique's one-man stand against her and what she represented reflected more on his stupidity than it did on her skills as a matador.

'He isn't another El Cordobés [Snr] either,' said someone I'd chatted to in Seville. 'El Cordobés was better – more passionate – when he wanted to be. Jesulín de Ubrique wouldn't have been allowed in the same city, never mind on the same cartel as the real El Cordobés in the 1960s and '70s, even when he was at his worst – and he could be pretty rotten sometimes too.'

Bill Lyons told me bluntly: 'I think people are generally losing interest in Jesulín – he was more of a personality than anything else; he wanted to be the El Cordobés of the 1990s, a sort of hayseed wise-guy, charming and unorthodox, and he was for a while. But he didn't have the real personality of El Cordobés the father.'

But I'd also heard other people say that Jesulín was almost single-handedly responsible for the new-found popularity of bullfighting. His I-don't-give-a-damn, wheel-them-out-and-I'll-kill-them attitude seemed to strike a chord with a lot of people. Maybe it was a sign of the times, one commentator said: people like to see violent films, smart-ass TV programmes, and pop videos are all about sex and money and not giving a damn – well, Jesulín was just another expression of that culture. He brought the kids in, was the claim, the kind who were unlikely to have been at a bullfight before and who were more interested in watching a Quentin Tarantino film. The promoters didn't care – their money was as good as anyone else's. But others disagreed and complained that he was bad for the industry. To kill the number of bulls he did, night after night, from one end of the country to the other, said one *aficionado*, he had to, just had to, be fighting crappy animals. It was an old complaint. Earlier in the century Hemingway noted:

> It is impossible, day in and day out, to fight bulls that are really bulls, huge, strong, fierce and fast, knowing how to use their

horns and old enough so that they have their full growth, with the technique that has been developed, starting with Juan Belmonte, in modern bullfighting. It is too dangerous . . .

I asked Francisco Rivera Ordoñez about Jesulín when we'd met in Aranjuez the day before. He rolled his eyes when his rival's name was mentioned. I pressed him for his opinion. He thought for a second or two then answered: 'Well, Jesulín has all my respect – anyone who stands in front of a bull has my respect – but he has another concept of bullfighting. I'm more traditional . . . Jesulín is more modern.'

'Can you elaborate?' I asked him.

'I'm like fine wine; he's like Coke . . .'

I hung around a busy bar inside Las Ventas until Maria arrived. It was packed inside. Hundreds of people milled around, scanning their programmes, eating and drinking and talking loudly. The air was heavy and it was very, very hot. The woman it had been arranged for me to meet arrived with her friends and family in tow. They were all dressed in expensive designer clothes and a few of them had kept their sunglasses on even though we were inside the building. They looked me up and down for a few moments and then mostly ignored me.

'I've got you a very good seat. It was *expensive*,' said Maria. She didn't smile when she spoke.

I nodded and showed her the ticket stub. I planned to pay her later when we were in a less public place.

'Is this a very popular way to spend an evening?' I asked her. I had to shout to make myself heard above the din.

'Oh, yes, young people are beginning to like the bulls again. We come here, spend an evening watching them, go on for a meal. It's a chic night out. Companies bring guests here. Like golf days. It's a very corporate thing to do. It goes on for hours. This is the best way to start off if you want to have a successful evening out with clients,' Maria told me off-handedly.

Bill Lyons had said something like this to me, that people went to bullfights to 'see and be seen – like going to Wimbledon'.

I asked Maria how often she came here.

'Every night there are bulls here, I am here.' She looked at me with a blank expression on her face.

'How long have you been going to the bullfights?' I asked.

'Just a couple of years.'

'Are you an *aficionada*?'

'Not yet. But I want to be. I need to see more *corridas* before I can call myself one.' She sounded a bit fed-up.

'So how many would someone have to see before they could call themselves a real *aficionado*?' I wondered.

'Oh, hundreds, many hundreds – over seasons.'

'People must have to be very rich to do that; to buy all those expensive tickets and travel all over Spain and not have any work to do which takes up your time,' I said.

Maria paused and examined her fingernails. That had not been a clever thing to say.

'I suppose . . .' She looked over my shoulder and stood up on her tiptoes to see if she recognised anyone.

'Do you work?' I asked.

'We must go in soon . . .' she said.

'How do you always manage to get tickets for the fights?'

'I have friends . . .' she said firmly.

'Friends?'

'Well, they aren't really friends. They're people who think they are my friends but I think of them as being *useful*. Do you understand?'

Her family and friends stared at me. I stared back at them. We went in to see the bulls.

It turned out to be a poor, disappointing evening.

I had hoped everyone was wrong and that the cheeky matador from Andalucia would surprise the sceptical crowd, me included, but he didn't. He came into the ring as the derided underdog and went out to muted, low-key applause. I'd spent a lot of money to see the slightly jaded, pockmarked Jesulín, who'd broken all sorts of records and fought 121 bulls in the 1996 season, and I suppose I expected something special for my cash. But Jesulín turned out to be a bit of a flop. Despite the glitzy white-and-gold suit of lights and his almost wig-like mop of thick black hair – which made him look like a runner-up in a Las Vegas Liberace-lookalike competition – he failed to set the crowd on fire.

We were crammed in, tens of thousands of us, cheek-by-jowl. Cigars were puffed, fancy clothes were worn, sunglasses were shoved back on heads and eyebrows were raised. When a matador did well, the atmosphere became truly electric. You were surrounded and overwhelmed by the sound and the excitement: it came from behind you, beside you, above you and across from you. It swept you along and it was hard, very hard indeed, not to feel part of it in some way. But when the spectators fell into silence, the atmosphere became oppressive, draining the energy right out of the very air you breathed.

As the night wore on and as Jesulín's performance went from bad to worse, he seemed to shrink, little by little, until he was lost in the golden sea of sand. But he carried on as if he hadn't a care in the world. He reminded me of some of the third-rate dreamers I'd seen back in Alcalá de Guadaira the night the rat ran across the sand. His endless theatrics fell flat, making him look cheap and in the end exposing his desire to please the crowd and be accepted by those he pretended to disregard.

Other matadors, although they were about to kill the animal, seemed to treat their bulls with a strange kind of respect during most of the fight. It was as if they acknowledged the fact the bull could have killed them at any moment if they'd got sloppy and it had got lucky. Jesulín wasn't like that at all; he seemed to enjoy belittling the bull and its efforts to catch the cape. He hopped on the bull, slapped it and then acted like a diva with a sore throat when it wouldn't die as quickly as he wanted it to. His *cuadrilla* and his henchmen all laughed like hyenas whenever he came back to the *barrera* to make wisecracks. Every so often, he'd wave and make faces at some girls in the crowd who shouted at him. He seemed to treat parts of the evening as a joke. He strutted around as if he were the only matador in the *plaza* and grinned when the bull came battering out of the Gate of Fear. Many bullfighters I'd seen refused to look at the gate when the bull was due to appear – John Fulton said he'd always stared at his shoes, until he heard the roar of the crowd telling him that the bull was in the ring. But Jesulín smiled his cocky smile and looked as if he couldn't wait to get his hands on the beast. He almost sneered at everyone else's apprehension.

By the time the matador killed his final bull of the evening he didn't seem to give a damn what anyone thought of him – either that or he was a very good actor. When he went in for the last kill of the *corrida* he launched himself into mid-air, his sword hand all over the place, both feet leaving the ground and his cape flapping in the wind like a loose sail. He looked like an anxious, hungry scarecrow trying to get the night over and done with as quickly as possible.

'What did you think of him?' I asked Maria as we were leaving after the final fight.

'I don't like him.'

'Why not?'

'He's vulgar, which is not good. He is also occasionally trying to fight with a classical style, which is even worse. He's from Andalucia as well which means he is backward when it comes to treating women with respect.'

'I heard he sings,' I said. One of the magazines I'd come across with Jesulín's photo on the front alluded to his alleged plans to launch himself as a rock star.

'No, he doesn't sing,' said Maria. 'He opens his mouth and certain noises come out.'

I smiled at her comment. She folded her arms and stared at me. She had beautiful large brown eyes, but they seemed cold.

'Now, can you pay me for the *corrida* tickets as soon as possible, please? I don't take cheques. I don't have a bank account. It's a long story. Cash would be better.'

I told her I didn't have any cash on me and that I had planned to give her a cheque later in the evening.

She rolled her eyes. 'I'll come by your hotel in a taxi in the morning. What time do you plan to have breakfast?'

Early next morning, as I was attacking a piece of toast, she turned up at my hotel. I quickly cashed a cheque at the reception and paid her for the tickets. I could tell that she didn't want to be kept waiting any longer.

'I have to rush,' she told me. 'I'm going to a town near the Portuguese border. The bullfight begins at half past six.'

Then she thanked me, kissed me on both cheeks and disappeared into a taxi she'd kept waiting. 'Look me up the next time you're in town' was the last thing she said to me.

TWELVE

A Sobresaliente in Burgos

Burgos was freezing. The temperature had dropped about 20 degrees in the space of 48 hours, and I had succumbed to a heavy cold.

But the drive up from Madrid had been something of a compensation. The golden fields, washed in sunshine, had given way to higher and greener pastures. There were more rocky hills too; in fact, parts of the road reminded me of the Scottish Highlands. It had become misty and wet by the time I stopped at an old abandoned bullet-marked church that was high in the hills. It was locked and barred. Crows squawked and crouched in the tower, watching my every move. The thick grass, all chopped and uneven, was soaking. The imprint of where a gigantic cross had once been nailed to a wall remained, the outline looking as if it had been burned into the plasterwork. A thick forest covered the slopes leading up to the church, grey and deep-green hills lay to the west. To the north and east, towards Burgos where I was heading, the weather looked misty and miserable.

I drove off from this haunted, silent old place of worship and joined the main road again. It took me another two hours to reach my destination. The city of Burgos, where General Franco had temporarily installed his fascist government during the Civil War, was also famous for being the birthplace of El Cid, the conqueror of the Moors. I passed his huge, inflated statue in the city centre on my way to a pharmacy for some cold medicine and throat lozenges. The image was terrifying and brutal – all flowing beard, muscles, sword and chain-mail.

Burgos has always had some slightly dubious military connections so I wasn't surprised to come across some nervous-looking young Spanish soldiers, fingering their automatic weapons, who were guarding a government building near by. One of them nearly had a fit when a tourist tried to park his car in front of where they were standing. He was told to get lost by the soldier. The tourist looked shaken and worried after the exchange. As I walked by, one of the soldiers stared at me. I smiled and nodded back at him. He automatically returned the gesture, then he caught himself and furrowed his eyebrows. Despite his crotch-thrusting macho pose, his state-of-the-art military gear and his steady gaze from under his precisely slouched beret, he succeeded only in giving the impression of slightness, immaturity and fear.

The streets were full of young people dressed in white clothes and wearing neckerchiefs of different colours. Bands tooted and banged their way down winding side streets, and children clapped and waved when a tiny parade of giant heads went by. The annual Burgos *feria* was in full swing. I was desperate to enjoy myself but I felt bloody awful.

I coughed and spluttered my way around the city following my little photocopied map, sweating and shivering by turns, until, cursing, I finally gave up and staggered back to my hotel. The suspiciously cheerful young man at the reception desk encouraged me to visit the city's cathedral. I tried in vain to tell him I wasn't up to it and that, anyway, after the cathedral in Seville, it was bound to be a let-down.

'Yeah, but we've got the Cristo de Burgos,' he told me.

'What's that?' I asked.

'An icon of Christ on the cross – copied directly from the real scene of the crucifixion.'

I raised my eyebrows.

'Well, that's what they say. And then there's the skin,' he went on.

'The skin?' I muttered.

'Yes, it's real. Also the beard and the fingernails. They need to be trimmed every eighth day.'

I left him and went up to my room. By mid-afternoon, doped up with cold medicine and several glasses of red wine, I collapsed on top of my bed and fell fast asleep.

A couple of hours slipped by. Then I awoke with a start.

A crowd of rampaging people were screaming and stampeding through my darkened room. A whole mob of them, right at the foot of my bed, were bawling, making the walls vibrate.

I snapped the bedside light on. The room was empty. The rumpus had stopped as suddenly as it had started. I looked around. A second later it started again. It sounded just like a shrieking football crowd, or a screeching audience at a rock concert. It came from every corner and part of the room, echoing and banging through the walls and filling the air. I grabbed the telephone and called the reception desk.

'There's a terrible commotion in my room,' I shouted. 'Listen, it's pandemonium up here!'

'Have you been to the toilet lately?' said the man on the other end of the line. He sounded very polite.

'No – why?' I snapped. Was this man a freelance doctor, moonlighting as a hotel employee?

The din continued in the background.

'Then that can only mean the gentleman or his wife in the room next to you may have had to go.'

'I don't understand.' The clangour stopped again and my voice suddenly sounded very loud.

'It is the lavatory, sir . . .' I heard him say. He started to say something else but it was lost in the bedlam which rampaged through the walls again.

I lay on the bed, my ears recovering. I reached for my guidebook and leafed through it until I found a mention of the hotel I was staying in. The small print said it was 'perfectly adequate' except that it had 'yesterday's finest plumbing'.

I could hear the gaggle of young girls before I saw them. They were gathered outside the *plaza de toros* in Burgos, waiting for the matadors to arrive. They clutched their small cameras tightly and showed each other signed programmes from bullfights that had been going on all week during the *feria*.

Suddenly a large blue minivan appeared, trailing a plume of exhaust behind it. A middle-aged man rushed out to meet it and stood waving at the van's occupants like a star-struck teenager. I could see Francisco Rivera Ordoñez in a blue-and-gold suit of lights sitting in the front passenger seat. He gestured at the driver next to him, pointing to the red gate which led into the matadors' entrance. But the way was blocked by hundreds of girls and even a few young men. They began to squeal and clap when Ordoñez's door opened and he stepped out. One of his men tried to distract the fans by holding up handfuls of free postcards and autographed photos of the matador but nobody paid any attention to him. Ordoñez smiled and shoved his way through. Camera flashes went off. His name was shouted. A swarthy man in a red jacket stood guard by the entrance gate; he beckoned the matador towards him and pulled him inside. Ordoñez's *cuadrilla* followed.

The shouting and clapping and screaming evaporated as quickly as it had started. A few giggles sounded. 'I rubbed his head! Look, smell my hand! You can smell his shampoo!' said one teenager excitedly. As her friends all sniffed her hand and scrunched up their noses, Ordoñez's driver, with a bored, patient expression on his face, began slowly backing the blue minivan out of the driveway.

I spotted the tall figure of John Fulton at the back of the crowd. He was standing alone.

'I'm waiting for Vicente,' he said. 'He's inside getting us some tickets for tomorrow night's *corrida*. We're tired – it was a long journey by train from Seville to here. He needs to get his rest too – if anything happens to the two bullfighters in the ring tomorrow, he's the guy who has to kill them all single-handedly.'

'And what are the chances of that happening?'

'Very remote. Still, he's got to prepare as if it's a possibility.'

Vicente appeared out the door, shoving past the people who were still hanging around hoping to catch a glimpse of one of the top matadors. He embraced me and gave John his tickets.

'*Mucho frio*,' he said, giving me another bear hug.

'I know, I wasn't expecting it to be so cold!' I laughed.

I was wearing a wool jacket I'd bought from some Ecuadorian natives who were selling shirts, jerseys and jackets all around Burgos. Everywhere you went in the city you could find them, at any hour of the day, laying out their wares on stretches of cloth. Their clothes had patterns of llamas and Aztec symbols sewn into them. They were hand-made, warm and cheap.

'What do you think of my jacket, Vicente?' I asked.
'Good. But for me, from Colombia, it's too *indigenous*.'

The bulls that evening were of a very poor quality. The crowd booed and whistled when one animal kept falling down. Eventually the president showed a green handkerchief. This indicated that the cowardly animal was to be led out of the ring and slaughtered immediately instead of dying at the hands of the matador.

When I'd first entered the *plaza* I was deafened by the noise of the local bands celebrating the fiesta. Everyone screamed, trumpeters blasted away, huge drums were thumped and their echoes made talking impossible. Everyone shouted to be heard. At various points in the evening the band tried to whip up some enthusiasm by bursting into life at the most improbable moments. Sometimes it worked; sometimes it didn't. Towards the end of the evening everything seemed to fall flat. The crowd was washed in weak sunlight, although it was cold enough to see your breath, and many were dressed only in shirtsleeves. They seemed to keep warm by bellowing at each other every so often and drinking gallons of wine.

Francisco Rivera Ordoñez fought two very overweight, unsteady animals which fell over several times. The crowd became silent whenever that happened. Ordoñez tried in vain to make up for the poor bulls by throwing himself into his performance but it fell flat. He looked like he was having to try, and the crowd could sense it.

The star of the evening was a matador called Jose Miguel Arroyo Delgado, known as Joselito. He was the crowd's favourite. He looked like an old-fashioned Hollywood movie star with his striking profile and slicked, jet-black, thick hair. He seemed very serious, concentrating on his actions more like an accountant than a bullfighter. He rarely showed any emotion beyond a furrowed, intense passion. Apart from at the very end of the *corrida* when he was given some awards I never saw Joselito smile once.

As he walked around the ring taking one of the few standing ovations of the evening, Joselito was watched from under hooded eyes by Francisco Rivera Ordoñez. Standing on his own, he hung over the fence, his suit of lights dulled by the shade, never taking his eyes off the other matador. Joselito was on the opposite side of the *plaza*, still picking up the cards, gifts and flowers that had been thrown to him by the appreciative spectators. He examined and touched each item before tossing it back into the cheering crowd.

Just as the applause was finishing Francisco rinsed his mouth out with some water, spat it out on the ground, then turned his back on the ring and slowly walked off through the matadors' exit.

I waited for Ordoñez at his five-star hotel on the outskirts of Burgos. He was staying in a place called the Landa Palace which was basically a modernised castle, with a swimming-pool and sports complex attached on to one side of it. Fifteen minutes after the *corrida* ended Francisco swept in through the hotel's front door. He was still dressed in his bloodstained suit of lights. We shook hands. His eyes were glazed and lost. I suggested we chat but he strode off, unwilling to talk or have his photograph taken.

'Did you have a good night?' chirped the woman at the reception. Her squeaky voice echoed around the vast hall, floating up to the high ceiling and the thick wooden rafters.

The matador walked right past her. He looked straight ahead, unaware anyone had said anything.

One of his men, wearing a green suede jacket, grimaced and leaned over towards the woman.

'No . . .' he whispered. 'Bad. It was a bad night.'

'It's Peruvian gold. Do you like it?'

I nodded.

'My father mined it.'

Magri pointed to a large gold lump of a pendant which hung between her dark breasts. She was from Peru and her family were very rich. She told me how they had made their money: mining and breeding horses. Now she spent 'the season' following matadors from one side of the world to the other. 'The season' wasn't an accurate term. Most seasons came to an end, whereas Magri's season just kept going. When the bullfighters finished fighting in South America they packed up and went home to Spain. Magri hopped on a plane and followed them. When they finished in Spain, she packed her bags and returned to South America and followed them around there too. And so it kept going. She'd been doing it for years, she said.

'I'm here to see Joselito,' she whispered in my ear. Then she jerked her head back and lazily watched my reaction. 'He was incredible tonight . . .' she cooed softly.

We were standing in the bar of a city-centre hotel. The place was packed with people who'd just come from the evening's bullfight where Joselito seemed to have triumphed.

'Wasn't it more a case of him having had the best bulls of a bad lot?' I asked Magri.

She frowned. 'No. He can make magic from anything. Even bad bulls in Burgos. That's why he's special.'

'Is that why you like him?'

'He's very handsome, too,' she said. Her eyes looked glazed. 'He's very bright. He's not a boy either . . .'

The air was thick with smoke and the bar staff had trouble keeping up with the amount of people who were trying to order drinks.

Heads began turning. I saw Joselito enter the room. He was wearing a businesslike blue pinstriped shirt and his hair had a newly washed sheen to it. Two very hard-looking women were behind him. They wore thick make-up and very bright designer clothes. Both were shrouded in heavy clouds of smoke from their long cigarettes.

When Joselito spoke to someone, he would look over their shoulder at someone else. He did this to everyone he talked to. When he was near other people, they did the same thing – except they all gazed at him.

I took some photographs and decided it was time to leave. One of Joselito's hangers-on told me the matador didn't want to give any interviews. I didn't care. I still had a cold and my throat was stinging.

As I was walking out of the room I said goodbye to Magri. She didn't reply. She was too busy trying to talk to Joselito who was gazing at her periodically with a jaundiced expression. She blinked, her eyes rolled and she threw back another drink.

By the time she'd swallowed it he was gone.

A few minutes later I breathed in the clear, cold night air of Burgos. I stood at the edge of the pavement outside the hotel trying to flag down a taxi. A group of people who had been walking towards me suddenly stopped directly behind where I was stationed. They were in their sixties, smartly dressed and clearly out for a night on the town. They'd come to an abrupt halt when they noticed the people in the bar I'd just left. Within seconds all of them had their faces pressed up against the dark glass trying to catch a glimpse of Joselito doing the rounds inside. They giggled and pointed when they spotted him.

Next to where they were standing I spotted a man holding a cleaning rag in his hand. He saw what they were up to, noticed me watching them and, when our gazes met, he shook his head. Then, pausing only to spit on the rag, he went back to what he was doing. In the dark of the night he was carefully shining up one of the matadors' minivans. The hotel lights illuminated the vehicle, which had the bullfighter's name emblazoned on the side of the door. The man, just a dark shape, wiped the cloth back and forth, cleaning the dirt off the paintwork, until it gleamed like something in the window of a car showroom.

I sucked on a throat lozenge and stared into space.

I was waiting back at the Landa Palace to see Francisco Ordoñez again. He was three hours late for our appointment. John Fulton had joined me for a morning trip to the hotel where I'd arranged to meet the matador for some photographs.

'I'm hoping to get Ordoñez involved in the benefit *corrida* I'm organising for Atsuhiro in Seville in the autumn. They want to help him all right but it's really hard to get matadors to commit to dates and places. Joselito, for example, said he might be on for it. I just can't pin him down, though,' John told me. He looked frustrated.

We sat for hours in the oak-panelled grandeur of the hotel. A picture of General Franco and the country's monarch Juan Carlos gazed down at us. A few yards away sat Ordoñez's manager, an older man named Camara. He patiently read the morning newspaper and sipped cups of scalding black coffee.

Another journalist appeared. She was wearing black leather trousers and very red lipstick. She paced up and down the stone floor with a severe expression on her face, her stiletto heels clicking and echoing everywhere.

She had her arms folded and looked as if she was in a very bad mood.

'French,' muttered John when he saw her.

'How do you know?' I asked.

'French.' He scrunched up his nose and nodded. 'Trust me. French.'

I asked Camara how long Ordoñez would be. He glanced at his watch, said, 'Not long', licked his fingers and turned the page of the newspaper he was reading.

I ordered more coffee.

An hour and a half later Francisco Ordoñez appeared in a cloud of aftershave. 'I'm sorry,' he said. 'I didn't know you were waiting.'

'I've been waiting longest. I want to interview him now!' said the woman who'd been pacing up and down.

Francisco looked at her, then saw the expression on my face and said he'd better go with me and John first. The woman looked hard at me when he said this.

We moved to a private area upstairs. Ordoñez and John chatted while I took some pictures.

'How's Atsuhiro?' asked Francisco.

John updated him on his friend's progress. 'Can you commit to fighting in our benefit for him in October?' asked John.

Ordoñez demurred. 'I've injured my knee and I need to go to Aspen in the USA for an operation at that time – I can't get out of it. Maybe I can help you some other way – donate a bull or two, or something. I want to help him. We all do.' He sounded sincere.

We shook hands and headed back down to the main hall. The woman in the leather trousers was still pacing up and down with her arms folded. The scowl left her face the instant she spied Ordoñez descending the stairs.

'Sorry I haven't longer to spend with you but I must speak to her,' Francisco whispered. 'She's come all the way from France.'

Two minutes later we stepped outside the hotel. The wind was blowing hard. We walked around the back of the castle and found our car. As we were leaving, John glanced up at the battlements, then at the fancy cars in the driveway. 'Like a young prince . . . eh?' he said to himself. Then he looked at his feet and shook his head.

*

Vicente Salamanca's name was at the bottom of the bill for that evening's *corrida* in Burgos. He was appearing, again, as the *sobresaliente*, the understudy to two other matadors who were going head to head in a *mano a mano* fight.

I met him and John in their hotel room at four o'clock. A fat local man, acting as Vicente's sword-boy for the evening, another man who was a driver and a smiling dark-skinned South American *banderillo* were also present. Everyone perched on the edge of the beds.

Vicente was doing a radio interview over the hotel telephone. He was naked apart from a thin pair of tights. As he chatted he glanced up every so often at us and at a TV which was silently showing a film with Ingrid Bergman in the role of Joan of Arc. Eventually he said goodbye to the journalist and began to get dressed.

It took Vicente over an hour to get ready for the *corrida*. Everything had to be done correctly and carefully. The atmosphere in the room was slightly tense. He had a difficult time getting into his pink and gold breeches – the *taleguilla*. 'We've both been eating pizza,' muttered John under his breath. Vicente bit his lip, sucked in his abdomen and pulled at the material as his sweating sword-boy hoisted the breeches over his thighs. At one stage he bent right over, doubling himself up like a man in pain, in an attempt to hook a button. Eventually he straightened up, his face coated in sweat, and fixed their tops in place with braces.

After catching his breath, Vicente reached into the crotch area of the breeches and hauled his genitals into a clump, shoving them down the side of his groin until he felt comfortable. He laced the breeches up with the help of an old-fashioned button-hook device, fixing them around his calf muscles. The bright white shirt was tied in place with a drawstring around his waist, then the thin black tie was fixed with a tiny enamel button showing an old matador. A sash was wrapped around his waist and then he pulled on a tight matching waistcoat. Finally he reached up high and slid into his heavily padded jacket, the *chaquetilla*. The whole outfit looked very constricting and tight.

He checked himself in the mirror. He walked around the room for a moment, pacing and feeling the outfit on his body. Then he sat down, the fabric creaking and straining. His fat sword-boy fell to his knees with a thud and proceeded to shoe-horn Vicente's feet into a pair of black slippers. Once they were in place the matador stood up and stamped his feet on the carpet, his toes wriggling around inside the thin leather.

He stretched and arched his body in an effort to make the suit feel comfortable. We all watched, saying little or nothing. Only John, who occasionally got to his feet to help, hesitated, made a suggestion, then sat down.

'How do you clean the suits if they get dirt or blood on them?' I asked him quietly.

'With a toothbrush in the hotel sink. I used to do Atsuhiro's every night during that last summer he was fighting. I was like an old lady scrubbing and worrying. He used to make fun of me being so particular about things.'

He smiled and shrugged.

'What happens if you need to go to the toilet?'

'You go. Or hold it in.'

I shook my head.

'Listen, I once accidentally ripped my suit of lights just as I was going out the front door of my hotel. I heard the damn thing tear as loud as anything. I couldn't believe it! We had only half an hour to go until the *corrida* started and there I was with a rip right up my crotch,' John told me.

'What did you do?' I asked.

'Well, there was panic in my *cuadrilla*. They weren't sure what to do. But I felt really calm and focused. I said, "Relax. Back up to the room everybody." So we trooped back upstairs, I undressed, got a needle and thread out, and ten minutes later, we walked out the door for the bullring.'

Vicente disappeared into the bathroom to comb his hair. He reappeared and, with aid of a mirror, a little elastic band and a clip, fixed his ceremonial pigtail – the *coleta* – in place on the back of his head. He glanced in the mirror again, then clapped his hat on.

A small wooden hand-made religious triptych stood on top of the cabinet near by. Vicente took a second to stand in front of it, his arms outstretched. When he was finished silently praying, he blessed himself. He turned around, his face serious, then broke into a big grin.

'Okay!' he said clapping his hands, 'it's time.'

The tension lifted, everyone stirred and John, eyebrows raised, gestured us all towards the door.

We departed, leaving the soundless TV playing to the empty room. Travel bags, piles of clothes and coffee cups were its only audience.

The last image I saw on the screen was of a beautiful Ingrid Bergman being burned alive at the stake.

The *corrida* in which Vicente was appearing as *sobresaliente* was trumpeted by the local press as being the finest bullfight of the *feria* and possibly even the whole season.

By the time I showed up to buy my tickets there were only two kinds left – the cheapest and the most expensive. Not wanting to miss Vicente's big moment and having seen him dress for the part, I thought it wise to blow my money on the best seats in the house.

The two bullfighters, Joselito and Enrique Ponce, were vaguely regarded as rivals. The press tried to whip this up into a full-scale battle similar to the alleged rivalry between Dominguin and Ordoñez back in the so-called 'dangerous summer' of '59, but the whole thing didn't really ring true. In fact, as someone pointed out to me, their styles of fighting weren't that different. But that didn't stop the two matadors from regularly appearing on the same cartel together. You couldn't blame them – their names were good for business up and down the country and in South America and had ensured them huge pay cheques, probably the biggest in all Spain, at the end of each evening's performance.

Enrique Ponce was regarded as being the number-one matador in Spain. His performances were described as being dependable and consistent. Ever since he was a *novillero* he was seen as something special – they said he dominated the bulls he fought with grace and elegance. Bill Lyons the Madrid-based American journalist, had told me that Ponce was 'very good – he wants to be successful with every bull . . . some say that he's got tricks up his sleeve, that he doesn't have the purist style, but Ponce is always interesting – he's very consistent'. Others I'd canvassed disagreed: they thought he was superficial and said he tended to compete in slightly less-than-memorable *corridas*.

Joselito, on the other hand, was apparently brilliant but unreliable. One critic said his problem was simply that he couldn't motivate himself before a bullfight. The matador himself said he would often prefer to stay in his hotel room reading a good book than have to put on his suit of lights and leave for an evening's work at the *plaza*. Even once he got into the ring the critics said he sometimes lost heart and couldn't be bothered trying. He was at his best in a *corrida* where he had to kill all the bulls himself, they said, because then he didn't have time to think or be discouraged. When he was on form, however, he was considered to be a genius and everyone agreed he always killed the bulls very well.

On a good day both Ponce and Joselito easily reached £20,000-plus per performance. Over a year they probably grossed more than a million pounds. For guys like Vicente at the other end of the scale, life was very different. Every time they managed to get themselves on to a halfway-decent cartel, they would be lucky to go home with more than a few thousand pounds. And, unlike the matadors at the top, they had to make their money stretch because, unless they were part of someone's regular *cuadrilla* doing the rounds across Spain and appearing in nightly *corridas*, they wouldn't know where their next pay cheque was coming from.

I'd bought tickets for the shaded side of the ring. In Spain, where it's usually very hot during the summers, this would normally have been a good idea. In Burgos's cold mountain atmosphere, though, it was a bad mistake and when I found my seat in the shadows it was freezing. Everyone sitting near by wore cashmere woollens to keep warm. Even before the bullfight began, people were throwing back sherry and gulping down wine in an effort to take the frost out of their bones.

The trumpets sounded high up on the stand opposite me. The pressmen ran out of the tunnel first, then the matadors' parade followed. Ponce, in royal blue and gold, looking sombre with dark shadows under his eyes, and Joselito, in emerald green and gold, still as handsome and uncertain as the night before, took their bows and acknowledged the applause. Vicente, their understudy, appeared behind them, walking easily in the tight-fitting suit of lights I'd watched him struggle into an hour earlier. He looked very serious. The stadium was full, with maybe 30,000 people packed into it. I wondered what it must be like for someone like Vicente to walk in behind the men he so desperately wanted to emulate and, for a few minutes, allow the wave of adulation directed at them to wash over his imagination.

The opening ceremony ended. The crowd shifted and settled into their seats. There was a lull in the charged atmosphere, a collective intake of breath. The matadors loosened up and shook the last fragments of pre-fight nerves away by making slow passes at one side of the *plaza* with their large bright-pink and blazing-yellow capes. Then the *corrida* began.

Someone once told me that one of the strangest things about bullfights was that you just never knew what was going to happen. It was part of the attraction said this *aficionado*. It was like live theatre in many ways: you were not watching something that was already filmed and edited, you were watching an event where only *some* of the variables were under control. It was like life without a script, where no one knew what was around the corner. That's what gave it its edge. So when you bought the cheapest seats in the plaza to the worst third-rate card, you might witness a fantastic *corrida*. Perhaps see an up-and-comer do something that had never been done with a bull before. On the other hand, just when all the signs pointed to the likelihood of a spectacular evening of top-rank fights, there was sure to be a hiccup.

And that's exactly what happened in Burgos.

The bulls which were brought out to fight that evening were poor creatures who did not seem to want to engage the matadors. They lacked what one journalist I'd spoken to had called 'fierceness'. He believed this characteristic had been systematically bred out of many Spanish fighting bulls since the late 1960s in an attempt to keep the managers and the matadors happy, alive and, therefore, in profit. A bull without ferocity, which was also overweight, under-exercised and generally unhealthy, didn't exactly look as if it was ready to take on the world, and I'd felt sorry for more than a few I'd seen on my travels. Indeed, the only decent-looking bull I'd seen so far was one of the animals Francisco Rivera Ordoñez had faced up to in Burgos. It at least looked and acted like the mythic Iberian fighting bulls which Hemingway said had been known to blindly attack trains and, in cruel circus freak-shows held in backwater towns a century ago, even kill lions and tigers. The bulls in Burgos, in contrast, looked awful.

On the evening of the Ponce/Joselito cartel, two of the six animals being fought were sent back to their corrals to be slaughtered immediately. The rest were reluctant to fight and, when they did get going, they were so out of condition that they either fell over or couldn't run for panting. I felt waves of guilt wash over me when I watched such scared and unfit bulls – both mentally and physically – enter the ring to face the hostile crowd and one of the great matadors of the day was being paid to perform the almost impossible task of killing it with some style. I naïvely thought that someone, somewhere, between the ranch and the *plaza de toros* should have spotted the bull's weakness before the fight and made sure it never made it on to the sand. Without a brave bull the whole spectacle became shameful.

As the *corrida* wore on, the crowd became increasingly angry. No one took any pleasure in seeing a frightened, unhealthy bull being toyed with. People shouted, they whistled, they booed. Their anger wasn't directed at the animal itself; on the contrary, it was directed at the president in his box and the anonymous managers, breeders and organisers scattered around the *plaza*. One man kept standing up and screaming at the top of his voice about how the bull-ranch owners should be brought out into the ring to face 'the *aficionados* of the city of Burgos' and 'the great matadors here tonight'. People laughed when he shouted and I could see his friend trying to pull him back down into his seat every time he drunkenly hoisted himself on to his feet.

Ponce's last bull, despite its generally poor physical state, was mentally very agile and, in spite of everything, proved to be one of the most dangerous and difficult I would see.

It trotted out of the gate very slowly and reluctantly. But, when the mid-evening sunlight hit its eyes, it stopped dead. The *banderillos* tried to get it to charge and, eventually, it did. It charged straight and several times smashed into the *burladeros*, the wooden shields around the openings to the bullring. It also rammed straight into the picador and his mount, almost knocking both to the ground. But when it saw the matador Ponce appear on to the sand with his blue-and-gold suit of lights shining and with the pink cape held out in front of his body with both hands, the bull backed away and stood across the ring with its back to the *barrera*.

Ponce shouted at it: it looked around.

He shouted again: it wouldn't move.

The crowd began a half-hearted, very slow hand-clap. The noise gathered and grew louder, echoing around the stadium.

The bull stared at the cape, the crowd, the matador. The blood ran down its back. Eventually it charged at Ponce a couple of times – low, jabbing and slicing efforts. But, despite all his skills and efforts, the matador could not get his passes to flow together. He knew straightaway that he had a problem. Every time the bull came lurching near him, it lifted and jerked its massive head at the end of the pass. Ponce kept jumping back out of its way. If his reflexes had been a split-second slower, he'd have had a horn straight through his shoulder, neck or head.

'It's actually defending itself very well,' said a young woman from Mexico City who was sitting next to me. She'd travelled all the way across the world to follow the bulls in Spain for part of the summer season. Her boyfriend was Italian and said he didn't know much about bulls. 'It's a smart bull, scared but very cunning,' she added, nodding her head in appreciation.

Ponce practically stood on his head trying to get the bull to charge his cape. When it did, it turned, made for the cape again, and returned to exactly the same spot it had just left. The animal was making Spain's top matador look awkward and unskilled.

I'd read about this phenomenon. The bull was taking up residence in one area of the ring – called the *querencia*. In this case it was near the Gate of Fear through which it had entered the ring. But a bull's *querencia* can be anywhere it wants – it's the place the bull feels most at home in, the spot it feels it can defend better than anywhere else in the *plaza*. Once he finds that place, it'll only leave it as a last resort and, even then, it'll head straight back to it at the first opportunity. Matadors sometimes notice this tendency and use to their advantage the bull's homing instinct for a certain area of the ring by making fast passes as the animal bolts towards it. On other occasions, as Ponce was finding out, the bull just wasn't playing ball. He tried waving his cape in front of it to lure it out; he tried dragging the cape along the sand to tempt it. But it wouldn't budge. The few times it did venture out it chopped and sliced at *him* – not the cape – with its horns. It had learned very quickly what was making the cape shake. It had decided the matador was its enemy, not the cloth he carried.

A few slow minutes slipped past . . .

The bull looked weaker and weaker. It had been bleeding from the wounds caused by the picador and the *banderillas* hung off its neck muscle in a bloody, feathered clump. It wasn't helped by the obvious fact that it had been clearly out of condition to begin with, and I found myself feeling sorry for it. It was a smart bull, although one which *aficionados* would have called cowardly. Ponce decided it was best to kill it quickly since its stubbornness and unwillingness to charge meant he couldn't get any linked passes out of it. The longer the situation went on, the worse it made him look. He lined it up, aimed his sword and, suddenly, the crowd started booing. People stood up and shouted at him, yelling at him to try more passes with the bull, anything, just make it work. They were trying to salvage something, no matter how little, from a very unsatisfactory evening.

'He should kill it,' said the Mexican woman. She shook her head as the whistling went on and the ferocity of the crowd grew stronger.

Ponce shrugged and put the sword away. I glanced over at Vicente who was watching all this from behind the *barrera* where he stood with a couple of *banderillos*. They rolled their eyes and shook their heads. John Fulton, who was acting as Vicente's manager, was standing in the passageway known as the *callejon* with the *plaza* officials, the vets, the managers, the sword-boys and the pressmen; he caught my eye. I shrugged and nodded at the action, or lack of it, on the sand. He raised his eyebrows.

Ponce tried a few more passes with the bleeding bull. He couldn't do much with the animal, since the moment it got close to him, no matter how graceful and disciplined his form, the bull went straight for *him*. He was constantly flung off balance, his cape flapping and his feet jumping around like a man walking on hot coals. He tried again, his frustrated expression betraying his mounting anger. The bull unenthusiastically charged a couple of times, then trotted back to its *querencia* again. Again the matador lined it up for the kill. The crowd was silent this time. Just as he was about to pounce at it, the bull, like a dying man pleading for mercy, fell to its knees. Ponce stepped back, looked accusingly at the crowd and shook his head slightly. There wasn't a sound. The matador looked straight into the faces in the stands: his expression was filled with fury, disgust and anger. By forcing him to keep going when he knew the bull was too scared and tired to perform, the crowd had let themselves down.

'He wanted to kill it quickly – now he has to watch it suffer more than it should,' said my neighbour. 'That's bad.'

The bull was eventually pulled to its feet by the tail. The matador lined it up with his sword and cape. The bull waited patiently for him; it had no choice. There was silence. With one flick of its head it could have killed him. But it didn't even have the strength or the will for that any more.

Ponce moved fast, lightning fast. He killed it instantly on his first attempt. The crowd clapped loudly when he finished the animal off but he ignored the applause and just strolled away from the bull staring at the ground with his tired, hooded eyes.

'He should never have listened to the spectators,' said the woman next to me after Ponce had left the ring.

All around me people were opening up bottles of wine, sandwiches wrapped in tin-foil and cans of beer. A man with a wooden leg hobbled around selling shots of whisky and peanuts. He couldn't reach all his customers, so whenever someone bought something from him he would chuck the bottle or the packet over to them. People in the crowd around me ducked and laughed as the glass bottles of booze and packets of peanuts flew over their heads.

'Why shouldn't he have listened to them?' I asked her.

'Because it's fiesta time – they're drunk. And, anyway, they're Spaniards. They think they know everything about the *corrida*. It would never have happened in Mexico,' she said, lighting a cigarette.

Joselito appeared at the side of the ring. Within five minutes it was clear to everyone that his final bull was every bit as troublesome as Ponce's. But it was the last fight of the evening, indeed the last fight of the fiesta, and the crowd didn't want the party to be over too quickly. As he tried to pull together a halfway decent *faena* – the work done with the small cape – the crowd shouted for music. They yelled and clapped: '¡Musica! ¡Musica! ¡Musica!'

'I wish they'd just be quiet!' said the Mexican woman

High up on the stands opposite us I watched the shining brass band break into a triumphant *paso doble* which filled the chilly air. Joselito, his face set in its customary scowl of concentration, waved angrily at the band in an effort to shut it up.

'About time,' said my neighbour, rolling her eyes.

The little conductor flapped his arms and put his hands on his hips. The music stuttered to a dribbling halt. The band leader hadn't had an easy night either. At one point earlier on, when one of the bulls was refusing to leave the *plaza* after the president had judged it unfit for fighting, the conductor had led his band into an upbeat version of 'My Bonny Lies over the Ocean'. He was drowned out in whistles and jeers and, from the way he ducked, it appeared some missiles may have been thrown at him from the cheap seats near by.

Down on the sand the bull faced Joselito, panting and uncertain. The matador had managed to force it out of its *querencia* and had manoeuvred it in such a way that it seemed confused and disorientated. It kept looking around instead of straight ahead at the red cape. Joselito lined it up quickly, the sun running down the side of his green-and-gold suit of lights, the sequins from his chest reflected on his face like the glimmer from the sea on a sunny day. Then he slowly teased the bull with the cape which he held down very low, until it was touching the sand.

'This could be interesting,' said the woman next to me. 'This bull is dangerous.'

Then it happened. The bull moved first . . .

In a heartbeat it suddenly seemed more focused, more concentrated on its target. It dug down deep, its head going straight for the red fabric of the *muleta*. As its head fell and it lunged at his cape, Joselito – all compact muscle and with the explosive speed of a lightweight boxer's jab – snatched towards its shoulder muscle, his sword instantly disappeared in a flash of sunlight, down into the blackness of the animal.

The bull trotted a couple of paces, turned, heaved and fell down.

Joselito stood still, watching the bull's laboured breathing slow to a final stop, then he went over to the animal and patted it on the head.

It was over. The last bull had been killed in the last *corrida* of the fiesta.

The matador turned and faced the crowd which had already

started cheering. For the first time in the whole *corrida* Joselito's tanned, square-jawed face relaxed, the tension instantly lifting from his brow. He smiled, wiped some sweat off his face, and walked over towards the *barrera* where one of his *cuadrilla* was waiting with a towel for him.

Vicente had watched most of the fight from the sidelines – either standing behind the *burladero*, leaning on the *barrera* or occasionally walking along the chilled, windy *callejon*. During the whole evening he'd only been able to get in one pass of his own with Ponce's second-last bull. His actual participation was over in a flash: I'd glanced at my watch and it had happened. I'd missed it. Apart from that, he'd spent the entire evening watching and waiting. I saw him every so often stand with his cape ready to take the bull away from the matador if he was required. But he never was. Other times he simply lifted his cape up, using his teeth to catch the top of it while he folded it over his arms neatly, when he realised his skills weren't necessary. A couple of times he stood chatting to Ponce or Joselito while they both watched the *banderillos* doing their work. Spain's top matadors seemed to like him. But often he just stood by himself, almost lost in his thoughts, but never for a moment taking his eyes off the action in the ring.

When it was all over I caught a glimpse of him walking off through the exit chatting to some fellow matadors. He looked animated, smiling and enthusiastic, happy to be doing what he was doing, if only for a short time, his pink-and-gold suit of lights disappearing into the shadows of the tunnel.

'He says his suit is almost hanging off him now, would you believe!' said John when I met him about half an hour after the bullfight had ended. I was giving him a lift over to a hotel in the city where some of the various *cuadrillas* were holding court, the same place, in fact, where I'd met Joselito the night before.

'It looked really tight when he first got into it,' I remarked.

'Yeah, that's what happens. You sweat a couple of pounds and the fabric stretches, it feels great – just when it's time to pack up and go home!' John stared out of the window at all the people streaming out of the *plaza de toros* and into the city streets.

'How is Vicente anyway?' I asked as we pulled up in front of the hotel.

'He's good,' said John, zipping up his windbreaker to shield him from the chilly breeze blowing up from the river. 'All the better for having chatted with Ponce's people. He reckons they're going to offer him the chance to tour with their *cuadrilla* in South America this winter. He's delighted. He gets to work and gets to go home too! Can't be bad. Maybe things will pick up for him, who knows? That's why appearing as a *sobresaliente* in Burgos tonight was good for him. He's in amongst the right people.'

We said our goodbyes and I thanked him again for all his time and help.

'What's next?' he asked.

A crowd of exuberant revellers passed by us, blowing trumpets and drinking wine from *botas*. I nodded towards them.

'Ah . . . following the fiesta north for San Fermines – I should have known!'

'Want to come?' I asked.

'Not this year. I've done that. It's good. Enjoy it. I'll be thinking about you.'

'You sure?' I asked.

'Yeah . . . another time. That's a promise. Remember and look up my friends. Tell them all I said hello. And check out Matt Carney's room too, if you get the chance.'

Matt Carney was another one of those larger-than-life characters that Spain and the world of bullfighting seems to attract like filings to a magnet. A handsome, roguish, Irish-American writer and sometime Paris-based model, Carney had adopted Pamplona as his second home. He was the leader of a gang of Americans who ran with the bulls every morning during San Fermines. John Fulton knew him well and I'd come across references to Carney in a couple of James Michener books – he'd been mentioned in glowing terms despite almost getting into a very public, very drunken punch-up with Hemingway one night in 1959. Michener subsequently based one of the fictional characters in his book *The Drifters* on Carney. At one time – especially during the '60s and '70s – John's buddy Matt Carney was a bigger draw in Pamplona during San Fermines than most of the bullfights. His image – stoically walking up a narrow street called Calle Estafeta wearing his 'USA' sweatshirt, people lying all around his feet, the human casualties of the bulls which had just thundered past – summed up the rakish appeal he was said to exude. That picture of Carney – the last man standing in Pamplona, the Irish Yank beating the Spaniards at their own mad game – was used for a poster advertising San Fermines. It became a world-famous image. He was everyone's lucky charm. John Fulton told me that Matt Carney died on Christmas Eve 1988, just three days shy of his 66th birthday, and that a friend of Matt's called Noel Chandler had a room in his apartment in the middle of Pamplona where he kept all Matt's running gear: 'It's like a shrine,' said John. 'You should check it out.'

I promised I would.

'And I'll say hi to Pamplona for you, John.' I'd enjoyed his company and I was genuinely sorry he wasn't travelling north with me.

'Sure, you do that.'

'And congratulate Vicente for me. Wish him good luck in South America.'

John nodded his head. I climbed back into the car. In the rear-view mirror I watched him walk towards the packed hotel bar. Just before I switched the engine on, I heard the sound of music and talk and laughter seep out into the air when he opened the lobby door and walked inside. The foyer, just as it had been 24 hours earlier, was already full of matadors, their families, their *cuadrillas*, their managers, their friends, their admirers and their countless hangers-on.

I drove back through the wide, busy streets of Burgos and parked my car as close to my hotel as I could. I was tired and my throat still hurt so I went to bed early.

I lay between the cool linen sheets of the high old bed which groaned and squeaked like a dying man every time I shifted or turned over. The plumbing exploded into life somewhere in the building every few minutes. Horns and trumpets and drums sounded down on the cold streets. I was too tired and cold-ridden to care. As I edged into sleep I caught snatches of the sharp, stuttering, deep blue reflections of exploding fireworks which filled my third-floor room.

Opposite my window, on top of the bell tower of an ancient church, there was a huge storks' nest. Every time a bright silver-white rocket exploded in the dark sky, a well-formed silhouette of the nest slowly shifted across the wall at the foot of my bed. I watched it for a few minutes until my eyelids became too heavy. Then I gave in. The cheers and clapping and raucous laughter from the spectators were the last sounds in my ears as my thoughts became fragments and the images of the day faded into the weight of the darkness.

THIRTEEN

¡Fiesta!

'The best place to see the running of the bulls is sitting in front of the TV screen.'

Dr Paul was on evening and night duty in the makeshift emergency medical centre in the middle of Pamplona and he wasn't too keen on the town's celebrated attraction: the running of the bulls. I'd heard that the city was a disaster area during the fiesta so I figured one of the best places to see what was going on would be at the front line where the casualties were brought in. The young doctor was depressed at the thought of spending a whole week patching up and mopping up after young drunks from all over the world who thought that Pamplona in July was some sort of drink-yourself-to-death-quick contest.

A young man lay opposite us on the floor. His arm was connected to a long, thin drip. Clear fluid was slowly filtering into the veins in his pale limb.

'What's wrong with him?' I asked.

'He's unconscious. Too much wine. He's been like that for an hour and a half. We're giving him insulin to help his condition. He'll have a hell of a hangover when he wakes up!' The doctor was only young, in his mid-twenties, but he spoke with an air of great world-weariness.

Next door I heard someone retching. I peered round a screen to see who it was. A teenage girl was lying on the stone floor, desperately trying to vomit. Her boyfriend sat beside her, a smile on his face. 'Stick your finger down your throat,' he said drunkenly.

'That'll do the trick!'

'Have you heard of the Angel's Jump?' asked Dr Paul when I sat back down beside him.

'No, what is it?'

'A fountain. It's just down the road there. A few years ago Australians began jumping off it. Their friends catch them at the bottom. It's really high, about 30 feet or so, I imagine. Anyway, they get really drunk, climb to the top of it and leap off into their friends' arms. Of course the people at the bottom doing the catching are just as drunk as the idiots at the top doing the jumping . . .' He took off his glasses and rubbed his face.

'What's all this got to do with bullfighting?' I asked.

'You tell me,' he sighed.

'What happens if the people at the bottom of the fountain don't catch the jumpers?'

He looked at me blankly. 'I get to meet them. Up close and personally.'

I nodded and looked around at some paramedics who'd just been called out on another emergency. Their radios crackled every now and then and the ambulance's lights silently lit up the portacabin in which I was sitting.

'Are you going to run with the bulls tomorrow morning?' he asked.

'No . . . I'm going to take some photographs,' I answered.

He stared straight ahead. The ambulance pulled out of its parking spot and switched on its deafening siren. It blasted its way off down the street. Streams of revellers staggered by.

'Do you know what we doctors in Pamplona call people who run with the bulls during the fiesta?' asked Dr Paul in a flat, weary voice as he slowly got out of his seat to get himself a coffee.

'No. What do you call them?'

'Organ donors.'

The running of the bulls started in Pamplona centuries ago when herders used to drive their bulls through the narrow streets of the old part of the city towards the *plaza de toros* on the morning of a *corrida*. Daring young men used to run ahead of the bulls – the most brave or insane, depending upon your point of view, running nearest the horns. It was just one more rural sport – like Basque tree-cutting – until Gertrude Stein told Ernest Hemingway all about it. After he wrote about it, it became a fad: a mad rite of passage; a worldwide 'dare'. Thirteen people have died this century taking part in the running – called the *encierro*, meaning 'enclosure' – the last fatality being an American in his twenties.

Like most fiestas, Pamplona's was religious in origin, celebrating St Fermin, a third-century bishop who was the patron saint of the Kingdom of Navarra and the diocese of his birthplace and home, Pamplona. Religious and cultural processions still form the core of the fiesta, especially for the local people – the giant heads and the processions of local bands, for example, appear regularly throughout the week; but the attraction of cheap wine, loud company, controlled mayhem and of course the running of the bulls, acts like a magnet for tourists from all over the world.

I'd read that over 200,000 people were expected in Pamplona for the Festival of San Fermines. The number of tourists had been steadily increasing ever since Hemingway initially wrote about the place after his first visit in 1923. One of his articles in the *Toronto Star* of that year began: 'In Pamplona, a white-walled, sun-baked town high up in the hills of Navarra, is held in the first two weeks of July each year the World Series of bullfighting . . .' He was probably one of only a handful of foreign tourists in Pamplona that summer. He came back several times in the years which followed, eventually immortalising the place, the events and the ambience in 1926 in his first novel, *Fiesta, The Sun Also Rises*. When that was published, the tourists started coming. And they've never stopped.

After a three-hour drive from Burgos I arrived in Pamplona on the day the fiesta started, 6 July. It was due to run for another seven full days, ending at midnight on the 14th. I'd dawdled on my drive north after leaving Burgos, taking in the magnificent mountain scenery, so I'd missed the midday opening ceremony at Pamplona's town hall by about an hour.

I heard later that local supporters of the Basque paramilitary group ETA had tried to hijack this event. Three people were arrested after they attempted to unfurl a banner in support of the outlawed organisation. Pamplona was allegedly one of the hotbeds of their support. On the way up from Burgos I passed lots of road signs in the Basque language, *Euskera*. It is unlike any European language I've ever seen and was apparently spoken as long as 5,000 years ago. The so-called Basque homeland – *Euskadi*, which means 'collection of Basques' – is really one nation in two countries. About three million people who claim the Basque identity are to be found in Spain's northern provinces, notably Navarra, Vizcaya, Guipuzcoa and Alava, as well as in three French provinces near the Pyrenees and the Bay of Biscay. I'd read that the Basque people are regarded by some as being the 'Aborigines of Europe', since they are supposedly one of the oldest peoples in the whole world. A traditional saying goes: 'Before God was God and boulders were boulders, the Basques were already Basques.'

Historically, the Basques had always been their own masters. Many never felt connected to Spain or part of the country. For centuries they ruled themselves with their own form of local government called *fueros*. But these were wiped out in the late nineteenth century. The terrorist group ETA – meaning *Euskadi ta Askatasuna*, 'Basque Homeland and Freedom' – emerged after the Basque people had endured long years of repression under General Franco. The dictator was determined to crush them and force them to submit to Madrid rule. During the Spanish Civil War he regarded the Basques as his enemies – although not all of them opposed him. His idea for bringing those who did support the Republic to heel was simple but not original – bomb them to hell and they'll give up their struggle. So on a bright, fresh Monday morning in April 1937, he enlisted Hitler's Luftwaffe with their squadrons of new Heinkel-111s and Messerschmitt-109s, and dropped thousands of pounds of bombs on the town of Guernica just off the Bay of Biscay. The German bombers killed hundreds of people. Those who survived the first wave of explosions that morning were meticulously picked off with machine-guns when the pilots swooped down for a second run. About 1,500 people died in a matter of minutes.

ETA's terrorist war began in earnest in the 1960s. The bloodiest year of all, however, was 1980 when they killed 118 people. Some limited autonomy was granted to the Basque region of Spain in the years which followed. During the '80s and in the early '90s many of ETA's leaders were rounded up and imprisoned after being caught hiding out in the South of France. Small pockets of support for their paramilitary strategy still survive in some places, Pamplona being one of them. In some small towns I'd passed through *en route* to the city, I saw large, hand-painted, brightly coloured ETA murals on the gable ends of houses. I couldn't help but think of similar scenes painted by supporters of Loyalist paramilitaries and the Provisional IRA in Northern Ireland.

After the failed attempt by the ETA supporters to unfurl a banner at the opening ceremony of Pamplona's fiesta, the crowd of tens of thousands began chanting: '¡*Fiesta, si!* ¡*Politicos, no!*' Then mass cheering broke out and everyone started to sing 'San Fermines, San Fermines' in unison.

I'd missed the opening ceremony, of course, and with it the ETA supporters' display of support for their radical cause. But it didn't take long for ETA to rear its head again. Just a week later the terrorists would again make their presence felt and this time in a much more brutally direct and bloody manner. Miguel Angel Blanco, a 29-year-old Basque town councillor, would be kidnapped and shot twice in the head by ETA. His death in hospital a short time later would lead to the running of the bulls being temporarily suspended by the Pamplona authorities as a sign of its 'sadness and indignation'. The news of his murder would hit front pages across the world. And tens of thousands of people in the town for the annual fiesta would storm the party's HQ to vent their fury on local ETA sympathisers.

But as I drove into Pamplona on the first day of the fiesta all this was still in the future . . .

As the revellers were downing their first glasses of the fiesta, I was still having difficulty finding my way into the town. I drove round in circles for a while, passing a huge mural of Che Guevara several times, before I finally got my bearings. Then I headed straight for the city centre. I knew I was in the right place when I saw hundreds of people streaming along the streets, every one of them wearing traditional Basque costumes of fire-red and communion-white.

Every shop window used the colours for their displays; it didn't matter what was on sale, the shopkeepers had managed to find a red and white theme. Cab drivers, florists, the man selling lottery tickets, TV and video salesmen, waitresses and thousands of ordinary people on holiday all wore red and white. They strolled along the streets which were sliced with bright, clear sunshine, taking their time and easing themselves into the week-long fiesta. It was strange to see so many people out on the streets when nearly all of the shops were closed. I slowly made my way through the town until I found one of the high, ornate fountains marked on my map. That was the landmark I needed to guide me to my bed for the next few nights.

I'd rented a room at short notice from an elderly woman called Maria Antonio. She lived in a quiet street off one of the main thoroughfares near the centre of Pamplona. An old woman, with the eye of a magpie, she let rooms every year to students and travellers who needed just the basics when they were passing through the town. Inevitably, the best time of the year for her was during San Fermines. Like a thousand others in Pamplona, she made a killing when the fiesta was on. Anyone with a spare bed would crowd around the tourist office, quietly pinning up notices for rooms to let in their homes. For the price of a good three-star hotel room with *en suite* bathroom and a decent breakfast thrown in, I got a small, cramped room and the use of the apartment's tiny bathroom.

Breakfast and all other meals were by my own arrangement. But the place was clean enough and I was lucky to find her. A handful of other guests also used Maria's place as a bolthole during San Fermines, but I never saw any of them. I only heard them as they staggered in through the front door, their key missing the lock and their giggles breaking the relative silence of the small hours. Maria herself came and went at will, appearing at the oddest times wearing heavy make-up and with her hair fixed up. She announced her presence by coughing loudly and turning the radio on in her little pantry. Then she marched around like a general on a surprise inspection of his troops.

A few hours after I first arrived, Maria cornered me in the hallway. Digging into the pockets of her worn cardigan she produced a ticket to a bullfight which was on later that evening. Such tickets were like gold dust in Pamplona – almost as rare as a room. It wasn't a great seat but it was cheap and she was asking for a fair price so I bought it. She took the money off me, stuck it in her purse and winked. 'My son gets tickets for his family but . . . well, it's yours now. Be a good boy and enjoy it.'

I left her apartment and walked a few streets to the medical centre. After I'd been led on a guided tour of the facilities by Dr Paul and his assistant, a heartbreakingly beautiful trainee-nurse named Olga, and been introduced to the numerous vomiting casualties, I made my way towards the old part of Pamplona in the early-evening sunshine.

I passed various posters along the road advertising the 'Twelve Colossal Polar Bears from Alaska and Tibet' which were also in town with a circus. The posters showed a painted polar bear standing next to a woman wearing just the merest hint of a bikini. Further along I saw the ambulance from the medical centre I'd just left – the paramedics were carrying a man into the back of the vehicle. He was too drunk to stand.

I made my way to the main square in the old town of Pamplona, the Plaza del Castillo. It was a sea of red and white. The collective noise of people excitedly enjoying themselves floated in the air I breathed like an intoxicating, slightly polluting, cloud: it was the sound of talking, of radios, of laughing, of castanets, of joking, of giggling, of singing, of trumpets, of shouting, of drums, of screams, of orders being taken, of car horns, of hawkers selling rubbish, of shoeshine guys offering, being refused, and then complaining, of flower-sellers, of children squealing and squawking and, above all else, of the rattle of a thousand glasses being banged with abandon on metal table-tops.

Every bar, no matter the prices, the decor or the atmosphere, was full; the chairs and small tables set up outside were packed and hundreds of figures staggered around in a semi-drunken haze. I passed three middle-aged women, dressed in red and white outfits, their huge melon-sized breasts swinging in time as they danced a flamenco down a side street. The sun shone through their thin peroxide blonde hair as they sang and waved red carnations at passers-by. Hundreds of people were in the balconies above the square, calmly watching the action below them. Crowds gathered on corners, all in the red and white uniform. They drank and laughed, heads back, cigarettes puffed, hands running through their hair, arms raised in half-dances; slowly, by the minute, letting their guard drop. Younger people staggered by, self-consciously washed in red wine stains from head to toe. Some looked like casualties from medieval battles. Quite a few more wore their hair in braids and flopped around in eastern clothes. They were already wasted and broke and Day One hadn't even reached its halfway point yet.

One guy had set up a game called 'Hit the Nail'. His livelihood was tied up in a piece of wood which he challenged the people of Pamplona to whack a nail into – with only one blow of the hammer. He offered prizes of wine, cider and champagne. When I asked him about it, he claimed to make £100 a day doing this.

Near by, two Japanese guys were selling mechanical shoes which danced the Lambada when you wound them up. The two of them grinned like maniacs when the shoes broke down, and offered potential buyers luminous yo-yos instead.

I passed a girl wearing a stained T-shirt showing a couple of bulls. 'When the Bulls Start Running – The Brave Go Drinking' it read.

Stallholders were selling other T-shirts too. I bought a red scarf and a T-shirt from one of them. These people worked furiously, throwing out their wares in plastic bags, the sweat running down their faces as they tried to make as much money in the short time available. A lot of stalls were set up near the tourist office which was situated just off the main square. The T-shirts had cartoons of bulls on them, as well as images stolen from Picasso, horns, ETA symbols and red-and-white photographs of Che Guevara which said 'Hasta! Victoria!'.

More stalls and fast-food caravans were set up near the bullring. The *plaza de toros*, in the old part of the city, was only a short staggering distance from everywhere else. Pamplona's fiesta revolved around it in a drunken whirl. Ticket touts, most of them were short men in caps who all seemed to know one another, grabbed my arm and waved overpriced tickets at me. When I refused they let me go and screamed in someone else's face.

The bullring was an imposing though ragged-edged building surrounded by thick trees in full bloom. Most of it was hidden in the shade. Paseo de Hemingway, a short narrow passageway, ran along one side of it. No more than 50 yards long, it was named in the late 1960s in honour of the author. I walked along it and found a strange bust of Hemingway on one side of the *plaza*. It looked lost and hollow. It showed the writer in his later years, with a healthy-looking beard and an unlikely mop of thick hair on his head. The statue's eyes seemed to have ash in them, as if someone had just stubbed their cigarette out in them. I was the only one looking at it, or paying any attention to it. An empty beer bottle stood at the foot of the plinth.

A few yards away three drunken young men were leaning on a portaloo. One of them was sitting on the sandy ground. He had his head between his legs and his white shirt was stained with faded red wine near the collar. He shook as he bent over, puking on to the ground. His arms and forehead shone with sweat as he retched time and time again. His two friends checked their watches and looked bored.

Queues were beginning to form for the first bullfight of the fiesta. The matadors appearing on the cartel were virtual unknowns. I watched the touts go to work as they tried to flog their tickets. As I sat on a bench, taking it all in, I was approached by a middle-aged nun dressed in a white habit. She looked around her, checking the coast was clear, before offering me a couple of tickets. She named her price and waved them under my nose. I told her I already had a ticket and said I didn't need any more. She stopped hustling, rebuked me and marched off in a bad mood.

I passed a sign on the way into the *plaza de toros* which warned: 'Throwing cushions into the ring is forbidden by law and punishable with immediate fines.' I climbed high up into the rafters to take my seat. An English couple from London sat next to me. They looked bewildered and claimed they knew nothing about Pamplona or San Fermines before they'd happened upon the town that afternoon.

'We're in Spain caravanning,' said the fat-faced solemn husband when I asked why they were in Pamplona. 'I wanted to see a bullfight, so give or take an argument or two, here we are.'

His thin wife looked shell-shocked. I asked her how she was doing. 'I can't wait to get the hell out of here. This place has ruined our holiday. And this is just sheer bloody cruelty.' She nodded towards the bullring beneath us.

They fell silent and didn't speak to me, or each other, again.

The bullfight itself turned out to be very poor. All the bulls in Pamplona, like most of the others I'd seen during my travels, were overweight and slow. The matadors were showboaters in the same mould as the young *novilleros* I'd watched in Alcalá de Guadaira outside Seville. They gave the crowd lots of theatrical drama but not much else. One dropped his cape and ran away when a fat bull charged at him once too often in a way he didn't like. It was eventually given the green hankie and led out of the ring before he killed it. Towards the end, the drunken crowd became restless and booed and whistled when one particularly slow animal lumbered reluctantly into the ring. When the bull saw the matador it freaked out and ran away. He shouted after the animal but it was already too late. The bull, horns down like a possessed demon, took fright and bolted straight for the red *barrera* fence which it charged at with all its might. The instant the tips of its horns crashed into the wooden planks, it dropped to the ground – stone dead.

A local man from Pamplona who was sitting next to me exclaimed, 'Wow! I've been coming here for 21 years and that's the first time I've ever seen a bull commit suicide!'

At the end of the *corrida* I left the *plaza de toros* and wandered back towards the mayhem in the main square.

John Fulton had given me the names of some people I had to seek out. They were older Americans and Britons who came to Pamplona every year to run with the bulls. I walked up to one likely-looking man who seemed to be holding court and asked him if he knew someone called 'Lord' Rex. He was wearing a baseball cap at a jaunty angle and a loose-fitting tracksuit. He eyed me up for a moment or two before replying. 'Depends who's asking, fella . . .'

I told him I was a friend of John Fulton.

'In that case you're looking at Lord Rex – take a seat.' He gestured to a drunken young woman who was sitting behind him. 'I'm explaining to this young lady how I knew and drank with Ernest Hemingway . . .'

The bug-eyed woman hung on his every word. She asked me who I was. Entering into the spirit of things, I explained to her that my father had known Hemingway well and that my mother had had the honour of washing the Nobel Prize-winning author's underpants. I asked her if she wanted his mobile-phone number. She nodded, seemingly accepting that this was entirely feasible.

'How long have you been coming here?' I asked Lord Rex after his friend had turned her attention to someone else.

'Decades – about 30-odd years, I suppose. Something like that. Saw Hemingway when he last blew in . . . in '59.'

'Are you a real lord?' I enquired.

'Was in the House once – answered questions on dog shit on pavements, actually, as I recall,' he said, looking imperiously around the square.

Suddenly a firm-figured woman with silver hair and dark glasses sat herself down in my lap. She squirmed her thighs into my crotch.

'Eamonn O'Neill, meet Frosty!' proclaimed Lord Rex.

'A pleasure!' said the woman. She kissed me on both cheeks then launched herself at an empty seat on the other side of the table.

'A woman of many talents is our Frosty,' said Lord Rex. He told everyone I knew John Fulton. They all nodded and asked me how he was: I was told to pass on their regards. Lord Rex announced a toast: 'John Fulton and absent friends!'

Everyone threw back their drinks.

'How long have you been coming here?' I asked Frosty.

She thought for a moment. Looked at Lord Rex. Winked at someone else. Then blew me a kiss. That was all I was getting out of her.

'And, on occasion, a woman of few words, I might add! Here's to Frosty! Cheers!' cried Lord Rex. Once again, everyone raised their glasses, including Frosty who raised hers and demanded more.

The crowds washed around us. We sat on metal chairs outside the Hotel La Perla, where Hemingway had stayed when he was in town. Parties were being held in some of the rooms, their French windows flung open above the square, and you could see people's shadows dancing and moving around inside. Below, where we were sitting, waiters were dodging in and around our table taking orders with lightning speed. People came and went, all in white and red, with the odd individual touch like a baseball cap, a name sewn into a T-shirt or a crazy pair of sunglasses worn at night.

A good-looking American named Mike appeared and joined our company. He was tall, well built and in his early fifties; when I asked him what he did back home for a living, he said he was in the 'retail end of the business'. I never found out exactly what 'the business' was. Two other men, a Jewish father and son from New York, arrived and promptly bought everyone drinks. The father was ill but seemed happy to be around his cronies. His son smoked a long, fat cigar and wore a black Basque smock. I asked him what he did back in the States.

'I restore eighteenth-century furniture,' he replied.

'Are you running tomorrow?'

By asking this I'd fallen into the same trap as everyone else in Pamplona: asking people you meet whether they are planning to run with the bulls. It was the natural question, the ice-breaker that loosened tongues between complete strangers.

'No, I'm not running,' the man replied. 'I get my kicks in Pamplona in other ways.' He winked and rolled his eyes.

I kept seeing people who bore more than a passing resemblance to Ernest Hemingway. I'd heard about this phenomenon. There was a competition in Key West, where the writer had lived for a time, for Hemingway lookalikes every year. I'd read that Pamplona was the same – people who looked like him gravitated towards it from every corner of the planet.

Ed was a teacher and writer from Florida. He didn't try to look like Hemingway but, when he was sitting down at least, he did. When he stood up it was clear he was too short, healthy and fit looking to be Hemingway. He had two huge unlit cigars in his top pocket when I met him. 'They stay that way until I get to a bullfight. Then I light 'em up,' he remarked when I pointed to them.

Jim from Boston was Hemingway's spitting image. He said he enjoyed wandering around Pamplona every year 'doing the Hemingway thing'. People constantly stopped him and took his picture.

'Why?' I asked.

'Oh, I don't know . . . what the hell. Lighten up, will ya! It's a laugh!' he boomed – then he gave me a bear hug.

'You running in the morning, young man?' asked Lord Rex. His eyes narrowed.

'No, just watching and taking photographs,' I said.

'Just checking in. Just checking in . . .' he nodded his head sagely.

"Cos if you need any advice, Frosty here is your woman. A lady of a certain age, she'll party all night, then run in the morning. Puts us all to shame, does dear Frosty. A legend.'

Frosty blew him a kiss then stood up and veered off to find a toilet. Everyone was drinking slowly, pacing themselves; they still had seven drunken nights to go. Pamplona wasn't a quick sprint, it was a painful, joyful marathon.

'You must try and find Noel,' Lord Rex told me.

I'd heard of Noel Chandler from John Fulton. He was the old salt who owned a flat in Pamplona on the Calle Estafeta, and who had kept a lot of Matt Carney's personal effects. Lord Rex stayed in that street, as did a few others, during the fiesta. It was one of the best-known places in the whole city; a narrow street with tall buildings on either side down which the bulls charge in the mornings before they turn into the bullring. Noel's hospitality and generosity to complete strangers during San Fermines was legendary.

'Do you know where he is?' I asked around the table. A collective laugh went up. It was the first day of San Fermines. Noel could be anywhere and everywhere, possibly at the same time.

'C'mon, I'll show ya where he'll be – well, where he was half an hour ago,' said Mike the wealthy American. He flung his arm around me and we walked off up a side street. Lord Rex and his pals waved us off.

Five minutes later we found Noel. He was propped against the front door of a bar. I introduced myself and mentioned John Fulton's name. Noel didn't say much – like almost everyone else in the city, he was too drunk for conversation – but he smiled and posed for a snap.

'Can I drop by and see Matt Carney's room?' I asked him. 'John recommended it.'

He staggered for a moment then smiled and said, 'Any friend of John Fulton's is a friend of mine . . . come by any time.'

We shook hands and I left him. He was blinking, swaying and laughing, almost doubled up at a joke someone had just told him. As I walked away I looked over my shoulder to try and see him again but he was gone, washed away in the sea of red and white.

It was late but the fiesta was just warming up. A disco in a nearby corral was going full blast. I saw some Australian girls diving off the top of a high wooden fence into the arms of burly men who were stripped to the waist. One had the words 'OUTBACK BASTARD' written in lipstick on his bare chest.

In the main square drifters of every nationality had found one another. New-age characters in dreadlocks, none of whom wore Basque red or white, hung around in groups looking the worse for wear. They had bongo drums, strange ethnic wind instruments and expensive public-school accents. They were the type that went to rock festivals all over Europe each summer. Someone must have told them Pamplona was the place to be in July, but they looked disappointed with what they had found. They turned their backs on the red-and-white partying and the T-shirt sellers and the mad exuberance going on all around them and instead focused in on themselves. Some drank. Others were doped into oblivion. Most of them looked cold and hungry. They seemed bewildered and out of place.

North African pedlars wandered around wearing Santa hats with fairylights on top, selling fake Rolexes and strings of pearls and water-pistols. They wore sandwich boards and were very serious about plying their trade.

I wandered off through the back streets towards my apartment. People strolled past, arm in arm, waving bottles and singing. There wasn't even a hint of violence in the air. Families walked along together, the children skipping and playing along the kerb where drunks lay in the gutter. Young people stood on the corners, kissing and cuddling. Music could be heard everywhere. All the bars were packed. Inside everything was washed red and white. Even the barmen were dressed in costume. Most were as drunk as their customers.

I walked off alone along quiet empty streets that weren't on the city-centre map. Slowly the crowds thinned out.

The street where I was staying was quiet in comparison to the old part of town. Not much was happening there. I turned the corner, walked up the deserted street and into the darkness. Just before I reached the flat, I heard some happy dance music.

I kept on walking, and around the block I found a small park in a square. It was full of elderly Pamplonians. Neat tables and chairs were set out, small stumpy wine glasses sat on clean tablecloths and baskets of bread lay to one side. Hundreds of people, all wearing red-and-white outfits, were dancing with each other to traditional Spanish music.

The street-lights flickered on and off as I sat beneath some thick trees watching the scene for what seemed like ages.

They waltzed round and round, old men holding their once young wives in their arms. Their faces were bright and happy, their feet light and free, elated to be on holiday for a week, pleased to be dancing to the music, delighted to be with their friends, each celebrating their own private fiesta.

'Don't come back here dead if you get killed running with those bulls!' My landlady Maria waved me off towards the running of the bulls at half past six the next morning.

The streets were already packed. The fast-food shop on the corner hadn't closed all night. The apron-wearing owner and a drunken man were dancing with each other when I passed by. People were alseep outside on the hard white metal chairs. Whiny dance music blasted out of a cheap radio.

Streams of people moved towards the old part of town. I had butterflies in my stomach. I knew this was the first day of the running of the bulls but I hadn't a clue what day of the week it was. The normal rules of the calendar had evaporated during the last 24 hours. Pamplona had its own time scale.

It was cold in the pewter shadows of the side streets. I passed dozens of cars with crumpled faces buried in sleeping-bags inside them. Their windows were washed white with the occupants' milky condensed breath. One large van, its windows covered in tinfoil, suddenly opened its doors as I approached it; six matt-black North Africans spilled out onto the street. They spent a minute or two organising their wares of pearls, hats and scarves in the early dawn light before joining the throng which drifted past.

I spotted two pretty girls hobble off between parked cars, their eyes vigilant for people watching, as they pulled their pants down. Then they peed for all they were worth, the steaming rivers of urine trickling out on the road and underneath the feet of those heading for the bulls.

The air was thick with anticipation and excitement near the main square. Everyone had a sort of mad wedding-day fever on their faces. They were gripped by the knowledge that something was about to happen. An event that would stretch and telescope time right before their eyes.

The grass in the main square was worn thin. Scruffy travellers lay in sleeping-bags on the bare patches, their matted hair in the dirt. A few were in the foetal position on wooden benches. Empty wine bottles were scattered everwhere. People who'd just woken up found themselves in the middle of a huge crowd.

I followed the throng down to Calle Estafeta. I wanted to take some good photographs but I hadn't a proper press permit so I had to busk it for a vantage point. Local workmen in blue boilersuits began putting huge planks of wood into prepositioned corrals. The police shoved bystanders out of the way. All the best positions were already spoken for by local photographers and TV crews. They'd been booked up months in advance. The atmosphere was excited and claustrophobic.

It wasn't even 7 a.m. yet.

It was chaos near the bullring. This was the spot where the bulls had to take a sharp left-hand turn. People were already climbing onto the wooden fences from which, a few hours earlier, I'd watched the Australian girls diving. The police looked very neat and well groomed in comparison to the half-drunk and scruffy visitors. I noted dozens of ambulance volunteers dotted at every corner. They were dressed in the Red Cross garb of red and white, so it was hard to spot them amongst the blood-and-dove-white masses.

I walked across the old town, down through the narrow side streets filled with ancient, tumbling hat shops and venerable family businesses selling expensive pastries. Noisy brass bands marched past, blasting out folk tunes to anyone who would listen.

Eventually I found myself opposite the ornate town hall of Pamplona. The route taken by the bulls cut diagonally across the square immediately in front of the building. TV cameras and police officers were everywhere. Tall buildings rose up on every side; people hung out of or clambered onto balconies and ledges. They draped themselves from high and low places – anywhere, really, which afforded them a view of the route the bulls would take. In the blue morning light of Pamplona they staked their claim for the morning's run. Then they waited – swinging their legs, whistling, waving and rubbing their arms to keep warm.

Pamplona-minutes tottered past in seconds; everything was rushing forward. I looked around quickly for a vantage-point. On one corner of the square I spotted a magnificent old building with brass balconies. A middle-aged, beautiful woman with big brown eyes and an early-morning hair-do was standing at a window looking down on the scene beneath. I waved at her and pointed to my camera. She smiled and looked away; I couldn't stop myself doing a pathetic little dance to try and attract her attention. She waved me away, laughing. I wouldn't give up and tried to look lost and sorry for myself. It worked. After what seemed like an age, she finally signalled for me to come up.

I pushed my way through the crowd of people and pressed the doorbell for the first floor. A buzzer sounded and I entered. As I opened the door half a dozen people tried to cram in at my back. I had to shove them all back out. Inside was complete darkness. A woman's voice echoed from above me and, as my eyes adjusted to the dim light, I saw her face appear around the corner of a wrought-iron spiral staircase. 'This way! Hurry! And close the door tightly!' She signalled for me to follow her up the stairs, where I was shown into a small, cramped flat. It had a few sticks of furniture and bare floorboards and looked scarcely habitable. I asked the woman if I could take some photographs; she agreed and showed me into a small room. About four or five other photographers were already on the balcony. They all looked bleary-eyed and tired. Every one of us was wearing a red San Fermines neckerchief. I joined them and waited.

For the next hour the room filled up behind us. Anyone who had a decent spot was frightened to leave it to go and do a pee. Nobody trusted anyone else. Eventually we brokered a deal in five languages which allowed each one of us to troop off in search of a lavatory.

The place became fuller and fuller. I got the impression the woman had taken pity on every journalist and photographer who passed by. We all squeezed onto the tiny balcony to get our pictures. More than one of us nervously voiced the possibility that the whole thing might collapse under our collective weight. The balconies

¡FIESTA!

above us were equally crammed. One entire family filled a brass balcony which was only an arm's length from where we perched.

While we all faced out on to the street, the flat behind us continued filling up with more and more people. At one point, two men wearing only their underwear staggered out of an adjoining room brushing their teeth. Unbeknown to the rest of us, the woman had rented out the tiny front room to tourists a few days before. While we'd been piling in for photographs, they'd been innocently trying to get some sleep. The two men looked annoyed for a few minutes before they too joined in the viewing.

Beneath us was an ocean of people in red and white. Someone estimated the crowd to be about 10,000 strong. The whole route of the running of the bulls – from the corral where they were let out at one end of the old town, to the bullring which they ran into at the other – was only about 800 metres in length. In theory it would take the bulls only a short time to run it.

The runners were packed into small spaces in a number of different places along the route. Lines of short-sleeved, blue-shirted officers held them back. The street in front of the eager runners was empty; washed in shafts of early-morning light, it looked safe and inviting. At a glance the participants had the appearance of red-and-white marathon runners. Many wore crazy hats. Most looked madly anxious. Each section of the crowd was corralled behind wooden fences and cordoned off by smiling and joking police officers. Some of the runners had clearly decided to forget facing the bulls and had begun shinning up lamp-posts and drainpipes instead. The policemen half-heartedly waved them back down. Some pretended to be deaf and stayed where they were. The rest were squashed in beneath them. Occasionally the runners began clapping and chanting, trying to summon up their courage, like would-be warriors before some hastily organised street battle.

Quite unexpectedly, in the middle of everything, a little street-cleaner appeared, driving a tiny buggy with vacuum brushes whirling underneath. Ignoring the 10,0000 open-mouthed characters standing in front of him, he stared intently at some scraps of paper lying on the ground, chasing them like a hound going after a fox, until he finally cornered them and sucked them up with a look of great satisfaction on his face. Then, as quickly as he had appeared, he vroomed down the cobbled street to a mixture of jeers and cheers before eventually vanishing up an alley.

At about ten to eight the lines of policemen abruptly melted away. The majority of the runners began to move forward. Some jogged, some walked. A few patted their friends on the back as if, by just being there, they'd already notched up some kind of achievement. Only a few dozen were left behind below our balcony, where two minutes before there had been thousands. A low mist hung in pockets hidden from the early-morning sunshine. One or two runners nervously moved around in it, sweating like racehorses after a hard gallop.

I glanced up at the town hall. On the roof the statue of a stone figure holding a trumpet was dipped in shadow. The clock beneath him said it was almost eight. A few minutes passed. Its chimes began to sound. The crowd grew quiet. It was odd to hear such a hush fall instantly. Then, like spectators at Wimbledon, everyone's head turned in unison towards the alley where the bulls were due to appear at any moment.

Suddenly there was a flurry of activity. Two policemen ran in amongst the runners and dragged out a guy who was too drunk to run. He was hauled out by the scruff of the neck and dumped outside the corral. He was so smashed he didn't even seem to know what was going on. I watched him trying in vain to sit up, before he slumped to the ground in a confused heap. Everyone laughed nervously. A few claps and tight-throated shouts could be heard.

In the balcony across from me a TV crew had its cameras firmly fixed on the alley that ran alongside the town hall. Beneath me hundreds of press photographers were looking down their lenses at exactly the same place.

A rocket whizzed up into the air. Thousands of heads jerked up to look at it. Starlings shot up from rooftops, slicing and swooping in all directions, like arrows from the ramparts of a besieged fortress. Then, just as abruptly, the heads snapped their gaze back downwards towards the street . . .

That first rocket was the signal that the bulls had started running. It was followed almost immediately by a second rocket, its puff of white smoke carrying a thin, white, streaking tail. This was the signal that all the bulls had left the corral. The closer these two rockets were together, the tighter the herd of bulls.

A panicky cheer went up from the crowd when the second rocket cracked into the cobalt-blue sky. The two clouds looked like flour-stains on a bakery floor. They hung in the air in wisps until the high cold air blew them away, strand by strand.

People began jogging slowly down the narrow, misty cobbled street towards Calle Estafeta. The hordes hanging out of the balconies cheered and waved off the mass beneath them. Some of the runners stopped and looked back every so often as they headed down the street, while a few tried to get up some speed but succeeded only in bumping onto the hundreds of runners in their way.

At the corner of the town hall where the bulls were due to emerge any second, a thick clump of runners were jumping up and down. They looked as if they were warming up for a sprint; in a sense they were, but the real reason they were jumping was to try and see above the oncoming runners' heads. They needed to spot the bulls' horns before they could begin running. These jumping-bean figures were the real, hard-core Pamplona runners.

Suddenly they sprinted forward with almost, it seemed, unnatural speed. It was speed driven by sheer fear and semi-controlled panic. Quite a few were completely out of control, and none ran in a straight line. The majority scattered forward, their legs taking them away from an unseen foe.

Then I spotted the bulls . . .

In comparison to the fleeing men who vanished like lightning, the bulls lumbered forward, almost unconcerned by all the fuss. They didn't look even slightly perturbed by the screaming little figures who threw themselves through gaps in the fences, between policemen's legs and up lamp-posts. The animals looked more intent upon getting to their destination peacefully and, strange as it may seem, with a certain degree of elegance.

I took some snaps of the bulls as they ran through the crowd, their mere presence instantly thinning the people in front of them. The leading bull was a heavily muscled chestnut-brown colour. It seemed confused but not frightened by the men who jostled, scattered and flung themselves out of its way.

Then a strange thing happened. Out of the corner of my eye I spotted something – a blotted object – run across my field of vision. I knew instantly that, whatever it was, it should not have been there. The bulls were *clearing* people out of the way. From the moment I'd first seen them, the pattern had been for the runners to dive away from them in every direction. Only a handful of mad characters in control of their legs snatched at the bulls' horns with rolled-up newspapers. Everyone else stayed well away from them. But this figure – this shape – looked like it was veering towards the bulls, heading straight into their line of sight.

It was a young man. He was clearly drunk. In an instant I watched what happened next.

He had been standing quietly at the side of the street. Just as the half-dozen bulls came battering down the street, he panicked and decided to cross the cobbles in front of them. Perhaps he hadn't even seen the bulls – he may well have been too drunk even to know what was happening. Either way, he walked straight into them. The morning light bounced off the whole scene, somehow making it look strangely beautiful.

The first bull, the brown one, rammed straight into the man just like an American footballer tackling his opposite number. He fell to the ground immediately. The second, angered at being separated from the first animal, tried to scoop him in its horns and toss him. The man flopped over, lifeless, like a thin scarecrow. Knocked off its stride by this unexpected obstacle, the bull fell down on top of him. I could see its thick veins and twitching slabs of muscle as it tried to right itself. Finally it got back onto its feet. It stumbled forward into a shaft of hot light, instinctively following the rest of the herd which had already caught up.

The figure on the ground looked small and naked and exposed. He lay there motionless . . .

The two or three bulls which had gone over him thundered down the street, their hooves kicking up small clouds of dirt. The fourth bull, separated from the leaders, became disorientated for a few seconds; then it was turned around by someone snapping a rolled-up newspaper at its nose. Instantly, it veered round like a trained polo pony and confronted its agitator. The guy froze with utter fear. He blinked. The bull was gone, lumbering after the others, before he realised what had appened. Only later would he shake with fear and realise just how lucky he'd been.

The fifth bull followed moments later. It stopped and thumped the figure on the cobbles with its horns then backed up and jumped over the drunken casualty. People screamed. Almost unbelievably, the man tried to get up but his legs wouldn't carry him. He managed to get to his feet and just stood there. Heads spun round to see where the final bull was. The spectators on the balconies shouted and squealed. The last bull, having been distracted by some runners, was a few seconds behind the rest of the herd when it spotted him. With the staggering runner in its sights, it charged straight for him.

'Oh, shit, no!' screamed a photographer beside me.

The bull hit him full on. His face exploded in blood and he spun round. People screeched like wounded, trapped animals. A second later it was over. The bull charged on after the others as the man fell to the ground, his hand clawing at his head. For a moment or two he lay motionless.

In that instant I felt the calm of the morning return. The running of the bulls had taken it away but, in spite of the man-made chaos, it was back again. The sunlight, the air and healthy feeling of early morning flowed through us all like a powerful river. I felt strangely detached. Then, a second later, I pulled myself back to reality. The injured man was still lying on the cobbles.

One or two runners jogged by him, shaking their heads. They chased after the bulls. A short man appeared with a team of oxen. He whipped them, making them follow the bulls to keep the latter together in a group. A few people, drunk with fear and booze, ran alongside the oxen, waving at their friends and mistaking the team for the real bulls which were long gone. They made faces as if to say 'Look! I'm running with the bulls in Pamplona! What's all the fuss?'

Another second or two passed. The guy still lay on the cobbles. A small, dark pool of blood grew beside him. Pamplona-time had stretched again: it felt like minutes had passed since he'd been hit, but in fact no more than a handful of seconds had trickled by.

Then the spell lifted. Everyone abruptly woke up at once. Suddenly it sank into the bystanders what had happened just feet from them. They dashed forward and dragged the injured man off to the side. People kept looking around warily as if they expected more bulls to come charging down the street. But they didn't need to worry. It was all over for another 24 hours.

I could see that the man's head was already puffy and smothered with red. A crowd surrounded him in a matter of seconds. Camera crews and photographers jostled to get a picture of the first casualty of the fiesta. Paramedics rushed to his side. The sun flooded the whole scene in gold. The medics lifted him gently onto a stretcher and placed him carefully in the back of a waiting vehicle. I saw his hand sticking out from beneath a red sheet. It looked small and white as he clutched the hand of the nurse who was gently reassuring him. People clapped and cheered when he was carted off.

'Man, I feel sick after watching that,' said Thomas, a photographer from Poland who'd been standing beside me on the balcony. 'I need to get out of here.'

Everyone who'd witnessed the accident, myself included, felt a mixture of exhilaration and nausea. We pushed out of the small room and headed downstairs to get some fresh air. No one said a word.

I wandered through the streets of the old part of Pamplona after watching the running of the bulls. It seemed as though everyone I passed was walking around in a semi-daze. It was as if we'd finally exhaled after holding our breath for ages. Street-cleaners in orange boilersuits were already out in force washing the wine-soaked cobbles down in an effort to keep one step ahead of the festivities. The sunlight bounced off the shining surface for a second or two, blinding everyone walking along it, until the heat dried out the pavement to a comfortable matt finish.

The deafening noise of mountains of glass bottles being stacked up, carted off or emptied into huge metal containers filled the air. My head thumped.

A crowd had already gathered for early-morning coffee in front of the Bar Txoko in the main square. I spotted Ed from Florida whom I'd met the night before. I joined him and ordered coffee. A post-mortem of sorts was being held.

'Were you out this morning?' I asked. It was the question on everybody's lips.

'Nah . . . but I was going to,' said Ed. 'I walked out on to the street to wait for a couple of young guys who'd asked me to run with them. I hung around for a while but they never showed up. I didn't feel right. I don't know what the hell it was – probably my imagination. But, anyway,' he looked around sourly, 'I decided to forget it. When I get a bad feeling like that about something I take a raincheck, you know what I mean?'

I nodded. My head was still full of images of that guy being battered by the herd of bulls. I kept seeing it in slow motion, the blood pouring from his face, the awful way he'd lain motionless and the strange pause before anyone went forward to help him.

We both stared into space for a few minutes. The crowd flowed around us.

'I saw a guy being hit this morning . . .' I said absently.

'Oh, no – was it bad?' asked Ed.

'Awful. I felt sick,' I said, grimacing. My stomach fluttered just thinking about it. I closed my eyes and leant my head back against the cold metal of the chair. The chill of the steel helped. Then I found myself wondering how my pictures would turn out: I'd photographed the whole incident. I felt shame and excitement in equal measures.

I opened my eyes and looked at Ed. He shrugged and I nodded. I swallowed some milky coffee and stared into space.

He pointed out Joe Distler, the man who'd taken Matt Carney's place as the 'lead' American in the running. The guy was wearing a red T-shirt with the sleeves cut off and white Levis. He had the build of a marathon runner. A distinguished professor of literature, Distler was also a successful businessman from Manhattan. He was talking to two young Americans who had just run for the first time that morning. One of them had slipped and cut his hand.

'Get that hand bandaged up, man. Get it seen to, have some iodine on it or something. I'm not kidding.' Joe was a good-looking man in his early fifties, very fit in appearance. The two young guys who were listening to him seemed impressed.

After introducing myself to Joe Distler I asked him the all-important question.

'Yeah, I ran. You betcha! Excellent! Felt great! Although I do more standing with the bulls these days than running. But, boy, at one point those horns were *that* close to the guy next to me, I thought, "Aw Jeez, I've had it!" Then the thing just turned and ran off...' He shook his head and rolled his eyes like a teenager who'd just survived a dare. You could see the buzz he obviously got out of the whole thing.

'How long have you been coming here?'

'This was my thirtieth year, man...' He nodded his head. 'I love it! I've never missed a single day.' A group of people were trying to drag him away from my table so he could talk to them. He shook hands with me after our brief chat and allowed himself to be hauled off by his friends.

Everyone who had taken part in the running was really pumped up and excited. They all smiled and basked in their collective energy.

'What about you, Ed? When did you first start coming here?' I asked.

Ed was reading a newspaper. He scratched his beard, folded the paper with a rustle and look thoughtful: 'I came years ago then I stopped for a while. I've been coming these last few years, though,' he said.

'Why do you come, though?' I asked him.

'Like everyone else here, I love Hemingway. And for other reasons too – personal stuff, I suppose. My birthday is on the first day of the fiesta and I got married here on that day too. Beat that!' he laughed.

I smiled. I'd only hooked up with Ed 24 hours previously but I felt like I'd known him for years. He was gentle and thoughtful, easy company to get along with.

Across the tangle of metal tables, amongst the hundreds of red-and-white costumes, I spotted Jim from Boston, another Hemingway lookalike. He was smiling and posing for some pictures. A handsome black American called Warren, an artist from Brooklyn wearing a baseball shirt, was also there. He was sipping coffee and talking to friends.

Ed, who was lighting one of his large cigars, turned to me between puffs and said: 'Are you going to run, Eamonn?'

A day or two earlier I'd have definitely said 'no' to this question. But after all the people I'd met in Pamplona, all the cronies of Lord Rex, all the characters outside the Hotel La Perla, an odd thing had happened. Because no one put any pressure on me to run, I began quietly and secretly to consider the possibility that I might just have a go. I'd met so many people who were relaxed about it and who seemed to know exactly what to do and what not to do. If anyone had suggested this might happen to me, I would have laughed in their face. Yet, it had. My mind had turned 180 degrees. John Fulton's 'bullfighting worm' had entered my brain. I was half-elated and half-ashamed – especially after seeing that guy being battered by the bulls less than an hour earlier. I thought I had the strength to remain apart from it all, but I didn't. I was being sucked into it by the minute. I was just the same as everyone else.

'I don't know, Ed,' I heard myself reply. 'But if I do decide to run, can I run with you? They say you should run with someone who knows what they're doing.'

He paused for a moment, squinting in the smoke, as he relit his cigar. 'Sure,' he answered, puffing on it. 'I'd be honoured.'

A few hours later I had lunch in a cafe overlooking the main square. The afternoon newspaper said five people had been injured in the running. The man I'd seen being tossed was from London. He was in hospital in a serious condition.

Across from where I was sitting, a woman with a harmonica was doing a raindance – or sundance – on the street. She jumped around, pointed at the sun which was breaking through the clouds, and played a terrible tune. Suddenly, out of nowhere, an odd-looking character dressed as Superman appeared. His costume was of the home-made, flung-together variety: a blue suit, a red tablecloth for a cape and a brown nylon wig which he doffed like a hat every so often. He danced around the woman, piling up metal chairs from a nearby cafe. People stopped to watch them. They looked like a couple from hell. Superman arranged the chairs like a hurdle and made gestures as if he was about to attempt to fly over it. The woman ignored him and blew her guts into the tuneless mouth-organ. The whole affair was building up to a mad climax which was halted only when a delivery van drove up. The woman stopped playing her instrument and walked off in a bad mood. Superman, noticing her absence, took off his wig and held it out, hoping for a spontaneous collection from the crowd. His bald nut-brown pate shone in the sun as he worked the onlookers. He gathered a few sympathetic coins before piling up more chairs. He was about to jump over them when a bored-looking waiter appeared on the scene and started retrieving the furniture for his customers. Superman, with a mad gleam in his eye, shrugged, waved at everyone then sprinted off down an alleyway like a man intent upon saving the world.

After lunch I wandered over to see Noel Chandler's place on the Calle Estafeta. Noel himself was still missing in action but Lord Rex was in residence and he let me into the apartment to see Matt Carney's old room.

'We renamed it "The Matt Carney Suite",' he said, pointing to a brass name-plate on the door.

I peered inside. The famous poster for San Fermines showing Matt striding up the Calle Estafeta while everyone else was collapsed at his feet, hung on the wall. A few other portraits of him were also on display.

'Did you know James Michener dedicated a book to Carney recently?' asked Lord Rex.

I said that I did. The book, a novella about bullfighting, was called *A Miracle in Seville* and John Fulton had illustrated it, even including a sketch of Carney in Pamplona on the dedication page. Matt had obviously caught the attention of the multi-millionaire author.

'We think about him a lot at this time of year – San Fermines. Cancer is a terrible thing, isn't it?' he said absent-mindedly.

I nodded silently in agreement.

'Ah, well,' sighed Lord Rex. He padded off to grab a boiling kettle which was whistling, leaving me alone in the room. Carney's famous 'USA' sweatshirt, white trousers, red sash and his flat white Jay Gatsby cap were hanging at the foot of the bed. It was as if he'd just stepped out of them that morning after another run with the bulls.

A photograph on the wall showed him standing with Noel, Lord Rex, John Fulton and all the other members of the gang I'd met. Matt Carney had run with the bulls countless times and he'd been battered by their horns more often than he cared to recall, but he'd always managed to come up smiling, wearing his flat white cap, his American sweatshirt and a determined, manic, never-say-die glint in his eyes. When he sat down for a few beers after running he would be surrounded by half of Pamplona. He looked handsome and mad – laughing his head off because he was doing something which the rest of the world thought was completely insane.

Lord Rex appaeared at the door. 'That's a picture of his grave.' He gestured towards a small photograph on the wall which showed an ancient-looking plot in a green field near a grey misty seashore.

'Where is it?' I asked.

'Near Galway in Ireland. That was his dying wish – to be buried in Ireland but facing America. And he got it. We miss the bugger.' He had tears in his eyes.

Later that night I scoured the square looking for Ed. I'd made up my mind I would run with the bulls the following morning. But I needed to find Ed quick so I could arrange a place where we'd meet along the route. I asked Lord Rex's crowd in front of the hotel if they'd seen him, but they hadn't. They waved me off and wished me good luck.

I weaved in and out of the North Africans who were still trying to sell their fake watches. Now they were wearing Mexican sombreros and shawls. Rain was forecast so they'd also instantly produce a new line in umbrella hats and plastic ponchos. But no one was buying. They looked fed-up and hungry.

I searched through endless bars and cafes, occasionally spotting a drunken face I recognised. I was certain Ed was just one bar or restaurant ahead of me.

Eventually I gave up looking for him. I ended up sitting at the cafe in the square where, earlier in the day, we'd chatted after watching the running. I drank some rough local red wine and watched the silver blasts of fireworks explode in the sky. Everyone around me cheered and pointed. Adults became kids as the rockets burst open. The bars were doing a roaring trade. No one gave a damn what time or even what day it was. It was fiesta time in Pamplona and that was all that mattered. For a couple of hours I watched the faces in the crowd swim by, hoping to catch a glimpse of Ed. Once or twice I thought I'd spotted him. I stood up on my seat and shouted out his name, but invariably it was just another Hemingway lookalike.

I sat for what seemed ages until I grew cold and tired and drunk. I kept looking and hoping. But it never happened. I never did find him.

My alarm clock went off the next morning at dawn. I got up with every intention of running with the bulls. I'd decided to take a chance and do my first run alone. I opened the window and looked out. The air felt heavy and damp. It had been raining all night and the surface of the street was shiny and soaking under the orange street-lamps.

I stood in silence weighing things up. That's when I felt it . . .

Something at the back of my mind told me not to run after all. It would be too dangerous. This sudden change in the weather was a bad omen or something, I thought to myself. I'd read of bullfighters who'd experienced a similar thing: if they saw a bull they didn't like the look of, they simply threw in the towel. They refused to fight because they trusted their instincts. And the Son of God himself couldn't have changed their minds. Other people had had similar experiences: as a child I'd once been told that sailors leaving from Irish ports for a month at sea would sometimes get the same feeling – a strange shifting in their senses when they approached the dock where their vessel was moored; it was a whisper in their minds telling them to walk back home – and most made a habit of listening to it. Their fellow crewmen understood, for they'd encountered it too. These were men who had never learned to swim: they believed it gave them more respect for the sea. The voices they heard belonged to their dead forebears, drowned in the oceans they now fished, and who were talking to the sailors, warning them not to venture out. If they listened to these voices they lived; if they didn't, the whole ship and its crew might go down . . .

I tried to blank out these thoughts but I couldn't stop myself feeling them. But I tried, I really tried my best.

I showered, dressed and stood in the silent darkness of the room wrestling with my mind. Outside, the sky was still gloomy, the mountain clouds jealously shielding the sun's weak rays. It was more night than day.

I hesitated and sat down on the edge of the bed. Ashamed of

myself, cursing my courage – or lack of it, as I thought – I lay back on the blankets, stared at the ceiling and, after a few minutes, fell into a fitful sleep. I was angry, knowing this was my last day in Spain and my one and only chance that summer to run with the bulls of Pamplona. But something had told me not to do it. The unsettling feeling was ultimately stronger than my equally strange urge to run.

So, in the end, I didn't take part.

Three hours later I was sitting in the main square of Pamplona having a quiet, subdued farewell lunch by myself. The place was surprisingly empty. All the new-age bongo-drum travellers had packed up and cleared off to their next port of call. Everyone else was in bed after the running of the bulls, probably nursing the early stages of a week-long hangover. The square looked lovely. The leaves on the trees glistened in the sun which periodically broke through and the air smelled clean and fresh.

A juggler appeared and tried his best to gather a crowd around him. He failed, packed up his suitcase and walked off with it on a trolley. People seated around me looked damp, bedraggled and fragile.

I was already regretting not running that morning. I felt left out and left behind – annoyed with myself in a childish way. I looked around for someone or somthing to distract me from my thoughts. The crew of a local radio station had set up shop near by. They were listening to interviews and reviewing tapes. I asked one of the reporters, a pretty woman wearing a leather jacket, how the running had gone that morning.

'Didn't you run?' she asked.

'No, I didn't,' I replied. She looked me up and down. I felt my face turn red, so I added lamely: 'But I might some other time.'

She knew I was talking nonsense but she said nothing and left my dignity intact.

'I was going to run this morning but at the last minute I changed my mind,' I babbled hopefully.

'Well, you were wise,' she said, shaking her head.

'Why is that?'

'You'll find out . . .' she said, arching one eybrow. Then she turned her back to me and put on a set of thick plastic headphones.

*

Before I left Spain a short time later I spoke to a few people in an attempt to find out what had happened in Pamplona that morning. Eventually, when I'd fitted all the pieces of the various stories and descriptions together, a relatively clear picture began to present itself.

Apparently the early-morning drizzle had caused a lot of the bulls and the participants to slip and fall during the running. Runners stumbled in front of the bulls from the moment they charged out of the corral. The image that was uppermost in people's minds was that the whole thing had been scary and messy from the outset. The cobblestones were greasy and wet as well as cold and hard when you cracked your hands or knees against them. Everyone was unusually jumpy and vicious with each other. Elbows went flying, punches flew and people shoved their neighbours out of the way.

But the real panic started when one huge bull became separated from the rest of the herd. It had turned round, becoming confused and scared. When it was separated from the rest of the animals, screams of '¡*Toro solo!*' went up all the way along Calle Estafeta. A *toro solo*, I was told, was the single most dangerous thing which can happen during the running in Pamplona: even veteran runners fled in terror. Things got out of control. Anyone with a plan or strategy threw it aside; they just ran for their lives.

The crowd scattered in all directions but that only upset the lone bull further. It lost sight of the other animals and could only see erratic figures darting in and out and around its field of vision. It felt hemmed in and threatened, so instinctively it lashed out with its horns. It charged at anything it saw, even the terrified onlookers standing like statues in the doorways and at the panic-stricken novice runners who threw themselves onto fences and who clawed and scraped their way up lamp-posts to escape.

In a very short space of time this *toro solo* had caused chaos all along the route of the running with its speed, power and sabre-sharp horns. Seasoned spectators had been shaken by its unearthly ferocity. It took the bull nearly eight minutes to reach the bullring.

Several people told me there had been a 'bad feeling' in the air before, during and after the running – something not quite right which they were unable to put their finger on. Some said they'd sensed this discomfort earlier in the morning but had decided to ignore it and take part in the running anyway. They weren't sure what significance to attach to the sensation but they recalled it quite clearly.

When the running of the bulls was over, the Calle Estafeta looked like the aftermath of a medieval battlefield: more than 50 people were treated on the streets by paramedics and 29 others had to be hospitalised.

The worst injury was to a runner from Britain who'd been badly gored by the *toro solo*. Battered, cut and bleeding heavily, he'd ended up in Pamplona's main hospital in what the media later reported to be a 'serious' condition. But in the days that followed, he eventually emerged in one piece, having defied all the odds. A picture in the newspaper from much later in the week showed him propped up in bed grinning and giving the thumbs-up sign to the photographer.

I stared at his face for a long time; his bright animated expression had a strange, slightly unsettling quality. It reminded me of the old black-and-white photos I'd seen of Matt Carney and John Fulton in their younger years, both running through the streets of Pamplona looking like a pair of God's madmen, each wearing the same look of sheer devilment. Several matadors I'd seen elsewhere had shared it too – grinning with wild-eyed relief at the end of a bullfight when, after a few close calls, they'd unexpectedly found themselves still standing, still living and breathing.

When I put the newspaper aside, I was uncomfortably aware that I knew that face in the article only too well. I'd glimpsed it more than once in my life: in fact, I'd seen it long before I ever set foot in Spain.

It was the face of someone who'd abruptly rediscovered the lunatic joy of simply being alive.

The face of a mortal who'd lived to tell the tale.

Acknowledgements

I'd like to thank the following people, in no particular order, for the assistance they gave me during the writing of this book:

Bill Campbell and Peter Mackenzie of Mainstream Publishing for commissioning the work and for their subsequent help during its writing; all their staff at Mainstream in Edinburgh; Philip Watson of *Esquire* magazine, formerly of *GQ* magazine in London, for originally sending me to Spain in the first place to cover bullfighting for his publication and for his professional loyalty, editorial judgement and valued friendship; to all the people I met in Alcalá de Guadaira, Córdoba, Seville, Madrid and Burgos – you know who you are; to Allen Josephs, President of the Ernest Hemingway Foundation and Society, for his time, insight and patience; everyone I met in Pamplona – especially Noel, Ed, Mike, Frosty, the Spicehandlers, Joe Distler and Lord Rex; Vicente Salamanca, *Matador de Toros*; the Bullfighting Club of London; Juan Carlos and Macu from Seville; to all the professional matadors I met on my travels, especially Francisco Rivera Ordoñez, Joselito and Enrique Ponce; John Fulton, artist and *Matador de Toros*, for his kindness, hospitality and grace – this book could not have been written without him and I'm in his debt; to Dan Buck and Anne Meadows of Washington DC for their friendship, hospitality and translating skills.

To my wife Sarah for her love, humour and companionship, a courageous and inspiring pal; special mention must be made of her mother and my mother-in-law, Esther Nui, and her husband, Jerry Carpenter, of Apalachin, New York, for their endless kindness, hospitality, unfailing humour, sheer generosity – material and spiritual – and for their ready supplies of Phil's Chicken which I shall miss almost, but not quite, as much as them. Thank you both.

And, finally, to my own family, especially my sister Kate, for first introducing me to Spain. It is to them, both individually and collectively, that I wish to dedicate this book.

Muchas gracias.